CHILD
PSYCHOLOGY

Terry Faw, Ph.D.
Formerly, Lewis and Clark College

Gary S. Belkin, Ph.D.
Long Island University

An American BookWorks Corporation Project

McGraw-Hill Publishing Company

New York St. Louis San Francisco Auckland Bogotá Caracas Hamburg
Lisbon London Madrid Mexico Milan Montreal New Delhi Oklahoma City
Paris San Juan São Paulo Singapore Sydney Tokyo Toronto

About the authors

Terry Faw is a clinical psychologist in Portland, Oregon, specializing in work with children and families. He formerly taught Child Psychology at U.C.L.A. and at Lewis and Clark College, where he was Chairman of the Psychology Department. He is the author of college level books and a variety of research reports focusing on child development.

Gary S. Belkin teaches at Long Island University's Westchester campus in New York, and is the author of several college textbooks. He also maintains a private practice in cognitive psychotherapy.

Child Psychology

Adapted from *Schaum's Outline of Theory and Problems of Child Psychology*. Copyright © 1980 by McGraw Hill, Inc. All Rights Reserved

2 3 4 5 6 7 8 9 10 11 12 13 14 15 16 17 18 19 20 FGR FGR 8 9 2 1 0 9

ISBN 0-07-020112-9

Library of Congress Cataloging-in-Publication Data
Faw, Terry.
Introduction to child psychology/Terry Faw, Gary Belkin
     p.   cm. — (McGraw-Hill college review books series)
     ISBN 0-07-020112-9
     1. Child psychology. 2. Child development. I. Belkin, Gary S.
BF721.F3823   1989
155.4—dc19   CIP

Preface

Child development is one of the most exciting and relevant areas of psychology. It is a scientific study, yet it focuses on topics that each of us is personally and intimately aware of: our own family background and its influences, our relationships with siblings and peers, our developmental strengths and deficiencies. It also helps us understand how our physical growth, language, thinking, personality, and adjustment problems evolved during the course of our lives. In short, the study of child development enables us to explain (or, at least, clarify) many of the mysteries that together comprise that perennially confounding question, "How did I become what I am?"

This book is directed not only to students enrolled in a child or developmental psychology course but also to teachers, parents, and professional psychologists whose daily activities are focused on the education, development, and well-being of children. For all these readers, it provides a clear understanding of the facts, principles, and theoretical explanations found in the leading texts. The material is neatly organized under a series of subheadings to facilitate study and review, whether the volume is used alone or in conjunction with a course text. A glossary provides an easy reference source for unfamiliar terms.

Interspersed in the text are examples drawn from research

literature and from the authors' own experience. These examples not only clarify the principles of child development, they also relate these principles to practical problems of child psychology encountered by clinical and counseling psychologists and by parents who must continually make decisions about the best way to interact with their ever-changing children.

For flexibility of study the book is divided into six parts. Part One presents a discussion of issues and methods in child psychology while Parts Two through Six each examines a different period in the development of the child. Within each of those parts is a chapter relevant to the various facets of psychological functioning—cognition, social interactions, and so on. Readers who wish to obtain a picture of the developing child from all perspectives should read Parts Two through Six sequentially. Readers who wish to focus their attention on a particular facet of development—such as cognition or social development—can do so by reading the chapter relevant to the topic in each of the last five parts of the book. Finally, concentration on a particular period of development can be achieved by reading only that relevant part of the book.

Terry Faw
Gary S. Belkin

Contents

PART I:
Introduction

As a discipline, child psychology is in some respects similar to other branches of psychology and in some respects different. Perhaps what distinguishes it most is its emphasis on development—those changes that take place in a human being over time. Wordsworth said, "The child is father to the man," implying that our adult personalities and behavior are strongly influenced by our childhood experiences. So too is our learning about the world and our ability to manipulate our environment.

Developmental psychologists are interested in how and when our various behavior patterns emerge and why these patterns change over the course of the life span. In other words, their goal is to understand how a person becomes what he or she is and what factors contribute to this process.

Depending on the goals of a particular psychologist and on his or her point of view, the subject of development can be approached in several ways. Chapter 1 of this book is an introduction to the major schools of thought that have influenced child psychologists and the assumptions they make about human development. Chapter 2 is a review of some of the basic experimental and observational tools that child and developmental psychologists use in their studies of human growth.

CHAPTER 1

Issues in Child Psychology

The discipline of psychology explores a vast number of processes that govern the functioning of the human organism. These processes include motor behavior, perception, cognition, learning, language development, and social processes, to name but a few. While many psychologists explore the functioning of these processes when they are fully developed, developmental psychologists focus on changes that occur in those processes from conception through childhood, childhood through adolescence, adolescence to maturity, and during the adult years into the years of old age. These are called developmental stages.

This chapter begins by looking at different viewpoints about the human organism, its growth and development. It then outlines the main theories of development: maturational, behavioral (learning), cognitive, humanistic, psychoanalytic, Adlerian (Individual), and Eriksonian.

The Nature of the Human Organism

One of the issues that dominates debates concerning human development focuses on the nature of the human organism and the role each individual plays in his or her own development. Two viewpoints in this debate predominate; one holds that the human organism is active, while the other sees humans as essentially passive reactors to their environment.

The Active Viewpoint

Some philosophers and psychologists view humans as active participants in their own development. These theorists maintain that the child brings to the environment his or her own program for development and uses the environment to facilitate the implementation of that program.

Psychologists who hold that humans are active participants in their development tend to seek an understanding of the characteristics that the individual brings to the developmental process and the ways in which those characteristics will influence development in a given environment. Those psychologists tend to explore the developmental patterns shared by individuals reared in vastly different environments.

Jean Piaget (1896–1980) emphasized the active participation of humans in their own development. Piaget held that human development results from the individual's attempts to maintain a state of equilibrium with his or her environment, to function effectively within that environment, and to reduce uncertainties in the environment. Children who are not able to use their capacities to fulfill those objectives reorganize their psychological processes so that they can adapt more effectively to the world in which they live.

Developmental psycholinguists, who emphasize the active role played by the child in the acquisition knowledge about language, often describe the patterns of language development common to children who speak different languages or whose language stimulation varies dramatically. They have discovered that children from different environments all begin to speak at about the same age. Furthermore, all children initially construct sentences in a similar way, despite the fact that they are from societies that speak different languages, such as Russian and English.

The Passive Viewpoint

Some philosophers and psychologists view humans as passive beings whose development is shaped primarily by environmental forces outside their control and their own bodies. Psychologists who adhere to this position tend to seek an understanding of the environmental conditions that cause a child to behave in a particular way.

These conditions may be internal (such as biological needs for food, water, companionship, and so on) or they may be external (such as previously experienced rewards and punishments). Those theorists who hold the passive viewpoint tend to emphasize the study of differences in the pattern of development for individuals exposed to different environmental influences.

The philosopher John Locke, writing in the late seventeenth century, was an early advocate of the viewpoint that humans play a passive role in their own development. For Locke, the child was born a *tabula rasa*, or blank slate. Development consisted of environmental experiences imprinting knowledge onto that slate. The child was like an empty container into which the forces of the environment—in the form of parents, schools, and social institutions—poured the knowledge and customs of the adult world.

Learning theory is a more current position that reflects the viewpoint that humans are passive participants in their own development. An early example of the learning theory perspective is found in the writings of John B. Watson (1878-1958), who once suggested that if he were given a group of children and the ability to manipulate their environment, he could develop adults who would be able to perform any role in society. In this statement, Watson emphasized the omnipotence of environmental agents in shaping the development of the child. Similar beliefs have been expressed by B. F. Skinner, a contemporary psychologist.

The Nature of Development

Two issues often debated concern the nature of the changes that occur in development and the factors that influence the end product of those changes. The two factors most often debated are the relative influences of heredity and environment.

Change: Continuous or Discontinuous?

Developmental Continuity

Some psychologists maintain that the psychological processes that mediate human functioning do not undergo fundamental changes during their development but instead change gradually in their efficiency or functioning capacity. A graph that reflects continuous development appears in Figure 1.1.

When children first begin to speak, they utter only short sentences of two or three words. Later, the sentences become longer and the structure becomes more complex. Psychologists who believe that development is continuous suggest that these changes reflect gradual increases in the child's ability to remember words and to use them in sentences. It is postulated that no fundamental change has occurred in the child's knowledge of language.

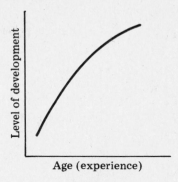

Fig. 1.1

Developmental Discontinuity

Other psychologists maintain that the changes we observe in development reflect fundamental changes in the psychological processes that mediate human functioning. These individuals see development as movement through a series of qualitatively unique stages, in which the evolution of one stage may depend upon the characteristics of preceding stages.

Figure 1.2 depicts the developmental process as it would be viewed by a stage theorist. When these stages are superimposed on one another, they produce a graph that is depicted in Figure 1.3. Note that at a given moment an individual may be functioning predominantly within one stage of development but retain some remnants of functioning from an earlier stage, and at the same time be beginning to evolve the characteristics of a later developmental stage.

Roger Brown, a contemporary psychologist, and his colleagues have proposed that in the process of language acquisition, the child progresses systematically through a series of five stages. Each stage of development is characterized by the acquisition of a new set of rules and skills, allowing the child to produce sentences exhibiting new forms and higher levels of

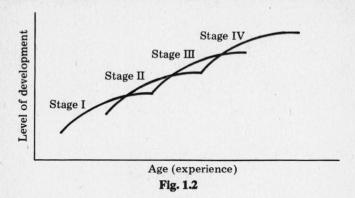

Fig. 1.2

A detailed description of this model of language acquisition may be found in Chapter 14.

Likewise, Jean Piaget maintained that cognitive development progresses through a series of stages. Each stage, Piaget discovered, is characterized by the acquisition of a unique set of cognitive processes that allow the child to think in identifiable ways. In the first stage the child's knowledge is restricted to that which can be gained by direct sensory and motor contact with the world around him or her. Subsequently, the child can form

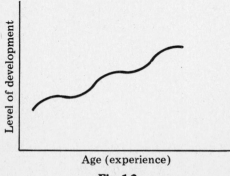

Fig. 1.3

internal representations of his or her experiences, and can think not only about present activity but about past activity as well.

Later, the child acquires an understanding of logical operations, which makes it possible for the child to solve concrete problems that theretofore could not be solved. Finally, the adolescent develops a unique set of logical operations, which allows him or her to think abstractly. (For a more detailed account of this developmental theory, see the section on theories of development below, as well as Chapters 8, 12, 17, and 21.)

Change: Nature vs. Nurture

Historically, a debate among psychologists centered on the relative importance of heredity (nature) and the environment (nurture) in determining patterns of human development. About a century ago, when psychology was under the strong influence of Darwin's evolutionary theory, it was believed that the primary influence on development was heredity.

This view was challenged in the early part of the century by environmentalists, led by John B. Watson (see discussion below), who believed that proper training can make any child into any type of adult. This notion of the importance of experiential factors had great appeal in a democracy, the credo of which was that anyone could work hard and rise on the socioeconomic ladder. The environmentalist view dominated American psychology for several decades.

Today, it is no longer argued whether one or the other of those factors is more important in determining developmental patterns. Instead, it is commonly agreed that environmental and hereditary factors interact with one another to influence development.

Heredity certainly influences development. Characteristics such as skin color, height and weight tendencies, and hair or eye color, which are all passed on from parents, may affect behavior.

For example, a seven-foot-tall boy might well become a basket-ball player, but not a racing jockey. Such a boy's self-image may also be affected by the fact that he is so much taller than all his peers. Heredity also directly influences such unwelcome traits as brain damage, mental retardation, color blindness, and other characteristics that are very likely to have significant effects upon the types of behavior a child will be able to engage in.

Environment, it is universally held, is also a potent influence, affecting every aspect of development and behavior from birth to death. The specific language that we learn, our religious and cultural values, many personality traits—all are influenced by environmental factors. Moreover, it has been suggested that such basic traits as intelligence, perseverance, and even creativity are largely influenced by environmental factors, including the parents, the socioeconomic group, the schools, and the mass media.

The influences of heredity and environment, it is generally agreed, interact. This means the behavior observed is the result of the combined effect of hereditary background and past or current environmental experience. It is generally believed, for example, that the relative amounts of each influence cannot be separated by percentage. Each influence may affect the other to produce a result that differs from a simple summation of the two influences.

Animal Behavior

A related area of investigation in developmental psychology is ethology, the study of how animals behave in their natural habitats. Evidence gathered by researchers such as Konrad Lorenz and Urie Bronfenbrenner through naturalistic observation indicates that evolutionary processes modify both the physical and behavioral attributes of organisms. The process may be viewed as a reciprocal one, in which the developing person and environment influence each other over time. These findings better help us appreciate the relative influences of heredity and environment in human development.

Evolutionary adjustments include the development of physical traits such as camouflage coloration, thick fur for warmth, and the development of a thumb that works in opposition to the other fingers of the hand. Perhaps the most dramatic example of a species' adjustment is the development of the human brain. The human brain has evolved into a structure that has tremendous capacity for sensory and motor functions, the translation of motivation and emotion, and a vast variety of learning skills.

It is particularly in their ability to learn that humans surpass all other organisms. The evolution of a highly elaborated brain with a massive cerebral cortex apparently enables humans to demonstrate advanced thinking, learning, and memory skills. Humans are especially distinguished from other species in their ability to depict the world symbolically by using language.

Theories of Development

There are seven classes of theoretical models stand out as significant contributors to the exploration of human development. Each class places emphasis on a different characteristic of the developmental process; thus, it is difficult to make comparative evaluations of their adequacy. In the remainder of this chapter, the basic assumptions of each class of theories will be briefly outlined, and some specific examples of theories representing each class will be provided. More complete discussions of the theories within each class and their contributions to our understanding of specific developmental phenomena will appear in subsequent chapters.

Maturational Theories

Maturational theories emphasize the active role played by the individual's biological systems in determining patterns of development. Some psychologists most notably Arnold Gesell (1880–1961) and his contemporary followers, Francis Ilg and Louise Bates Ames have emphasized that developmental changes are promoted by two conditions: (1) by the inherent predisposition of the organism to develop; and (2) by the spontaneous development of the neurological, muscular, and hormonal systems of the body that mediate motor and psychological capacities. In other words, a person's development in many different areas depends on the body's physical abilities, such as nervous system development, muscular development, and so on. For example, bowel and bladder control will emerge when the child's biological systems have developed to the level that the child can detect the need for waste evacuation and control the muscles of the anus and urethra. Training before this time is an exercise in futility.

Development, these theorists agree, may be inhibited by severe environmental deprivation (such as malnutrition or lack of stimulation), but follows its normal course when the individual is provided a minimum amount of environmental support. A child who does not learn to walk at the same period as other children may learn it later, when the environment is suitable and the child's motor abilities are ready (that is, sufficiently mature).

In a study reported by Arnold Gesell, one member of a set of twins was given training in stair climbing, while no such training was given to the second child in the twin pair. In spite of the training given to the one twin, both children mastered stair climbing at the same age. This observation emphasizes the importance of maturation in the development of early motor skills. Because of the emphasis placed on biological determinism by the maturational theorist, research undertaken within this theoretical framework often attempts to describe the normal pattern of growth, which is viewed as inherent in the human organism. Little effort is expended to explore the factors that accelerate or inhibit that growth, nor is there much effort to determine the specific mechanisms that trigger changes in the individual.

Behaviorism and Learning Theories

John B. Watson established a system for the study of behavior in which only the observable responses made by the subject were relevant. The system came to be known as behaviorism and was characterized in the beginning by an interest in the muscular movements and glandular responses of the subject. Behaviorists denied the concepts of "mind" and "consciousness" because a mind or consciousness could not be observed.

Behaviorists were interested only in observable phenomena. A strict behaviorist would not describe a person as "happy" because happiness is a state of mind, and a mind is not observable. Instead, the behaviorist might describe the person's smile or laugh, or some other observable response to a stimulus.

Although the system soon found much criticism, it did point out the possible futility of trying to describe nonobservable activities of the subject and helped psychology confront the ideas of stimulus control and determinism of behavior. Direct concern with the stimuli and consequent responses has become an important part of several psychological positions. These are salient in understanding the two types of conditioning often used to account for aspects of human development: classical (respondent) conditioning and operant (instrumental) conditioning.

Many theories share the common assumption that the significant changes we observe in the course of development can be attributed to learning. The principles that form the foundation of learning theories are discussed throughout this book, but here we will outline some of them briefly.

Learning theories differ in just how they explain the learning process and in the kinds of learning they emphasize as being the most important for development. However, all learning theories are similar in at least the following four ways:

1. *Emphasis on Behavior.* Because the mental phenomena of thinking and feeling cannot be directly observed or measured, learning theories do not emphasize their development. Learning theorists do emphasize the development of behavior that can be directly observed and measured, such as aggressive acts, speech, and motor responses.

2. *Anything Can Be Learned.* To the extent that an individual is physically capable of producing a behavior, any behavioral pattern can be learned if the appropriate environmental conditions exist. This assumption leads the learning theorist to reject the belief that development must occur by passing through an invariable sequence of distinct stages. It places those theorists in the position of assuming a continuity in the developmental process, with the potential available for many individual differences in patterns of development.

3. *Role of Reinforcement and a View of Humans as Passive.* Learning theorists emphasize the roles played by positive (reinforcing) and negative (punishing) consequences of behavior in the developmental process. Whether these reinforcements or punishments are externally administered or the individual engages in self-reinforcement or self-punishment, the learner is viewed as a passive participant in the developmental process. His or her behavior is shaped by the forces of the environment.

4. *Use of the Experimental Method.* In their attempts to understand the developmental process, learning theorists tend to invest the majority of their energy in undertaking empirical research in which environmental conditions are manipulated and

observations of the impact of those manipulations on behavior are made. It is assumed that the principles of behavioral change generated by those experiments are the same principles that govern behavioral changes during the natural course of development.

Classical Conditioning

Classical conditioning is a process in which an organism learns to respond in a particular way to a stimulus that previously did not produce the response. This stimulus, which was once "neutral," becomes response-producing because it is paired (or associated) with another stimulus that does produce the response.

Classical conditioning is also called respondent conditioning or Pavlovian conditioning. The term "respondent" implies that the learned response is elicited involuntarily from the subject rather than produced by the subject in a voluntary (or operant) manner.

The term "Pavlovian conditioning" gives credit to the Russian physiologist Ivan Pavlov (1849–1936), the first person to investigate classical conditioning extensively. Pavlov devoted over thirty years of his career to the study of this type of learning.

With classical conditioning, a stimulus that is originally neutral and comes to be response-producing is called a conditioned stimulus (abbreviated as CS). The stimulus that produces the response on the first trial and each trial thereafter is called the unconditioned stimulus (UCS). The response elicited by the UCS is called the unconditioned response (UCR). Eventually, the same type of response will occur at the presentation of the CS; this response is called the conditioned response (CR).

In his original investigation, Pavlov used dogs as subjects. He found that presentation of meat powder (UCS) would cause the dogs to salivate (UCR). Pavlov then paired the ringing of a bell (CS) with the presentation of meat powder. This pairing soon led the dogs to salivate at the sound of the bell (CR). The CR in this situation occurred in the first few trials, when the dogs turned their heads in an attempt to determine where the bell was located.

Operant (Instrumental) Conditioning

Instrumental conditioning is a learning process that involves changing the probability of a response by manipulating the consequences of that response. An instrumental response is defined most simply as a response that leads to a goal.

Instrumental conditioning is also called "operant" conditioning or Skinnerian conditioning. The term operant is used because instrumental responses are frequently operations upon the environment. The term "Skinnerian" gives credit to the work of B. F. Skinner, a leading investigator of the many principles of instrumental conditioning.

Instrumental conditioning is concerned with the acquisition and retention of instrumental responses as well as the elimination of undesirable responses. An instrumental response is a voluntary response made by an organism. These responses may be learned in a sequence (or chain of behavior) so that the end result is attainment of a desired goal.

Generally, instrumental conditioning occurs in situations where the actual delivery of a reinforcement depends upon the appropriate responses being made. This is called the contingency of the reinforcement upon the response.

Suppose, for example, a fourth-grader is told that he must show a certain number of "Excellents" on his report card before he will receive the new computer game he wants. This is a contingency situation. The attainments of "Excellent" grades comprise the instrumental responses, while the computer game is the reinforcement, since delivery of the game is contingent upon the successful completion of the task.

One learning theory of child development has been proposed by Sidney Bijou and Donald Baer. They suggest that an analysis of child development should begin with a description of the responses made by a child and the environmental conditions under which these responses were made. Subsequent analysis should list the ways in which responses are attached to new stimuli—and are detached from old ones—through the processes of respondent conditioning and extinction. This would also include listing the ways in which responses are strengthened or weakened through various reinforcement contingencies. Bijou and Baer believe that such an analysis yields a rather thorough account of the child's motor, perceptual, linguistic, intellectual, emotional, social, and motivational repertoires.

Albert Bandura has emphasized the role played by observational learning in the child's social and psychological development. His research on the development of aggression suggests that aggressive behavior can be learned by observing the aggressive behavior of others.

Cognitive Theories

The work of the Gestalt psychologists in perception, thinking, and problem solving foreshadowed the development of another school, known as cognitive psychology. Cognitive psychologists disagree with the main assumptions of behaviorism. They feel that stimulus-response theory cannot explain all behavior, because the mind plays an active role in processing information from the environment, thus influencing an individual's response.

The cognitive position emphasizes the mental processes that influence behavior. These include perception and interpretation of environmental events, belief systems, thinking, planning, problem solving, and other processes crucial to understanding the individual's responses to environmental events. One of the leading cognitive theoreticians was Jean Piaget, a Swiss developmental psychologist, who developed a highly original theory of the stages of intellectual, perceptual, and moral development, based on the development of a person's thinking processes.

More than 80 years ago the philosopher-psychologist John Dewey argued against behaviorist theory, because he felt that the attempt to categorize reality into "stimuli" and "responses" was a faulty endeavor. Dewey pointed out that there could not be a "pure stimulus," since the influence of any event on a living creature depends on that creature's perception and interpretation of the event. The same event is not the same when it is experienced by a different person, because each person brings unique feelings, motives, and thoughts to the event, and therefore interprets it in a unique fashion. This is the foundation principle of all cognitive theories.

Cognitive theorists emphasize the active role played by the child in his or her own development. The child is viewed by these theorists as continually striving to reduce uncertainty in his or her world, and in so doing to function more effectively in it. Through this effort, the child develops more efficient ways of exploring all aspects of the environment, thinking about experiences, and responding to the demands placed upon him or her.

There are numerous developmental psychologists whose viewpoints fall into the class of cognitive theories, but the work of Jean Piaget is the most prominent in the field. In subsequent chapters concerned with cognitive development as well as in the discussion of moral development in Chapter 19, the details of Piaget's theory will be described.

The Cognitive Theory of Jean Piaget

Piaget believed that development is stimulated by the inherent drive of humans to reduce the uncertainties that confront them and, in so doing, to adapt to their environment. This adaptation function remains a constant objective of development throughout life. However, the mechanisms used to adapt to the world change as a person has increasing interactions with the environment.

The Adaptive Structure—The Schema. The psychological structure that mediates a person's adaptation was called the schema by Piaget. He defined a schema as an organized system of actions. These actions may be overt motor behaviors, in which case they are called sensorimotor schemata, or they may be internalized, in which case they are called cognitive schemata. The schemata possessed by individuals constitute the basis for their understanding the world with which they have had contact and the basis for their understanding new experiences they may encounter.

For example, a six-month-old infant looks at his mother and listens to the sound of her voice. Both actions involve activity on the part of the child. It is this organized pattern of activity that constitutes the child's knowledge of his mother, his schema of mother. Because the schema is based on overt actions—eye movements and listening—the schema is sensorimotor.

A row of six checkers is placed in front of a child of eight. An adult spreads the row apart so that the checkers cover more space on the table, and then asks the child, "Are there more checkers now than before, fewer checkers now than before, or the same number of checkers now as before?" The child responds that there are the same number of checkers as before because none of the checkers were removed and none were added to the table. (A younger child might report that after the manipulation there are more checkers.) Taking away or adding elements to a group are both organized systems of action. Being able to engage mentally in those actions is fundamental to understanding the meaning of the concept of number and quantity. Thus, the understanding of the concept of number reflected in this child's response exemplifies the use of a cognitive schema.

The Process of Adaptation: Assimilation and Accommodation. An individual exposed to environmental stimulation will attempt to understand that experience, to adapt. Two processes allow this adaptation to take place. An individual who incorporates the experience into one of his or her schemata is said to have assimilated the experience. Sometimes, however, an experience is so incompatible with one's current understanding of the world that it cannot be directly assimilated, nor can the characteristics of the experience be distorted to allow a distorted form of it to be assimilated. Under this condition, the individual restructures his or her current system for understanding the world so as to adapt to the new experience. This process is called accommodation. It is the process of accommodation that leads the child to develop new and typically more adaptive schemata.

An eighteen-month-old child has a schema for animals that adults label "cat." Whenever a catlike object approaches, the child recognizes it and calls it "kitty." This assimilation process is applied to animals that are really cats, but on occasion to animals such as rabbits or dogs, which are novel to the child, are also assimilated into that schema. The properties of these animals are distorted in the thoughts of the child so that the uncertainty of this novel situation may be reduced.

At two years of age, the child described above is taken to the zoo, where she sees an elephant. This is a novel experience, one involving a stimulus so different from the schemata she possesses that she must create a new schema within which to incorporate the experience. This change on the part of the child represents a form of accommodation.

An infant learns to suck effectively at her mother's breast. Her pattern of sucking defines for her the concept of the breast. Later the child finds her hand in her mouth, but discovers that the pattern of sucking used with the breast works well with the hand. She changes her sucking response to adapt to this new object. This accommodation of the sucking response is not only adaptive, but also results in the subsequent discrimination of two objects: hands and breasts.

Piaget's Stages of Development. According to Piaget, children's experiences of uncertainty and their attempts to adapt their understanding of the world in order to reduce those uncertainties result in systematic progress through four stages of development. Each stage evolves from the experiences that the capacities of the child allow in the preceding stage. Progress through these stages is reflected not only in the child's intellectual functioning, but also in his or her language capacities and social and emotional development. The four stages are:

1. The *sensorimotor stage*, in which the child's understanding of the world is contained totally in the child's sensory and motor interactions with it, and the child's schemata are all organized systems of overt behavior

2. The *preoperational stage*, in which the child can symbolize sensorimotor schemata and, in so doing, can think about those schemata without actually engaging in the sensorimotor activity

3. The *concrete operational stage*, in which cognitive operations develop to allow logical thinking about experiences that are happening in the here and now

4. The *formal operational stage*, in which cognitive operations develop that allow the individual to think about abstract problems

A detailed discussion of each stage of development can be found in Chapters 8, 12, 17, and 21.

Other Cognitive Theories

Although Piaget's theory of human development has had the greatest impact on psychology, other theories share his basic assumptions concerning the active role played by the child in development and the inherent forces that motivate the child to reduce uncertainty in the world and adapt effectively to it. Some theorists, however, do not agree with Piaget's description of the processes that underlie developmental changes or with his assumption that one must progress through an invariable series of unique stages in the course of development.

Jerome Kagan suggests that cognitive development is a reflection of the child's acquisition of better "executive capabilities" to organize and direct the use of cognitive skills, such as attention, memory, hypothesis generation, and the evaluation of hypotheses. (See Chapter 17 for a complete discussion.)

Unlike Piaget, in his all-encompassing theory, some cognitive theorists restrict their discussion of development to only one domain: cognition, social development, or language acquisition. *Lawrence Kohlberg,* for example, has emphasized the role played by cognition in the development of the child's moral reasoning. (See Chapters 15 and 19 for a complete discussion of Kohlberg's work.)

Humanistic Psychologists

At midcentury, when behaviorism and psychoanalysis were the two major forces dominating American psychology, a new movement came into existence, which was referred to as the third force. This term applies to humanistic psychology, which emphasizes the study of the individual as a whole person rather than just sensations, reflexes, thinking processes, or habits. The individual under study is looked at as a total integrated person, unique and motivated to fulfill his or her potential for creativity, dignity and self-worth—to become what humanists call self-actualizing. In contrast to the study of behavior, this approach emphasizes a person's feelings and self-awareness.

Psychoanalytic Theories

Psychoanalytic theories, derived from the work of *Sigmund Freud* (1856–1939), address primarily the emotional development of the child. Little attention is paid to the child's cognitive, perceptual, linguistic, or behavioral development.

Freud believed that personality has three basic components: the *id,* the *ego,* and the *superego.* The personality is motivated throughout life by the fundamental drive called *libido.* Libido provides psychic energy that is devoted to the achievement of goals. The essential feature of libido is that it has a sexual quality that, because of social restrictions, cannot be expressed directly. Instead, libido has to find release in substitute or indirect fashion. These expressions begin in the first year of life, but change radically as the child matures and passes through what Freud called the psychosexual stages.

The Dynamics of Development

Psychoanalytic theories view the process of development as a dynamic interaction between environmental forces and the needs and drives inherent in the individual. The former is embodied in societal norms that establish parameters within which those drives may be expressed and the needs satisfied. The individual plays a passive role in this interaction.

Freud's Stages of Development

One of the identifying characteristics of classic psychoanalytic theory as it was articulated by Sigmund Freud is the belief that before reaching maturity, children pass through five stages of psychosexual development. Each stage is defined by the dominant source of gratification for the instinctual needs of the individual. The end product of development, as viewed from this theoretical position, is dependent upon the extent to which that gratification is frustrated by factors in the child's environment and by the responses of the child to the frustrations encountered.

Oral Stage. During the first year of life, the child receives its pleasure from sucking. An infant whose need to suck is satisfied and who obtains from that sucking experience the pleasurable sensations that accompany the satisfaction of hunger develops a trust in the environment as a source of need satisfaction. Those infants who are frustrated in the satisfaction of this need may continue to seek pleasure through the use of their mouth. Psychoanalysts, for example, would postulate that smoking, overeating, and nail biting may be behaviors whose origins are found in the lack of early oral gratification.

Anal Stage. The second stage of development is the anal stage, during which the center for pleasurable experiences is fixed on the anal region of the body. The child receives pleasure from the ability to control his or her bowels and bladder. Much of this pleasure derives from the response of parents to the child's newly acquired skill; however, sensory pleasure is also derived from the acts themselves. Persons who are frustrated in their quest to derive pleasure during the anal stage of development may continue to seek pleasure by controlling their own behavior or the behavior of others. They are thought to be compulsive and/or domineering.

Phallic Stage. During the phallic stage of development, the child's source of pleasure centers on the genitals, and according to Freud, the child's interests focus on sexual pleasure. During this period of development, there is an exaggerated focus on the mother as a love object, by both girls and boys. The frustrations that stem from this mother-child relationship are seen by psychoanalytic theorists as the origins of sex-role identification and moral development. (See the discussion of these frustrations in Chapter 15.)

Latency Stage. The intense conflicts of the phallic stage of development are followed, between the ages of five and twelve, by a calm period in which the intense needs for pleasure are suppressed. It is during the latency period that the child acquires the culturally valued skills and beliefs that will allow him or her to adapt to society.

Genital Stage. With the emergence of adolescence, the sexual drive is once again kindled. However, during adolescence the object of need satisfaction is not the mother but others in the society. The genital period ushers in the development of adult heterosexual relationships.

Defense Mechanisms of the Ego

Freud proposed that actions or events that offend the superego and do damage to one's self-image result in anxiety in the ego. To keep this damage and anxiety to a minimum, a person develops and uses ego defense mechanisms as a way of protecting the self. Some examples of ego defense mechanisms follow.

Repression. The most common defense mechanism is repression. In its most basic form, repression simply means forgetting. Whatever was once part of consciousness, but no longer is, has been repressed. We repress both feelings and situations, thoughts and occasions, using as our guiding principle the reduction of anxiety. Whatever causes us pain or provokes anxiety becomes a likely candidate for repression and is then no longer accessible to our conscious mind.

Reaction Formation. Reaction formation is a defense mechanism that is often difficult to recognize. Simply stated, this mechanism involves acting in a way that is in total contradiction to the way one unconsciously feels. While the individual is acting in this way, however, he or she is not aware of unconscious feelings and is therefore unable to recognize the mechanism at work.

Let us say, for example, that a woman is experiencing some unconscious hostility toward a friend but that her ideas about what friendship should be preclude such feelings from her conscious mind. "If you like your friends, you will never feel angry at them," the unrealistic expectation goes. One way of handling this unconsciously is to react to this anger. She may, for instance, feel compelled to buy her friend an expensive present, one well beyond her means–a present given not for love, but rather for self-protection. The giving of the present is a direct reaction to the unrecognized feelings of hostility.

Projection. Projection, another common defense mechanism, is the process of attributing to another person or to an object in the outside world, feelings that really come from within oneself. A person who feels that no one likes him, for example, may be projecting internal feelings of hostility onto all the people around him. Projection protects the ego by attributing to others the unacceptable feelings of the self. For instance, paranoid individuals tend to project their hostility onto others, imagining a conspiracy of forces against them, or against someone else.

Intellectualization. Intellectualization is a defense mechanism that makes itself felt when a person understands something intellectually but not emotionally. Examples of intellectualization include describing a person in technical, non-emotional language or relating to others through planned, impersonal techniques rather than through spontaneous and genuine feelings. Intellectualization is a means of avoiding the reality of another person by seeing him or her as an object.

Denial. The defense mechanism of denial is sometimes confused with repression and reaction formation because of the similarities among the three. Denial, in its most general form, is when the conscious mind denies feelings from within or situations from without that prove threatening to the ego. A husband, for example, may fail to recognize that his wife is experiencing hostile feelings toward him, thereby blocking out of his perceptual world an important part of their relationship. Parents are sometimes prone to deny their children's angry feelings toward them. Sexual feelings are a class of feelings that are often subject to denial.

Regression. Regression means "returning," particularly returning to an earlier stage of emotional or intellectual development. When a person becomes overpowered by feelings he or she can no longer handle, one way of dealing with the situation is to return to an earlier level of development in which one was able either to avoid confronting such feelings or to feel comfortable with them. Older children often resort to "baby talk" following the birth of another child in their family. Direct attack toward the new baby would be inappropriate, but the regressive behavior may attract the parents' attention and thus help the older children maintain their feelings of self-worth.

Rationalization. When a person uses rationalization, he or she develops a false explanation for actions, or attributes false, overly favorable motives to explain behavior. Commonly referred to as sour grapes, rationalization is illustrated by the famous Aesop fable of the fox who tried repeatedly, without success, to get at a bunch of grapes. Failing time and again, the fox finally gave up his attempts, rationalizing that the grapes looked sour anyway. The person who rationalizes his or her problems defends himself or herself from real feelings by creating a false version of motives and causality.

Displacement. Displacement involves the shifting (or replacement) of the object of a feeling or drive. A man employed in a personnel department, for example, may take out some of the aggression he feels toward his supervisor by displacing it onto clients who are safer objects for his wrath. In general, displacement involves shifting to a safe object feelings unconsciously held toward a more dangerous or threatening object. Since there is an imbalance of power in many interpersonal relationships, the use of displacement can make the person in the lesser-power position a victim of the other. We see this all the time when one person says to the other, "Why are you always picking on me for things I didn't do?"

Compensation. Someone who feels deficient in some way may defend himself or herself by emphasizing some behavior that "covers up" the deficiency. This is called compensation, and it may take two forms. Using direct compensation, the person will emphasize behaviors that are specifically meant as contrasts to the felt deficiencies. Using indirect compensation, the person will stress behaviors that are not associated with the felt deficiency, but rather are substitutes.

Introjection and Identification. Introjection and identification are two mechanisms that are often confused with each other. Introjection occurs when an individual's personality incorporates part of another person. For example, the student may introject a part of the teacher, that is, take on some of the teacher's values and beliefs–which can be educationally productive. Freud initially used introjection to explain the learning of values by the child. A child introjects–takes inside–its parents' system of values, and they become a part of the child.

Identification is the process whereby an individual confuses his or her identity with the identity of someone else. With identification, the person may either extend identity into someone else, borrow identity from someone else, or fuse his or her identity with someone else's. A common form of identification is identification with the aggressor, where an individual exposed to an aggressive, threatening person feels endangered, and therefore begins to act and feel as aggressive as the threatening person.

While all of us at times make use of these various defense mechanisms, they do present difficulties for us (especially when used excessively) in living healthy lives. Defense mechanisms distort perception and block off part of the world. Theoretically, the better-adjusted an individual is, the less need he or she will have for defense mechanisms. But even the best-adjusted person will at times resort to using them.

Adler's Individual Psychology

Some theorists have accepted many of the fundamental principles of classic psychoanalytic theory but placed less stress on the stages of psychosexual development as being fundamental to human development. Alfred Adler (1870–1937), for example, stressed social motivation rather than strictly sexual drives. Adler's view is sometimes referred to as individual psychology.

For Adler, the key to personality is a striving for superiority. Every child is born helpless, dependent on others, and, therefore, overwhelmed by feelings of inferiority that he or she must struggle to overcome the rest of his or her life. People do this by striving for superiority, which becomes a major motivation in a person's life. In the healthy individual, the striving for superiority is in accord with the needs of the society, and the person acquires such traits as courage, independence, and a healthy sense of ambition. If development is not normal, a person may grow up with feelings of inadequacy, implied by the term "inferiority complex."

The process by which a person overcomes these feelings of inferiority is called compensation, which plays a crucial role in personality development. For example, an individual who is constitutionally weak may compensate by developing the body, perhaps by studying karate. Or, a child who stutters may grow up to become an actor or singer.

According to Adler, each person has a unique lifestyle that enables him or her to compensate for inferiority feelings and to strive toward superiority. The style of life is formed very early in childhood, by the age of four or five, and is determined largely by one's experiences within the family. Adler pointed out that the position a child occupies in the family—in terms of birth order and chronological distance between siblings—influences his or her personality development and style of life. This factor is known as ordinal position.

Erik Erikson's Theory

Another prominent theorist is Erik Erikson (1902–), who postulated that the drives inherent in humans lead them to confront a series of personal conflicts in life. For Erikson, the personality of an individual is a reflection of the way in which each conflict is resolved. Although Erikson noted that the conflicts of life are never fully resolved, he suggested that the maximum potency for certain conflicts to influence personality development occur during the following age periods:

Age	Conflict
0–1 year	Trust vs. Mistrust (Can I or can I not trust others?)
1–2 years	Autonomy vs. Shame, Doubt (Can I do things by myself, or should I feel ashamed of my independence?)
3–4 years	Initiative vs. Guilt (Can I initiate roles for myself, or must I do only what others want me to do?)
Middle Childhood	Industry vs. Inferiority (Can I do some things well, or am I a failure?)
Adolescence	Identity vs. Identity Confusion (Do I know who I am, or am I confused about who I should be?)

Early Adult   Intimacy vs. Isolation (Can I intimately share myself with others, or must I remain alone?)

Adult   Generativity vs. Stagnation (Can I maintain my creative productivity, or must I become bored with life?)

Aging   Integrity vs. Despair (Do I feel good about the life I have lived, or am I in despair over the life that has passed me by?)

CHAPTER 2

Methods in Child Psychology

In many respects the methods of child psychology are similar to the methods employed in any psychological research. In this chapter we will see how independent, dependent, and other variables are used in the experimental method. We will also look at different types of psychological studies, including the longitudinal, cross-sectional, and combined studies. Finally, we will consider some practical and ethical issues in research.

Independent and Dependent Variables

Basically, a research psychologist is interested in the relationship between two variables—for example, between the amount of praise a child receives from the parent and the extent to which the child feels good about himself or herself. To study this relationship, the psychologist observes changes in one variable, called the *independent variable,* and deduces how these changes in the independent variable are associated with changes in the second variable, called the *dependent variable.*

In a typical research study, for example, a psychologist might identify two groups of children, one whose parents provide much praise, and a second whose parents rarely praise their children. The identification of these two groups would be accomplished as the psychologist uses the method of observing systematic changes in the independent variable, the amount of praise.

The psychologist would then measure how the children in each group feel about themselves; this is a measurement of the dependent variable. Appropriate analyses could then be made to determine how changes in the amount of praise given to a child are associated with different feelings experienced by the child. In studies of this sort, it has been observed that children who receive much praise from their parents tend to feel better about themselves than those who receive little praise.

Experimental Methods of Studying Development

In experimental studies of development, there are two methods of manipulating the independent variable: by the correlational method and by the strictly experimental method.

Correlational Method

In some research studies, subjects are assigned to groups on the basis of characteristics they possessed prior to being included in the research; the investigator does not systematically change anything about the environment or the experiences of the subjects. When this procedure is employed, the independent variable is said to be varied using a correlational method.

In the research study mentioned above, children were assigned either to a high-parental-praise group or a low-parental-praise group on the basis of how much praise the experimenter observed the parents giving to the children. The amount of parental praise given to a child was a characteristic possessed by that child prior to the research. Thus, the independent variable was manipulated using a correlational method.

Drawing Conclusions Using a Correlational Method

When a correlational method is used to change an independent variable, and the psychologist finds that the manipulation of that independent variable results in corresponding changes in the dependent variable, it is legitimate for the investigator to conclude only that changes in the independent variable are associated with changes in the dependent variable. It is not legitimate to conclude that changes in the independent variable cause changes in the dependent variable.

Why is this restriction necessary? When a correlational method of changing an independent variable is used, two explanations of the relationship observed—in addition to the independent variable causing the change in the dependent variable—may be postulated.

First, it must be considered that changes in the dependent variable may cause a change in the independent variable rather than vice versa. In the two examples given above, it might be that children who feel good about themselves tend to behave in a manner that stimulates their parents to praise them. In this case, praise does not cause the child to feel good about himself or herself; instead, the good feeling causes the praise.

It must also be noted that a third variable might cause simultaneous changes in both the independent and dependent variables. For instance, looking again at the examples above, we might find that children who are bright and attractive tend to feel good about themselves because of their performance in social and academic situations. Furthermore, parents tend to praise children for their attractiveness and intelligence. In this case, the intelligence and attractiveness of the child causes both the parental praise and the positive self-concept. Changes in the independent variable do not cause the corresponding changes in the dependent variable, nor do changes in the dependent variable cause changes in the independent variable.

Experimental Method

When an independent variable is varied experimentally, subjects are assigned to groups at random, and the experimenter systematically introduces a change in the experiences or environment of the children in at least one group. There is nothing about the individual subject that determines the group into which he or she will be assigned. Everyone has an equal opportunity of being in any group. This is the basis of the experimental method, probably the most commonly employed method in psychological research.

Refer to the first example above. Instead of manipulating the independent variable of parental praise using a correlational method, we might change the method of manipulating the independent variable as follows. Forty children in a fifth-grade class all receive the permission of their parents to participate in an experiment and themselves agree to do so. Twenty red balls and twenty white balls are put into a box, and each child draws a ball. The parents of children who draw white balls are contacted and asked to make a special effort to praise their children daily during the next month.

The parents of children who draw red balls are asked to refrain from commenting on their children's praiseworthy actions during this same month. At the end of the month, the children's feelings about themselves are measured. It is found that the children who have been praised by their parents feel better about themselves than the children who received limited amounts of praise.

In this experiment, children are not assigned to low-praise

and high-praise groups on the basis of the amount of praise they received before the experiment or on the basis of any other characteristic they possessed before the experiment. Each child has an equal opportunity to be assigned to either group. Thus, the independent variable is manipulated using an experimental method.

Drawing Conclusions Using an Experimental Method

When an experimental method is effectively used to manipulate an independent variable, the psychologist can conclude that changes in the independent variable cause changes in the dependent variable.

Confounded Independent Variables

Unfortunately, a problem can arise in the manipulation of an independent variable that results in a psychologist being unable to determine clearly what caused changes in the dependent variable. That problem stems from the confounding of variables. Two variables are confounded when the manipulation of one variable is systematically associated with changes in the second variable. When the manipulation of an independent variable is confounded with the manipulation of other variables, it is impossible to determine which of the variables causes the observed changes in the dependent variable.

Let us say that each time the instructed parents praise their children in the experiment above, they also suggest that the child go to the park to play. Children whose parents do not praise them are not sent to the park. The variables of parental praise and park recreation have now been confounded. We cannot tell from this experiment whether it is the parental praise that causes the increase in the positive self-concept of the children or the fact that they are able to make many social contacts with other children at the park—contacts not made by the children in the low-parental-praise group.

Multiple Independent Variables: Factorial Design

In some research studies, psychologists are interested simultaneously in examining the relationship between more than one independent variable and some dependent variable. As noted in the preceding section, it is important that the independent variables not be confounded when they are simultaneously manipulated. The unconfounded simultaneous manipulation of more than one independent variable can be accomplished by first forming groups of subjects that allow one independent variable to be manipulated, subdividing each of those groups, and, for each of the original groups, manipulating a second independent variable across the subgroups. This experimental design is referred to as a factorial design.

Suppose a psychologist is interested in studying simultaneously the relationship between a child's age and intelligence. These are two independent variables. He will measure intelligence through the child's performance on a learning task, the dependent variable. The experimenter first selects children in three age groups: six-year-olds, ten-year-olds, and fourteen-year-olds. He randomly assigns half the children in each group to a subgroup whose members will receive candy each time they make a correct response on a test, and assigns the other half in each age group to a subgroup that will not receive candy. The design used in this experiment is a factorial design.

Note that in a factorial design, the two independent variables are not confounded. In each group used to manipulate one independent variable are represented all levels of the second independent variable. Changes in one independent variable do not correspond systematically to changes in the second independent variable. Because the simultaneously manipulated independent variables in a factorial design are not confounded, it is possible, through appropriate analyses of the results from such a study, to examine separately the relationship between each independent variable and the dependent variable.

In addition, the unconfounded simultaneous manipulation of more than one independent variable allows a psychologist to determine how changes occur in the relationship between one independent variable and a dependent variable as changes are made in a second independent variable. When the effect of one independent variable is dependent upon the quality of a second independent variable, the two are said to interact.

Refer to the example above. Assume that when six-year-olds are given candy for correct answers they tend to learn faster than when no candy is given. In contrast, the receipt of candy for correct answers has little effect on the learning of fourteen-year-olds. The variables of age and receipt of candy rewards interact in determining the speed of learning. Only by using a factorial design that allows the unconfounded simultaneous manipulation of the two variables could a psychologist determine that the relationship between one independent variable (receipt or nonreceipt of candy) and the dependent variable (performance on the learning test) changes with changes in a second independent variable, age.

Other Psychological Methodologies

Some psychological information cannot be obtained by using the experimental method. Psychologists also use techniques such as naturalistic observation, clinical case histories, and testing and surveying as means for gathering information. These techniques may not be as precise as the experimental method but they do give psychologists additional ways in which to gather and analyze information.

Naturalistic Observation

Naturalistic observations are careful, unbiased examinations of events that occur in a basically unmanipulated environment.

The psychologist does not control the circumstances in order to force or select a particular response from a subject. Instead, the psychologist conscientiously records whatever the subject does. For example, a psychologist who is interested in studying children at play might observe several children together in a playroom. Using a one-way mirror (or perhaps videotape equipment), the psychologist could then observe and record the children's activity without making her or his presence known. In this way, the psychologist could minimize the influence an "adult presence" might have on the children. The children could do as they wish, unless for some reason the psychologist halted their play.

Clinical Case Histories

The primary purpose of a counseling or clinical psychologist is to help people overcome their personal problems. In the course of treating someone, a counseling or clinical psychologist may make a record of problems, insights, and techniques that were important in the treatment. Such reports are called clinical case histories. They are often studied by other psychologists because they may expose some factor that has general significance for the understanding of behavior. Usually the information presented for the first time in a clinical case history is subject to skeptical questioning; more controlled investigation may take place before a clinical case history is accepted by other psychologists.

Suppose a five-year-old girl is brought to a psychologist because of her very aggressive behavior patterns, which have alarmed her parents and teachers. The psychologist suspects that the aggressive behavior is the result of frustration brought about by a recent change in the family's attitude toward the girl. To summarize and clarify this belief, the psychologist writes a clinical case history, describing in detail the girl's aggressive behavior and her family's frustrating situation.

At the conclusion of the case history, the psychologist may suggest that the problem can be lessened with appropriate alterations of the family's behavior. However, the psychologist might also want to investigate the frustration-aggression relationship in a more systematic manner. Both the case history and investigational records might be useful to psychologists for future reference in the treatment of other people with similar problems.

Tests and Surveys

Psychologists often obtain information about behavior by asking the subjects to respond to specially designed tests, surveys, interviews, and questionnaires. All of these provide stimuli to which the subjects react. Psychologists study these reactions in an attempt to find out more about a particular subject's or group's behavior.

A test or survey technique has been designed to investigate almost every aspect of behavior, including personality, intelligence, attitudes, and aptitudes. Tests and surveys have basically two advantages: they allow for the rapid collection of information, and they give the psychologist the ability to compare a subject's responses with those of thousands of others who have taken the same test. (One disadvantage of tests and surveys is that a subject may purposely give misleading responses.)

The analysis of the information thus obtained is accomplished by the use of statistics. Statistics is the discipline that deals with the collection, analysis, interpretation, and presentation of numerical data.

Age as a Variable

Child psychologists are often interested in one particular

independent variable—age. Age, by its very nature, is an independent variable that must be varied using a correlational method. A person brings to the research the age he or she possesses; a psychologist cannot arbitrarily assign an age to a person. Because age is an independent variable manipulated using a correlational method, one cannot conclude from research concerned with age that age alone causes change in a dependent variable. More likely, age is confounded with some other variable that causes the change in the dependent variable. One interest of child psychologists is to discover psychological processes in which the development accompanies age changes and is also the direct cause of changes in the dependent variable.

Older children seem to be much more concerned about the impact of their behavior on others than are younger children. One might conclude that age causes this change in attitude. However, as children grow older, there is typically a change in their ability to understand how others view situations. This change in the ability to understand how someone else feels is confounded with the change in age and is probably the direct cause of the observed changes in attitude. If an individual's ability to take the role of another person did not develop, concerns about the impact of one's behavior on others probably would not change, despite changes in age.

In addition to the aforementioned concern, there are at least four questions child psychologists ask about age:

1. What behavioral changes accompany changes in age? A psychologist is interested in how children's play activities change as they grow. The psychologist observes a large number of children of different ages and records the number of different children with whom each of the subjects interacts during the course of a day at nursery school. This psychologist could describe the play characteristics of children at different ages.

2. How do other independent variables interact with age to influence changes in a dependent variable? A psychologist is interested in determining how children at different ages will react to pressures from their peers. It is found that fifteen-year-olds have a greater tendency than do ten-year-olds to change their answers to questions in order to conform to the answers given by peers. Peer pressure has a different effect on the behavior of ten- and fifteen-year olds. Peer pressure interacts with age to influence conformity.

3. What effect do experiences at one age have on the behavior of children at a later age? A psychologist is interested in understanding the impact of living without a father on the social development of adolescent girls. The psychologist discovers that girls raised in homes where the father has died early in the child's life tend to be more uncomfortable around men than girls who grew up with fathers in the home.

4. How are characteristics possessed by a child at one age related to characteristics that the individual may exhibit at a later age? A psychologist may be interested in determining whether or not children who are said to be hyperactive when they are six and seven years old continue to exhibit hyperactive characteristics when they are twelve and thirteen years old. The investigator finds that the children identified as hyperactive by their first-grade teachers are also identified as hyperactive by their teachers six years later.

There are three primary methods used to manipulate age as an independent variable: the longitudinal method, the cross-sectional method, and a combination of the two.

The Longitudinal Method

In some studies, the same child or group of children is observed at different ages. This method of recording behavior at different ages is called the longitudinal method. The longitudinal method may be used to answer any of the questions posed by psychologists concerning age as an independent variable.

Starting at birth, each individual in a famous research study at the Fels Research Institute was tested at intervals throughout childhood and adolescence. Among other things, the researchers observed the level of "affectional dependency": the extent to which the individuals sought support from adults. It was observed that children who exhibited high levels of affectional dependency in the preschool ages were the same ones who exhibited affectional dependency later in childhood and on into early adolescence. This consistency was more marked for girls than for boys.

Advantages of the Longitudinal Method

While the longitudinal method may be used to answer any question concerned with child psychology, its unique quality is its ability to allow a psychologist to answer questions about the evolution of behavior within an individual, to examine the stability of behavior for an individual as he or she grows older, and to examine the impact of early events in a child's life on subsequent behavior patterns.

Disadvantages of the Longitudinal Method

First, because of the length of time often required by a study using the longitudinal method, there may be a problem of expense. An institution or an individual involved in a lengthy longitudinal study must be financed for the duration, whatever time period it will take to complete the study.

The second and more critical problem, however, is that of subject loss. Our society is mobile, and the initial group of individuals included in the longitudinal study may include persons who will move and be difficult to observe at later times in the study. This loss of subjects raises the question of whether the sample of subjects observed at later ages is similar to the original group, or whether it contains only those individuals who are stable in their movements.

A third problem centers on changes that may occur in the way variables are measured. As time passes, innovations are made in measuring techniques. Can the measurements taken using one technique be compared with those made using a second technique?

A fourth problem centers on the planning of the study. The questions that are of interest to psychologists at one time in history may be of little interest ten years later. When the longitudinal method is used, researchers must carefully plan their work to insure that the questions the study is designed to answer will be of interest when the study is completed.

Fifth, and finally, there is the question of whether the results from longitudinal studies can provide information applicable to understanding development in a world quite different from the world in which the individuals observed in the study grew up. For example, can the development of children raised between 1950 and 1965 be compared to the development of children who are just now being born?

Case Histories

One particular form of longitudinal study is the case history. In the case history only one individual is observed over a length of time. The problems characteristic of the longitudinal study also apply to the case-history method. However, an additional problem is posed by the use of a single individual: it is often difficult in a case history to differentiate which patterns of development can be generalized to other individuals and which patterns are unique to the individual being studied.

A variety of contributions have been made to the study of psychology by case-history reports. Charles Darwin undertook a systematic observation of his nephew and reported that developmental case history in a baby biography. It was one of the first systematic accounts of child development, and it stimulated the empirical study of child psychology. Another observer of individual cases was Sigmund Freud. His case histories of adults and children led to the development of a general theory of human psychosexual development. More recently, Jean Piaget reported his observations of the cognitive development of his own three children. These case histories were the foundation stones for his extensive theory of cognitive development.

Cross-Sectional Method

A second method of manipulating age as an independent variable is to select different groups of individuals representing each of the ages of interest. This method is called cross-sectional.

For example, a psychologist is interested in examining the ability of children to be classically conditioned. The psychologist selects a group of infants who are two months old, a second group of infants who are six months old, and a final group of infants who are one year old. The experimenter attempts to condition each group to respond with an eye blink to the sound of a bell. He finds that the two-month-olds do not respond to the conditioning at all and that the six-month- and one-year-olds exhibit conditioning, but the one-year-olds do so after significantly fewer presentations of the conditioned and unconditioned stimulus pair. The comparison of classical conditioning potential across ages was made using a cross-sectional method.

Advantages of the Cross-Sectional Method

The advantage of the cross-sectional method is that the psychologist can collect data quickly, without having to wait for children to pass through all of the ages of interest. This method can be used effectively to study questions concerning behaviors that characterize different age groups, and questions concerning changes in the relationships among age, a second independent variable.

Disadvantages of the Cross-Sectional Method

The cross-sectional method cannot be used to examine the stability of behavior over time, nor to examine the impact of early experiences on subsequent behavior. These questions cannot be examined because the same child is not observed at different ages; they can only be answered using the longitudinal method or a variation of it.

Normative Data

One specific use of the cross-sectional method for age comparison is to describe the developing child and to establish norms for development. This research is often called normative, or descriptive, research. A norm for development describes the average age at which a characteristic is seen to develop and the variability in the developmental emergence of that characteristic.

For example, by recording the weight of many newborn infants, it has been found that while weights differ by several pounds across newborns, the mean weight across newborns is 7 1/2 pounds, and approximately 90 percent range in birth weight from 4 pounds to 8 pounds. Similar measures of weight at one year of age reveal that the average child weighs approximately 22 3/4 pounds and that approximately 90 percent of children weigh between 19 pounds and 26 1/2 pounds. The research used to establish this figure is called normative research. The description of the average weight of children at different ages and a description of the variations in children's weight at each age is called the developmental norm for weight.

A now-classic study reported by M. E. Smith in 1926 has served for years as the basis for describing the development of vocabulary in children. In the collection of that normative data,

**Table 2.1 Average Size and Change in Size of Vocabularies
of Children at Various Ages**

Age Year–Month	Vocabulary Size	% Change in Size
8	0	0
10	1	1
1–0	3	2
1–6	22	19
2–0	272	250
2–6	446	174
3–0	896	450
3–6	1222	326
4–0	1540	318
4–6	1870	330
5–0	2072	202
5–6	2289	217
6–0	2562	273

Source: M.E. Smith, "An Investigation of the Development of the Sentence and the Extent of Vocabulary in Young Children," *University of Iowa Studies in Child Welfare, 5: 3, 1926.*

Smith tested 278 children representing age groups ranging from eight months to six years of age and estimated each child's total vocabulary from his or her ability to understand the meaning of a selected group of 203 words. The average vocabulary size for each age group comprises a norm for that age group. (See Table 2.1.)

Uses of Normative Data. First, it enables child psychologists to obtain a picture of a point in a child's life when dramatic changes take place. Note, for example, the dramatic increase in vocabulary from ages two and one-half to five years and the relatively smaller increases occurring before and after that period. By knowing these important periods of development, the child psychologist can assess more easily when to study the development of those characteristics.

Professional child psychologists, pediatricians, and child specialists have a second use for normative data: It serves as a scale against which to assess whether a child is developing in a normal way. If, for example, a child is not speaking at age one and one-half, a psychologist would not be overly alarmed. However, as Table 2.1 indicates, no speech in a four-year-old child is a very unusual situation and requires some concern and treatment.

A third use of normative data is to provide parents with guidelines for observing their own children. Normative data allows parents to anticipate the behaviors they can expect from their children at different ages.

Limitations of Normative Data. One problem with normative data is that it describes for us only the sequence of development and the time at which behavioral characteristics emerge. The results of normative research cannot define the processes that underlie the emerging development, improve our understanding of why those behaviors emerge, or help us to understand the reasons for the variations in development that occur from one child to another.

A second problem in using normative data is that a child's development may be compared to norms that have been established from data collected by observing children representing a group of people very different from the group of which the child is a member. For example, normative data collected from children in the 1940s might produce norms of development that are not appropriate for children born in the 1970s. Similarly, norms based on data collected from middle-class children may not be appropriate to use in examining the development of children who are born and raised in a lower socioeconomic environment. Thus, it is important for users of normative data to be aware of the characteristics of the population on which the norm is based.

Cross-Sectional/Longitudinal Method

A compromise between the longitudinal and cross-sectional designs of examining age as an independent variable is found in the cross-sectional/longitudinal method. In this research design a psychologist interested in comparing children at three ages, A, B, and C, would observe one group of children at ages A and B and a second group of children at ages B and C.

For example, a psychologist is interested in changes in the patterns of moral development exhibited by children at ages six, eight, and ten. Rather than comparing the moral judgment of three separate groups of children representing those three ages (a cross-sectional design), or observing the same group of children over a four-year span (a longitudinal design), the psychologist observed one group of children who were six years old and another group consisting of eight-year-olds. Two years later, she reobserved the groups, who were now eight and ten years old respectively. This is a cross-sectional/longitudinal design.

Advantages of the Cross-Sectional/Longitudinal Design

First, the design allows one to compare the patterns of behavior for different age groups just as could be done in a cross-sectional or a longitudinal design.

A second advantage is that it is possible to draw conclusions concerning the continuity of behavior from one period to another.

And third, from a practical standpoint, the design allows one to collect data in half the time required for a full-scale longitudinal design; thus, it saves money and alleviates the problems resulting from subject attrition.

Disadvantages of the Cross-Sectional/Longitudinal Design

The major difficulty with the design occurs if one finds that the children observed initially at age B differ from the children observed on the second occasion at age B. If this situation should arise, it suggests that the testing process itself had an influence on their development or that some environmental event occurred in the interval between testings that might account for a general change in behavior for children of the age observed in the study. Of course, either of these occurrences would play havoc with the interpretation of the longitudinal data.

Where Research Will Be Undertaken

Another important consideration in the design of research in child psychology is a determination of where the research will be undertaken. Three types of location are most often chosen: a laboratory, the natural environment of the child, or a cross-cultural setting.

Laboratory Research

Laboratory research is defined as research undertaken in the controlled environment of a laboratory or similar facility.

Advantage of Laboratory Research

The major advantage of research undertaken in a laboratory is that the experimenter has maximum control over the variables that are manipulated in the research. Thus, the relationships observed in laboratory-based research are often the easiest to interpret.

Disadvantage of Laboratory Research

The major disadvantage of research conducted in a laboratory setting is that the results observed may not be applicable to predicting or explaining behavior that takes place outside the laboratory. This lack of generalization may be due to the fact that often a different set of demands is placed upon a person in a laboratory setting than is placed upon a person in the outside environment. For example, children in a laboratory may be forced to choose which of two pictures they prefer to view; in the outside environment, such choices are seldom demanded, and when choices must be made, they often involve a greater number of alternatives.

Natural Environmental Settings

Some research in child psychology, as we pointed out above, is undertaken in the natural environment of the child. Children are observed during their spontaneous classroom or playground activities or during their interchanges with parents or siblings.

Advantage of Natural Setting Research

The advantage of research undertaken in the child's natural environment is that the results obtained cannot be attributed to the artificiality of the experimental laboratory. Those principles of child psychology that are derived from such research can be generalized to the day-to-day life of the child.

Disadvantage of Natural Setting Research

The major problem with research conducted in the natural setting is the control of extraneous variables. All too often, two or more variables are confounded with the independent variable in such research. Thus, the interpretation of research undertaken in a natural setting can sometimes be difficult.

Cross-Cultural Research Settings

Cross-cultural research settings are used basically for two purposes. First, psychologists, anthropologists, and sociologists may simply be interested in describing the behavior patterns of individuals from various cultures. Secondly, a cross-cultural research setting may provide investigators with a unique method for observing an independent variable. If two cultural groups differ in some characteristic (the independent variable), a psychologist could compare individuals from the two cultures and assess the relationship between that characteristic and some dependent variable.

Advantage of Cross-Cultural Research Settings

The primary advantage of cross-cultural research settings is that they provide the opportunity to observe variations in some independent variables that might be impossible to manipulate within a single culture. For example, suppose the independent variable of interest was the presence or absence of puberty rites. It would be difficult, if not impossible, to manipulate such a variable within a single culture. However, by comparing individuals from two cultures similar in every respect except that one utilized puberty rites and the other did not, one could reach tentative conclusions about the effects of puberty rites.

Disadvantages of Cross-Cultural Research Settings

The primary problem with cross-cultural research is that its very nature requires the use of a correlational method for manipulating an independent variable; thus, conclusions regarding causation cannot be made. Furthermore, it is very difficult to equate two cultures with regard to all but one characteristic. Thus, the potential for confounding independent variables is extreme.

The Ethics of Research

While an investigator must select appropriate methods to use in undertaking research in child psychology, an equally important consideration is that the research conform to ethical guidelines that insure that participants are not subjected to potentially harmful experiences or denied their human rights. Some of these rights are discussed here.

The Right of Consent

Before participating in research, individuals should have voluntarily given their consent to be used as subjects. In the case of children and others who may not be legally, intellectually, or emotionally able to provide that consent, parents or legal guardians must provide consent.

The Right to Be Informed

Research subjects have the right to be informed about experiences that may be encountered in the research. When an investigation is undertaken using school children as subjects, for example, the investigator initially sends to the parents of each child a letter describing the research and asking for their written consent to have their child participate.

The Right to Withdraw

Subjects should also have the right to withdraw from the investigation at any time they choose. In an investigation requiring adolescents to fill out a number of personality tests, one subject stopped midway through the testing session and said to the investigator, "This is stupid. I really don't want to fill these tests out." Without hesitation, the investigator thanked the student for her honesty and informed her that she would not be expected to complete the tests if she so chose.

The Right to Confidentiality

The subjects should have the right to confidentiality. An investigator administered a self-perception questionnaire to a group of students. Later, a school counselor asked to see the results of one student's questionnaire. The counselor explained that the child was experiencing difficulty in school and that information from the questionnaire might provide insight into the cause of the problem. Despite the counselor's good intentions, the investigator could not share the questionnaire results without first obtaining permission from the child and the child's parents.

The Right to Protection from Traumatic Experiences

Subjects should have the right to protection from traumatic or potentially harmful experiences. On occasion, this guideline poses difficult interpretation problems. For example, a film produced by the American Psychological Association depicted the following research method: A child was instructed to guard an investigator's very special pet while the investigator was out of the room. While guarding the pet, the child was distracted from the task by attractive toys. Once the child was momentarily distracted, an apparatus was activated that made the pet disappear through a trap door.

The purpose of the investigation was to observe children's responses when they discovered the pet was missing. As you can imagine, the children felt guilty and responsible for the loss. The film depicts one child running frantically from the room and withdrawing in an anxious state to the playground. The results of this research were valuable, and the investigators made every effort to show each child that the missing pet was subsequently found and returned to its cage so that no harm was done to it. However, because of the traumatic experience of the child mentioned above, it is doubtful that with current ethical guidelines the research could be undertaken today.

PART II

Prenatal Development and the Newborn Child

The development of the child begins long before birth. From the moment of conception onward, the human organism proceeds through a complex pattern of developmental stages. The newborn, or neonate, enters the world with many characteristics that will determine, in part, the way the child will interact with the environment. In addition, the first month of life is a period during which the foundation of future social relationships is laid.

Fundamental to those relationships is the development of trust in the adults who serve as caretakers for the newborn. The following three chapters will explore these early developmental processes. Chapter 3 begins by examining the prenatal development of the child. Chapter 4 is a discussion of the physical and motor capacities of the neonate. Finally, Chapter 5 examines the perceptual, cognitive, and social responsiveness of the child in the first month of life.

CHAPTER 3

Prenatal Development

Approximately nine months before a person is born, sexual intercourse between a male and a female—the parents—results in the combination of the father's sperm cell (spermatozoon) and the mother's egg cell (ovum). This combined cell, formed from the union of the two reproductive cells—sperm and egg—is a unique product in nature, unequaled in its potential for growth. It is called a zygote.

During the forty weeks after conception, the human organism's development occurs in the uterus of the mother (in utero). Like the first space-walking astronauts who were supplied oxygen and other life-maintaining essentials through a cord attaching their space suits to the mother ship, the human organism during the prenatal period is completely dependent on the mother for its life-maintaining sustenance. Like the astronauts, the human organism at first receives life-sustaining substances through an umbilical cord connecting its body to that of the mother.

During this prenatal period, the child in utero develops all

*the physical and biochemical systems necessary for it to survive
independently outside the uterus. In this chapter, we will examine
the stages of development through which the human organism
evolved in utero, some of the variables that influence the
progress of development in utero, and the dysfunctions that may
result from inappropriate prenatal development.*

The Stages of Prenatal Development

Although the prenatal period is short, it is so complex that it
has been divided into several stages. The first of these is conception, followed by the germinal stage, which covers the first
two weeks after the egg is fertilized. This stage is followed by
the embryonic stage, which lasts for about six weeks. The final
stage, from about eight weeks until birth, is called the fetal stage.
The total gestation period—what we call the length of a woman's
pregnancy—usually lasts about 280 days from the beginning of
her last menstrual period.

Conception

Once every approximately twenty-eight days, a mature
female human releases an *ovum* from one of her two ovaries. The
ovum is a reproductive cell that may be thought of as an egg. It
is sometimes referred to as a female *germ cell* or *gamete*. The
ovum, about the size of a pinhead, moves slowly from the ovary
through the *fallopian tube,* connecting the ovary to the uterus.
While in the fallopian tube the ovum may be penetrated by a
sperm cell. A sperm cell is the male sexual reproductive cell,
which may also be referred to as a male germ cell or gamete.
Sperm cells are discharged in the female's vagina. From
there they move by means of swimming-like undulation up the
vagina and through the uterus to the fallopian tubes, where one
may penetrate an ovum if it is available for fertilization. The

penetration of the ovum by a single sperm cell constitutes *conception*. At the moment of conception, the ovum and sperm combine to form what is now called the *zygote*. This is the first step in human development.

The Germinal Stage

The germinal stage begins at the time of conception and lasts approximately two weeks. During that time the zygote moves down the fallopian tube into the uterus and attaches itself to the uterine wall. The zygote is now a physiological part of the woman and totally dependent upon her for its life support.

Spontaneous abortions may occur during the germinal stage. There are a number of reasons for these spontaneous abortions. The zygote may possess a severe defect that would hinder its normal development, or the interior lining of the uterus might be unreceptive to the zygote and thus deny it its needed support from the mother. In either of these cases, the rejection of the zygote would take place within two weeks of conception, and unknown to the woman, the zygote would be discharged in the regular menstrual flow.

The Embryonic Stage

The embryonic stage begins with the attachment of the zygote to the uterine wall and continues for approximately six weeks. Two important groups of events occur during the embryonic stage.

The Uterine Environment

First, the uterine environment in which the prenatal child will develop, is established. The structures necessary for the support of developing life are formed during this time. First, the *placenta* forms on the uterine wall at the point where the embryo and the uterus are attached. The placenta is the structure that exchanges oxygen, nutrients, and other elements from the blood of the mother to the blood of the child, and similarly exchanges excrements from the child's blood to the mother's. This exchange involves only elements from the blood of the two individuals and does not involve an exchange of the blood itself. Another structure that evolves is the *umbilical cord*, which connects the child directly to the placenta. Finally the *amniotic sac* develops, which will house the developing child in utero, and its watery contents, *amniotic fluid*, in which the developing child will float until born.

The Organism Develops

The second group of developmental events that occur during the embryonic stage involves the differentiation of physical structures within the organism itself. During the cell division that occurs in this period, three layers of tissue evolve from the zygote. The *ectoderm*, or outside tissue, forms the foundation for hair, nails, skin, the nervous system, and other structures. The *mesoderm*, or middle tissue, forms the foundation for the developing muscles, bones, and circulatory system. The *endoderm* forms the foundation for internal organs such as the gastrointestinal tract, the lungs, and the liver.

The initial differentiation of all these organs is completed by the end of the embryonic stage in approximately the eighth week of pregnancy. At this time it is possible to hear the primitive functioning of the heart and to observe that the physical characteristics of the embryo resemble those of a human being.

During the embryonic stage, the initial development of many vital organs of the child take place. Thus, any abnormalities that occur in the developmental process during this period may result in fatal dysfunction of a vital organ, such as the heart or stomach. For this reason, spontaneous abortions occur most frequently during the embryonic period. Furthermore, the impact of maternal disease, drug intake, or other events harmful to the developmental process have their greatest negative effect at this time.

The Fetal Stage

The fetal stage extends from about the eighth week after conception until birth occurs, approximately 40 weeks after conception. This stage is marked by continued growth and refinement of the structures for which foundations were established during the embryonic period. During this slow growth and refinement, the bodily structures of the organism, as well as its nervous and circulatory systems, become more capable of self-maintenance and of responding independently to the environment. While the normal gestation period of the human being is 40 weeks, the fetus is sufficiently developed by the twenty-eighth week that children born after that time have been known to survive.

Both mothers and fathers are often surprised at the amount of activity that appears to go on inside the uterus beginning with the third month of pregnancy. Fathers may be kicked by their as-yet-unborn child as they lie next to their wives at night. Mothers may note a complete distortion of their abdomen as the unborn child stretches vigorously within the uterus. Some fetuses develop hiccups, which are perceived by the mother as a systematic pushing sensation on the abdomen occurring at regular intervals. All these signs exemplify the increased physical capabilities of the fetus.

During the fourth month of pregnancy, doctors will typically ask expectant mothers if they wish to hear the heartbeat of their child. A sensitive stethoscope or sonar device can detect the heartbeat of the fetus at this stage. The heart rate of the fetus is considerably faster than that of the human adult, averaging approximately 140 beats per minute in comparison to the male adult's average of 70 beats per minute.

One question often posed by parents is "When is the sex of my child determined?" As we will see in the section on genetics, the genetically defined sex of the child is determined at the time of conception. However, the external sexual organs of the child develop approximately eight to nine weeks after conception. Interestingly, the initial sexual characteristics of all children are female. Male sexual characteristics evolve only if specific hormones manufactured in the male testes are present at the time of sexual determination. If the testes are removed prior to the development of the reproductive system, or if for some other reason the hormone is not produced, the child will develop the reproductive system of a female regardless of its genetically defined sex.

The Birth Process

Forty weeks following conception the child is born. Of course, in some cases this event occurs prior to the expected date, and in some cases the birth is late. A few days prior to the actual birth, the event is anticipated by the dropping of the fetus's head into the lower portion of the pelvis near to the cervix. This *engagement* is typically accompanied by a feeling of reduced pressure on the mother's lungs and stomach and is referred to as *lightening*.

Labor

Labor is divided into three stages. The first stage is by far the longest, lasting sometimes up to 20 hours, although typically more like 8 to 16 hours. During this stage, the narrow opening at the neck of the uterus, called the *cervix,* must expand, or dilate, to allow the baby through. Since the measurement is usually made by inserting the fingers into the vagina, it is sometimes expressed in finger-widths, although more correctly it is measured in centimeters. At first it is fully closed, then gradually it dilates one finger, two fingers, three fingers, four fingers. At about 10 centimeters, or 4 inches (five fingers), the baby is ready to pass through.

In the second stage of labor, the baby, expelled from the uterus by muscular contractions, makes its way down the birth canal. This can last anywhere from half an hour to 90 minutes or more. As the baby's head begins to emerge from the vagina, in what is sometimes called *crowning,* the doctor may make a small incision in the woman's perineum to ease the baby's passage. This is called an episiotomy; in most hospitals it is not standard procedure for all deliveries, but is rather evaluated on a case-by-case basis.

Finally, the third stage extends from the birth of the baby through the expulsion of the afterbirth, the placenta, along with all the accompanying material, including the roots of the umbilical cord. This final stage of labor usually takes only a few minutes.

Complications in the Birth Process

Complications in the birth process may result from physiological difficulties suffered by the mother. Complications may include toxicity, a cervix that does not dilate adequately, or the development of the placenta in such a way that it covers the cervix and does not allow for the delivery of the child prior to the delivery of the placenta itself (this is called *placenta previa*).

Complications may also occur as a result of the positioning of the fetus. In some cases, a child is positioned so that it will be born feet first, a *breech delivery.* In other cases, the umbilical cord may wrap around the neck of the child, causing strangulation during the birth process or *anoxia,* a lack of vital oxygen to the child. In many cases, these complications can be circumvented by the use of obstetric forceps to guide the child into a position appropriate for birth. At other times, the complications are circumvented by use of a cesarean section, or surgical delivery. Cesarean sections account for approximately 24 percent of all children delivered in the United States.

Social Aspects of Childbirth

While the biological process of childbirth is the same across all societies, the actual way it is handled varies greatly from society to society. The approach to childbirth varies in three areas particularly: where the baby is delivered, who assumes what responsibilities in the delivery, and some of the specific procedures relating to delivery and childbirth.

Where the Baby is Delivered

In the United States, the large majority of women deliver their babies in hospital facilities. This practice has been considered standard and desirable since the 1930s, when at-home deliveries, which were a common practice before then, came to be viewed as hazardous. If asked, most women will admit that they chose the hospital not only because they thought it a safer environment but because they never thought they had a choice. Part of the reason for this is the attitude that has taken hold: that giving birth is automatically treated as a sickness and that we need the "safety" of medicines and mechanization in order to deliver our children. Our own bodies have ceased to provide a sense of security to most Americans living in the second half of the twentieth century.

Such an attitude is a reflection of our general beliefs about the efficacy of the medical profession and the sanctuary of the hospital in particular. Of course, contemporary obstetric practices have enabled thousands of mothers and babies to survive who could not have done so otherwise. Moreover, the growing pediatric specialty of neonatal medicine today saves many babies who a dozen years ago would have died within weeks. Still, between 1980 and 1988, at-home deliveries increased significantly, as more women, especially those with previous deliveries, chose to have their babies at home. This increase may indicate a change of attitude, one that more nearly reflects the millions of years of human experience with childbirth.

Who Delivers the Baby

The second cultural factor determines who delivers the baby. If a prospective mother in the United States is asked who will deliver her baby, she will probably without hesitation name her doctor, never considering that for centuries doctors were only called into the delivery situation when there were medical complications. Yet in most societies throughout history, the mother or some other older woman managed the delivery and aftercare.

Midwifery, an ancient profession, has been a common practice. A midwife is a person trained in the art of assisting the woman at deliveries. Traditionally the midwife has been a woman, although there are now also male midwives. In the United States, a male- dominated medical profession exerted enormous pressures to prevent lay midwifery. Only those licensed as nurses or employed by a hospital—in either case under the control of the medical profession—are typically allowed to assist at deliveries, whether in the hospital or at home.

Childbirth Practices

Finally, we come to specific childbirth practices. These practices, of course, are related, directly or indirectly, to the "who" and "where" discussed above. There are many different ways to give birth, and the method a woman chooses may be strongly influenced by her physician or friends. Rarely does a woman objectively choose what is right for her while recognizing the forces of these outside influences.

First, the prospective mother is faced with the question of natural versus medically directed childbirth. Natural childbirth can be defined as labor and delivery without the use of anesthetic, forceps, or labor-inducing drugs such as oxytocin. A common form of natural childbirth in the Unites States is done in hospitals, with doctors and nurses present. In this form, the medical profession may be called upon to "deliver" or "intervene." To understand the full implications of what "natural" really means, it is necessary to understand what in our culture have been the accepted medical procedures used in uncomplicated childbirths. It is equally important to understand that many of these practices were not absolute necessities, but had been deemed so by our medically oriented culture.

If the mother has not chosen to follow certain breathing techniques such as those taught in the Lamaze method, she may be anesthetized at some stage during labor in order to cope with the pain of contractions. Anesthetics used during labor might include injection of a painkiller (a narcotic), injection of a local anesthetic in the cervix (called a paracervical block) or a continuous lumbar epidural (which is a regional, not a local, block). The fetus's journey, so to speak, is made neither more nor less difficult by these practices. Delivery, however, is a different story.

Anesthetics may also be used during the delivery process, which occurs after labor (although a laboring mother who has chosen to follow breathing exercises may choose not to be anesthetized during delivery). Anesthetics that might be used during delivery include local injections (e.g., directly into the perineum), continuous epidural (a regional block) or—rarely today—a general anesthetic. A local anesthetic does not interfere with the mother's ability to bear down and push the baby out; a general anesthetic always does.

There has been much discussion concerning the use and abuse of oxytocin. Oxytocin is a natural hormone secreted by the pituitary gland (it is even secreted by the fetus). Currently, oxytocin is used in two ways: to induce or start labor, or to stimulate or speed up a natural labor that is abnormally slow (a natural labor is not necessarily a normal one). There are pros and cons in any discussion of the use of this substance, because it can be (and has been) abused. Too much oxytocin, for example, can make contractions of the uterus occur so frequently that oxygen supply to the fetus can be reduced.

More important, however, than these specific differences is the implicit attitude underlying the natural method. With the medically directed method, the implicit attitude is "Just leave everything to the doctor who knows what's best for you." The natural method, on the other hand, says, "Only the woman can really know what's happening in her body, and she must therefore become totally familiar with and actively involved in the processes of pregnancy, labor, and delivery. Since the father is a very interested participant—and since he is the father!—he should be there all along, to help his partner, to coach her in her breathing and pushing, and to comfort her and cheer her on."

Whereas a decade or two ago, the natural method was quite controversial and was perceived as a rebellion against established medical practice, nowadays it is much more widely accepted, and many physicians encourage their patients to take the Lamaze natural childbirth course or some variation. Whereas a decade ago, young physicians advocated this method, while older, more conservative physicians generally did not, nowadays that generation gap appears to have been bridged. The natural method has found wide acceptance in the medical profession, and we may now find physician, expectant mother, and prospective father all knowledgeably working together for the best delivery possible.

Treatment of the Newborn

Cultural factors also play an important role in how we treat the neonate, or newborn infant, immediately after delivery. In some societies, following delivery, the baby was physically separated from the mother, who was not allowed to see or touch it. The baby was exposed to loud noises and harsh lights for a few moments. Finally the baby collapsed from shock and was removed to an area some distance from its mother, who was viewed as unfit to touch her baby. Other interested parties could view the baby from some distance, through glass.

This "horrible" society, of course, was our own some years ago. The practices discussed were standard hospital hygienic practices, which had become widely accepted since women began relying on hospitals for delivery. Some aspects of these practices have changed dramatically.

Our attitudes about the birth experience are in the process of undergoing important changes. Early psychologists, such as Sigmund Freud and Otto Rank, emphasized the trauma of birth, arguing that it was such a difficult experience that its aftereffects would actually last one's entire lifetime. But while this attitude told us how difficult a process it was, it told us little about how to improve it. Anthropologist Ashley Montagu points out a changing social trend in our perception of birth, one that does help us make it a less traumatic experience for the newborn. Whereas we used to think of birth as the end of the period of gestation and the beginning of independent functioning, we now recognize that a newborn child is almost as dependent on the mother as he or she was before birth. This realization is influencing our view of how to deal with the child immediately after birth. Specifically, we try to minimize the immediate separation.

The revolutionary concept of birth without violence was introduced by the French obstetrician Dr. Frederick Leboyer, whose book *Birth Without Violence* has had a wide social impact. His basic argument is that the first few minutes of life are critically important and that since the newborn baby is hypersensitive to the new extrauterine environment, it should be born in a quiet, unobtrusively lighted, pleasant environment. More significantly, Leboyer and others advocate strongly that at birth the baby be placed right beside the mother, so that she and her new baby can begin to get used to each other. This view is directly contrary to the former practice of separating mother and child at birth, but this innovative practice is receiving increasing acceptance today.

More and more mothers, even those who are not using the

Leboyer method for their deliveries, now expect to have contact with their baby at birth. The practices of mother-child interaction at birth, once viewed as medical decisions, are now more appropriately considered as being culturally, rather than medically, determined.

Genetic Influences on Development

Genotype

At the moment of conception, the genetic foundations that will direct much of life development are established. The genetic pattern inherited from the mother and father is called the *genotype* of the child.

A genotype is determined by the 23 chromosomes contributed to the organism by the male germ cell and the 23 chromosomes contributed by the female germ cell. Because the specific "genetic messengers" in 23 chromosomes differ among germ cells produced by the same individual, it is virtually impossible for children conceived from separate matings of the same two individuals to have identical genotypes. This is why siblings and nonidentical twins differ from each other in so many ways.

Genes and Chromosomes

The basic elements of genetic transmission are the genes. Chemically, genes consist of *DNA* (deoxyribonucleic acid). Each DNA molecule stores information in the form of a code, which is copied by a related nucleic acid, *RNA* (ribonucleic acid). The RNA molecule directs the synthesis of the proteins that form the body and guide its functioning. A chromosome is a large collection of genes; nearly 20,000 genes combine in a chain to form a single chromosome.

With one exception, every part of the normal human body is

formed from cells containing 46 chromosomes. Those chromosomes can be arranged into 23 pairs, one member of each pair contributed by each parent at the time of conception. These cells are called *autosomes* or *body cells*. The cells directly involved in reproducing new organisms—the sperm of the male and the ovum of the female—are the exception. These mature reproductive cells, called *gametes* or *germ cells*, contain only 23 chromosomes.

Cell Division and Development

At the time of conception, a male and a female germ cell, each containing 23 chromosomes, join to form a *zygote*. That zygote contains a total complement of 46 chromosomes. The process by which that single cell reproduces itself through cell division is called *mitosis*.

During mitosis, each of the 46 chromosomes duplicates itself within a single cell. The two identical sets of chromosomes thus produced move to opposite sides of the cell, and the cell parts in the middle to form two cells, each possessing an identical set of 46 chromosomes. (See Fig. 3.1.) Beginning with a single zygote, the process of development consists of the continual repetition of this division. Thus, each autosome in the body contains an identical chromosome pattern.

Reproductive cells are generated by a unique process referred to as *meiosis*. In that process, cells in the reproductive organ of the individual divide without first reproducing their chromosomal pattern. (See Fig. 3.2.) One chromosome from each of the 23 pairs becomes part of the newly created germ cell. Thus, each mature germ cell contains a unique pattern of 23 chromosomes.

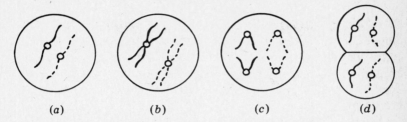

Fig. 3.1 Mitosis *(a)* Cell with representative chromosome pair; *(b)* Duplication of each chromosome; *(c)* Separation of original chromosome from duplicate and movement of chromosomes to opposite poles of the cell; *(d)* Cell division leaving two cells each with a chromosome pair identical to that in cell A.

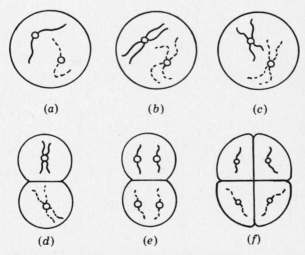

Fig. 3.2 Meiosis *(a)* Cell with representative chromosome pair; *(b)* Duplication of each member of the pair; *(c)* Movement of chromosome and duplicate to opposite sides of the cell; *(d)* Cell division leaving two cells, each with a single chromosome and its duplicate; *(e)* Separation of the original chromosome from its duplicate in each of the two cells; *(f)* Cell division resulting in four cells, each with one half the number of chromosomes as the original cell in A.

Fraternal Twins

Consider the situation when twins are born. Despite their identical ages, they may be no more similar to one another than a brother and sister. Such twins are referred to as *dizygotic*, or fraternal, twins. Their creation is the result of two ova being fertilized by two separate sperm. Because each ovum and sperm contains its own unique chromosomal pattern, each of the fraternal twins possesses a unique genotype.

The genotypes of fraternal twins are no more similar to one another than are those created when an interval of years separates the fertilization of two ova. Mathematically, the simple process of meiosis in germ cells, coupled with the combining of male and female germ cells to form the zygote, is estimated at having the potential for the creation of 64×10^{12} unique genotypes. This number of potential genotypes far exceeds the number of individuals alive in the world. Thus, it is highly unlikely that two individuals who did not develop from the same zygote would have the same genotype. Each individual who is not a monozygotic twin is unique. Twinning occurs in approximately 2.2 percent of births, and approximately two-thirds of those twin pairs are fraternal.

Identical Twins

In contrast to fraternal twins, whose development is initiated from two independent zygotes, identical, or *monozygotic*, twins possess identical genotypes. Identical twins are the result of a single fertilization; that is, a zygote, in its initial act of cell division, created two cells that continued to mature independently into two fully developed organisms. Because the initial cell division resulted in two cells with identical chromosomal patterns, the offspring generated from those two cells possess identical genotypes.

Phenotype

The term *genotype* refers to the genetic makeup of a cell or individual; *phenotype* refers to the actual characteristics exhibited by an individual. It is interesting to note that even individuals with the same genotype may exhibit different phenotypes, depending upon the environment in which they are reared. On the other hand, different genotypes may manifest themselves in identical phenotypes. (See the discussion of recessive and dominant genes.)

Although the height of an individual may be dictated in part by the genetic makeup of that individual, if two identical twins were reared under different nutritional plans, the one with the better nutrition would grow taller than the one provided less nutritious food. The height actually attained by the individual would be the phenotype.

It has been shown, for example, that schizophrenia, a form of psychopathology, can be transmitted genetically. However, even if a genetic propensity for schizophrenia exists, individuals may or may not exhibit schizophrenic behavior, depending upon the environment in which they live and the psychological stresses to which they are subjected.

The Transmission of Traits via a Single Gene

For the sake of simplicity, we will examine the process of genetic transmission for traits whose genetic definition is based on the action of a single pair of genes. In most cases, however, human traits are determined by the combined action of a number of genes.

Genetic Alleles

Genes, like chromosomes, act in pairs. A gene pair consists of the genes situated at identical locations on the two members of a chromosome pair. One gene in each pair was contributed by an individual's mother and the other by the father. Each gene may exist in two or more states. These states are called the alleles of the gene.

For example, the color of a person's eyes is basically determined by a pair of genes located at a particular place on a particular pair of chromosomes. (Several other gene pairs may affect the tone and distribution of pigments in the iris; see Codominance below.) Each gene whose function it is to influence the color of an individual's eyes may carry a code for either brown eyes or for blue eyes. The two colors are the states the gene may possess and are called its alleles.

An individual gene pair is said to be homozygotic when the two genes in the pair possess identical alleles; a gene pair is said to be heterozygotic when the two genes possess different alleles. If both eye-color genes described above were for blue eyes, an individual would be homozygotic for eye color. If one gene was coded for blue eyes, while the other was coded for brown eyes, the individual would be heterozygotic for eye color.

The phenotypic representation of a genotype is dependent not only upon the alleles forming the basis for genetic transmission but also on the way in which those alleles interact with one another.

Recessive and Dominant Genes

When the allele coded in a particular gene is manifested directly by an individual only when the individual is homozygotic with respect to that gene pair, the allele is said to be recessive. When the allele coded in a particular gene is represented phenotypically in both homozygotic and heterozygotic genotypes, the allele is said to be dominant.

Blue eye color, for example, is a recessive trait. For an individual to exhibit blue eyes, the allele for both genes must be blue. If one gene of the pair possesses a nonblue allele, the individual will not have blue eyes. Or consider phenylketonuria

(PKU), a genetics abnormality that results in the body's inability to metabolize phenylalanine, an amino acid. Accumulations of that acid in the system result in destruction of the nervous system and corresponding mental retardation. The transmitter of PKU is a recessive allele. A child exhibits PKU only if the critical gene contributed by the mother and the corresponding gene contributed by the father are both characterized by the defective (PKU) allele. If one or the other parent contributes a normal gene, one not characteristic of PKU, the abnormality will not be manifested. Fortunately, our current understanding of PKU allows infants to be tested for its presence at birth. If its existence is noted, the child can be placed on a special diet to alleviate the effects of PKU by reducing the intake of foods that create phenylalanine.

Codominance

Codominance refers to alleles whose traits may be manifested simultaneously in the same heterozygotic individual. The most striking example of codominance occurs when one sees an animal, and sometimes a human, with different colorations in their two eyes. Less striking are individuals who have flecks of one color in eyes that are predominantly a second color; for example, flecks of blue in a brown-eyed individual.

Intermediate Expression

The phenotypic expression of a heterozygotic genotype may also express itself as a value intermediate between the two alleles. This phenomenon is called intermediate expression. Skin color is a characteristic determined by an intermediate expression of alleles. If a dark-skinned individual mates with a light-skinned individual, the offspring will typically have a skin color that is brown—an intermediate between the two parents.

Sex-Linked Genetic Transmission

Chromosome pairs are distinguishable on the basis of their size. Geneticists number the pairs from 1 to 23, giving the smallest pair the number 1 and the largest pair the number 23. One pair, the twenty-third, is unique in its physical characteristics and is the pair that determines the sex of the offspring.

Chromosomes in the pair 23 may be of two types. A large, fully developed chromosome is labeled X and is called a female chromosome. A male chromosome, labeled Y, is much smaller and is thought to be nearly barren of genes. The difference between these two chromosomes results in a unique pattern of genetic transmission referred to as sex linkage. Characteristics transmitted by genes located on this chromosome pair are called sex-linked characteristics.

Sex Determination

A sexually normal female organism results from the presence of two X chromosomes in chromosome pair 23. A sexually normal male organism results from the presence of one X chromosome and one Y chromosome in pair 23.

Recessive Sex-Linked Characteristics

Recessive characteristics transmitted by genes located on the sex chromosome are more prevalent among men than among women. Unfortunately, these recessive characteristics are often defective ones that result in organisms functioning at a less-than-optimal level. The abundance of recessive sex-linked characteristics in males is the result of the genetically barren Y chromosome possessed by all males but not possessed by females. If the mother of a female child contributes a recessive allele on the X chromosome, the father of the child may contribute a dominant allele on the other X chromosome. The homozygotic female child will, in that case, exhibit the dominant characteristic.

It is only when both the mother and father contribute the recessive allele to the female child that the recessive allele will exhibit itself phenotypically. In contrast, the male child whose mother contributes a recessive allele on the X chromosome has no potentially counteracting gene on the barren Y chromosome contributed by the father. Thus, if only the mother contributes a recessive allele, that sex-linked characteristic will manifest itself in the phenotype of the male child.

Hemophilia, the "royal disease" as it is sometimes called because it affected male heirs to several European thrones, is a sex-linked recessive characteristic. It is manifested phenotypically by the individuals tendency to bleed internally in joints and muscles and to exhibit poor clotting of the blood. A male need only receive the allele for hemophilia from his mother to possess the trait. A female, however, must receive the allele from both her father and mother to exhibit the trait. Thus, a girl can develop hemophilia only if her father himself was a hemophiliac. Figure 3.3 depicts the family patterns of hemophilia.

Genetic Mutations and Birth Defects

In addition to abnormalities that are the direct result of genetic alleles, defective phenotypes may result from mutations of genes and chromosomes. A mutation refers to a change in a gene or chromosome. Mutations in genes may occur spontaneously, but the prevalence of such mutations is small and only minimally accounts for changes in gene frequencies across a population of individuals. Spontaneous mutations in the characteristics of chromosomes occur more frequently. When they do occur, they are the result of a dysfunction during meiosis.

Additional Chromosomes

One type of chromosomal mutation is the addition of one or more chromosomes beyond the normal 46. When a single chromosome is added to a pair, it is referred to as *trisomy,*

Fathers

Father $X_H Y_o$ M(H) / Mother $X_H X_H$ F(H)

	X_H	Y_o
X_H	$X_H X_H$ F(H)	$X_H Y_o$ M(H)
X_H	$X_H X_H$ F(H)	$X_H Y_o$ M(H)

Father $X_h Y_o$ M(h) / Mother $X_H X_H$ F(H)

	X_h	Y_o
X_H	$X_H X_h$ F(H)C	$X_H Y_o$ M(H)
X_H	$X_H X_h$ F(H)C	$X_H Y_o$ M(H)

Father $X_H Y_o$ M(H) / Mother $X_H X_h$ F(H)C

	X_H	Y_o
X_H	$X_H X_H$ F(H)	$X_H Y_o$ M(H)
X_h	$X_H X_h$ F(H)C	$X_h Y_o$ M(h)

Father $X_h Y_o$ M(h) / Mother $X_H X_h$ F(H)C

	X_h	Y_o
X_H	$X_H X_h$ F(H)C	$X_H Y_o$ M(H)
X_h	$X_h X_h$ F(h)	$X_h Y_o$ M(h)

Father $X_H Y_o$ M(H) / Mother $X_h X_h$ F(h)

	X_h	Y_o
X_h	$X_h X_H$ F(H)C	$X_h Y_o$ M(h)
X_h	$X_h X_H$ F(H)C	$X_h Y_o$ M(h)

Father $X_h Y_o$ M(h) / Mother $X_h X_h$ F(h)

	X_h	Y_o
X_h	$X_h X_h$ F(h)	$X_h Y_o$ M(h)
X_h	$X_h X_h$ F(h)	$X_h Y_o$ M(h)

Mothers

First Descriptive Line Signifies Genotype:
X female chromosome, Y male chromosome, H nonhemophilia allele (dominant), h hemophilia allele (recessive), o barren gene (no allele)
Second Descriptive Line Signifies Phenotype:
F female, M male; H no hemophilia, h manifested hemophilia; C carrier of hemophilia allele who does not manifest hemophilia

Fig. 3.3 Patterns of Hemophilia Transmission Occurring from the Mating of Individuals Possessing Various Genotypes

meaning three chromosomes. A number is added to the term to denote which pair of chromosomes has evolved abnormally.

One of the most common dysfunctions caused by the inclusion of one additional chromosome is trisomy-21. As the term implies, the abnormality is the result of an additional chromosome in the twenty-first chromosome pair. The common name for the phenotype of this chromosome mutation is Down's syndrome. Individuals exhibiting *Down's syndrome* are usually quiet and limp during the early weeks of life and exhibit skin folds of the upper eyelid similar to those found in Oriental peoples. This latter characteristic is the basis for the term "mongoloidism," the name formerly given to the condition. While there are other physical characteristics prevalent in Down's syndrome, the most severe dysfunction is a pattern of mental retardation.

An abnormal number of sex chromosomes produces a variety of phenotypic abnormalities. *Klinefelter's syndrome* is a specific example in which a male typically possesses one additional X sex chromosome. Thus, the genotype is XXY. It should be noted that this syndrome is sometimes found with other genotype abnormalities, but all involve the addition of abnormal numbers of X chromosomes. Individuals with Klinefelter's syndrome are male, possess small testes, are mentally retarded in about half the cases, and frequently exhibit a variety of personality and psychiatric problems.

Causes of Mutations

While spontaneous mutations do occur, evidence exists that outside environmental influence may increase the probability of mutations occurring. Sources of these influences, called mutagens, include high radiation, heat, and drugs.

Individuals subjected to high levels of radiation from radioactive fallout accompanying the atomic bomb blasts at Nagasaki and Hiroshima at the end of World War II, for example, exhibited chromosome abnormalities and higher incidences of leukemia and other forms of cancer than individuals not exposed to those high levels of radiation.

Early experimenters who studied x-rays to assess their value as diagnostic and therapeutic tools for medicine were often subjected to high levels of radiation because of their ignorance of its potential negative effects. Those individuals suffered from chromosome abnormalities, which probably accounted for many of their deaths from cancerlike illnesses at an early age.

It is interesting and important to note that evidence concerning the effect of radiation on chromosomes does not suggest that exposure to radiation has an effect on the unconceived child. The radiation appears to influence only the individual who is actually exposed. However, the effect of radiation, drugs, and other external influences can affect the child while still in utero.

Environmental and Other Factors Influencing Development in Utero

While genetic factors present at the time of conception play a major role in determining the development of the child both in utero and postnatally, a variety of environmental influences may interfere with development while the child is unborn.

Maternal Disease

For many years, it was believed that no elements from the blood of the mother crossed the placental barrier to enter the circulatory system of the child. However, while the whole blood of the mother does not mix directly with the blood of the unborn child, certain elements can and do cross the placental barrier and can in turn affect the unborn child.

A variety of disease-causing viruses fall into this category. Thus, it is possible for a child to be infected with a disease while still in utero. Probably the most often-cited disease that can have negative effects on the in utero development of the child is *rubella* (German measles). When contracted during the period of embryonic development, the rubella virus can cause abnormal development of various sensory systems, resulting in blindness or deafness.

Venereal diseases such as syphilis and gonorrhea can afflict an unborn child. These diseases affect the fetus and may cause mental retardation, blindness, or spontaneous abortions. Women treated for venereal disease before the critical period of its impact on the developing fetus can avert these negative consequences.

While not diseases, certain factors in the blood of some women are incompatible with the blood of their offspring. The *Rh factor*, when negative in the mother and positive in the child, may cause the destruction of oxygen-transmitting red blood cells in the child and result in death from an inadequate supply of oxygen. Fortunately, the problem of incompatible Rh factors has been alleviated by techniques of early detection, in utero blood transfusions, and maternal inoculation that reduces the mother's sensitivity to the child's Rh positive blood.

Drugs

Drugs, like some diseases, can cross the placental barrier and influence the development of the child. These drugs include not only some used illegally in our that society, but also ones normally used under medical prescription. The effect of the drug may be either directly related to the physical development of the child or similar to its effect on the adults—for example, addiction. *Heroin, methadone,* and *morphine*—all drugs addictive to adults—can be addictive to the unborn child whose mother is a user. Children of addicted mothers are often found to suffer severe withdrawal symptoms immediately following birth.

Tetracycline, a commonly used antibiotic, has been found to influence negatively the skeletal growth of an unborn child when ingested by the pregnant mother. Similarly, birth defects have been associated with the ingestion of *quinine,* a substance used in the treatment of malaria. For fourteen years following 1947, *DES (diethylstilbestrol)* was prescribed frequently to pregnant women as an aid in reducing miscarriages. In the late 1960s, it was found that the female children of women who had ingested DES were developing vaginal abnormalities and cervical cancers at abnormally high rates. It is interesting to note that the impact of DES did not manifest itself until after the children had reached adolescence.

Maternal Nutrition

While there is a controversy as to the exact effects of maternal diet on the unborn child, there is considerable evidence to suggest that a deficiency of important vitamins, iron, and proteins results in an increased incidence of premature births, smaller children, and potential neurological deficiencies.

Maternal Emotional States

Evidence concerning the effects on unborn children of the emotional states of their mothers is also controversial. It is reported that women who experience severe anxiety and stress during pregnancy are more likely to have complications during delivery, bear premature children, and have children who both in utero and as infants are above average in their activity levels. Some researchers have speculated that stress states in the mother during the first trimester of prenatal development may result in the transmission of excessive amounts of adrenalin to the blood of the child, which in turn increases the child's activity levels. The altered biochemical state, they think, might have negative effects on the normal development of the embryo or fetus. However, the complications observed after birth may be the result of parenting patterns associated with the anxiety of the mother rather than the biological characteristics of the child.

Consider this example: Mrs. J. and her husband were having rather difficult adjustment problems in their marriage when their child was conceived. During the course of the pregnancy, the marital situation continued to worsen, and Mrs. J. was constantly anxious and under stress. When their child was born, he was fretful and exhibited autistic characteristics. Some people suggested that stress during pregnancy had hindered the development of the fetus and resulted in the child's abnormal behavior. Interestingly, when the marriage ended in divorce three months following the birth of the child and all was peaceful for both mother and child, the abnormal behavior ended. Often the tensions experienced by a mother result in an uncomfortable relationship between her and the child, which in turn stimulates a child's abnormal behavior. Removal of the source of mother's tension eliminates the abnormal behavior in the child.

Temporal Determinants on the Effects of Environmental Influences

The influences of outside agents on the development of the child in utero depend on the point in the developmental process at which the child is affected. Some environmental influences hinder normal development only during the embryonic stage, some only during later fetal development. The particular impact of an outside agent also depends on whether the structure or system of the organism is in a critical phase of development at the time the child is affected. If the visual system is developing at the time a child contracts rubella, then the child may be born blind. By contrast, if the auditory system is in its crucial phase of development, the same virus may cause deafness.

Toxoplasmosis, an infection often carried by cats and transmitted in their feces, has no apparent effect on the child after birth but can cause brain damage and damage to the visual system of the child during the fetal period. Earlier exposure may have little impact on the child.

Maternal Age

Mothers bearing their first child after the age of 35 are likely to have significantly more difficulty in pregnancy and childbirth than are younger mothers. Furthermore, there are significantly more children with developmental disabilities born to women over 35 years of age.

The ideal age for childbirth is between the ages of 20 and 35 years. Interestingly, the incidence of dizygotic twins increases significantly as a women gets closer to the age of 35. It has been speculated that the reproductive system is beginning to lose its functional capacities at this time; thus, there is a greater chance for mutations during meiosis, as well as the multiple release of ova.

The proportion of children born with Down's syndrome is 0.31 in 1,000 births for women between the ages of 15 and 24 and increases to 9.99 in 1,000 births for women between the ages of 45 and 49. The chances of bearing a Down's syndrome child increase significantly when women are older than 35 years.

CHAPTER 4

Physical and Motor Capacities of the Newborn

The stages of prenatal development we looked at in the previous chapter are invariant throughout all cultures and from one person to another. In the same way, certain growth processes after birth seem to be relatively independent of environmental factors, occurring in a predictable sequence. For example, children develop the capacity first to lift their heads, then to sit up, later to stand, and finally, to walk. It would be impossible for the child to develop the ability to walk before he or she could roll over or lift up his or her head. The orderly sequence of events and the readiness to master certain tasks are integral to the concept of maturation.

Maturation always involves physical capacities. The child cannot learn to read before he or she has the ability to recognize letters, cannot learn to walk before the legs are strong enough to support the body, and so on.

The development of physical and behavioral capacities in a fixed sequence is due primarily to genetic factors but may require a normal environment. The rate of maturation is likely to vary from person to person because of inherited individual differences and because of influences in the environment, such as nutrition, physical care, and climate, that can either slow down or accelerate maturational processes. In this chapter we will look at the earliest process of maturation: the physical and motor development of the newborn child.

Physical Characteristics of the Newborn

Although the average newborn infant, or *neonate*, is similar in physical structure to that of human beings of any age, its physical characteristics are somewhat distorted at birth.

The Skeleton and Muscle Structures

In comparison to those of the older child, the muscles of the neonate are soft, small, and poorly controlled. The bones, too, are soft and flexible, consisting mostly of cartilage.

Parents are often distressed by the misshapen appearance of their newborn's head. The misshaping of the head may appear to be a birth defect. In reality, however, the shape of the head has been naturally distorted to facilitate the birth process. Within a few days, the head's soft structure will reestablish itself to the normal oval shape.

Of particular concern to some parents are the "soft spots" on the head of the neonate. These six fontanels occur where the bones of the skull have not yet knitted together, but the fontanels are covered by a tough membrane and are not as sensitive to stimulation as is often believed.

The flexibility of the skeleton at birth has been used by various cultures to allow for the creation of specific physical distortions that in those cultures denote social status, beauty, or simply membership in the society. Indians of the Pacific Northwest secured a board to the head of each newborn infant in order to produce a long, slanted forehead and pointed skull. This characteristic denoted membership in that particular Indian nation.

In some Asian cultures, small feet were viewed as symbols of femininity and high social status. Consequently, the feet of newborn females were bound in such a way as to inhibit their growth and development. Unfortunately, this binding procedure crippled the girls as they grew older.

Weight

The child at birth is smaller than most people imagine. The average weight of the newborn is 7 1/2 pounds (3,375 g), with 95 percent of newborns weighing between 4 1/2 pounds (2,025 g) and 8 1/2 pounds (3.825 g). The record books report that the smallest and largest babies born alive weighed 10 ounces (280 g) and 24 1/4 pounds (10,900 g) respectively. Surprisingly, newborns typically lose weight in the first few days after birth. While the average weight of the newborn is 7 1/2 pounds (3,375 g), the average weight of the baby leaving the hospital at the age of 3 days is 4 to 5 ounces (112-130 g) less than his or her birthweight. This weight loss is not harmful and probably occurs because so much of the newborn's energy is directed toward adjusting to life outside the uterus. The initial weight loss is not maintained and by the end of the first month the average weight of a child is 9 1/4 pounds (4,150 g).

Premature Births

Until the late 1960s, prematurity was typically defined by the birthweight of a child. Newborns weighing less than 5 1/2 pounds (2,500 g) were said to be premature.

More recently, however, it has become customary to consider two dimensions in defining the maturity of the child at birth: the birthweight and the gestation period. The normal gestation period for the human organism is 40 weeks. Children are referred to as short-gestation or preterm infants if they are born less than 40 weeks after conception. It would be expected that a preterm infant—for example, one born only 35 weeks after conception—would normally have a lower birthweight than a child born at full term.

Full-term newborns who weigh less than 5 1/2 pounds (2,500 g) are called low-birthweight infants. The impact of low birthweight for a full-term infant is quite different from the low birthweight of the short-gestation infant. There is evidence to suggest that low-birthweight infants do make rapid catch-up growth gains during their early development. However, even as children and adults, they typically do not achieve the height and weight of individuals who weighed more at birth.

Short-gestation infants often lack the protective layer of fat that emerges in the last stages of fetal development. Consequently, they are more susceptible to negative environmental influences than are full-term infants. For this reason, hospitals typically retain short-gestation-period infants in their care until they weigh 4 to 5 pounds (1,800-2,250 g) and have matured physically to a point where they can combat the threats of the environment.

Evidence also suggests that throughout life, low-birthweight infants perform less well, on the average, than their normal-birthweight counterparts on various tests of ability, such as tests of intelligence and school achievement. These impairments increase as birthweight decreases, with a large portion of infants having a birthweight below 4 1/2 pounds (2,000 g) exhibiting neurological and/or cognitive dysfunctions. For example, it has been reported that among children experiencing learning disabilities in school, 11.5 percent were premature. In contrast, only 4.6 percent of those children not experiencing learning disabilities in school were prematurely born.

Length

The average newborn is 20 inches (51 cm) long, a little under 2 feet. It is very hard to obtain an accurate measure of length for infants because their legs tend to flex up under them into a squatting position. Thus, during those first months, physicians are not likely to use length measurements as a diagnostic sign of developmental problems. If one desires to obtain an accurate measurement of body length, it is best to do so when an infant is asleep and relaxed. As anyone who has observed the speed with which newborns outgrow their clothes will attest, the length of the newborn increases rapidly. By the age of one month, the newborn, on the average, will have grown about one inch (2-3 cm).

There is little variability in the length of newborns; consequently, their length is not a good predictor of their adult height. The correlation between length at birth and adult height is approximately .25. However, a rule of thumb suggests that the newborn has achieved a little over 30 percent of his or her adult height. More accurate predictions of adult height can be made by knowing the height of the child at his or her third birthday.

Body Proportions

At birth, the human child is top-heavy. The head of the newborn constitutes one-quarter of the total body length, in contrast to an adult, whose head constitutes only one-seventh of the total length. In addition to the disproportionately small body trunk, the hands, arms, and legs of the newborn are small relative to the total body size. This disproportionate body structure accounts, in part, for the poor coordination of the infant—poor coordination that is evident even at age one or two. One can characterize the process of growth as developing legs and arms to fit one's body, and developing a body whose size will be compatible with the size of the head.

Neurological Characteristics of the Newborn

The nervous system of the human organism controls all its activities. Many developmental changes we observe throughout life are the result of changes in that neurological system. Thus, an understanding of the newborn's nervous system is essential for understanding both the child's limitations in functioning and the processes of development that are observed during the first months and years of life.

Anatomical Characteristics

The brain of the newborn more closely approximates its mature weight and size than does any other organ in the body. At birth, the weight of the brain is approximately 25 percent of its adult weight, and by the age of six months, it has achieved fully half its mature weight.

Lower Brain Structures

At birth, the most highly developed portions of the central nervous system are the *spinal cord, midbrain, pons,* and *medulla.*

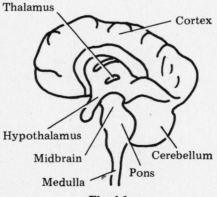

Fig. 4.1

This fact is not surprising when one realizes that those lower, or subcortical, brain structures maintain the vital reflex functions of the infant, for example, heartbeat and respiration. These vital structures constitute only about 1.5 percent of the total brain volume throughout life, although some changes are observed with development.

The major development of the midbrain, pons, and medulla takes place prior to birth. Other vital lower brain structures, the *thalamus* and *hypothalamus*, also differentiate anatomically prior to birth but grow much more rapidly during the first few postnatal months. During the first month, their growth is more rapid than that of any portion of the brain. Among the functions served by these structures are the maintenance of homeostasis, for example, temperature control and food intake, as well as fundamental sensory processes.

The Cortex

The cortex of the newborn is thought to be poorly developed at birth. The *neurons* that make up the cortex of the adult are nearly all developed at birth, but their *axons* and *dendrites* have not yet grown to produce the complex network of connections observed in the adult cortex. The development of the cortex involves the growth of those axons and dendrites as well as the development of a protein covering (myelin), which covers the axons to varying degrees. This *myelin sheath* facilitates neural transmission.

Although the cortex develops rapidly during the first months after birth, that development is not uniform across all cortical systems. The primary motor areas of the cortex, whose function is to control movement of the upper limbs and trunk, develop very soon after the birth and are followed in their development by the primary sensory areas. Later, the motor areas responsible for lower limb control develop, and still later, the association areas of the cortex emerge.

The Cerebellum

The function of the cerebellum is to coordinate cortical activities, which influence balance and muscle tone. Of particular significance is its role in motor coordination. At birth the cerebellum is very immature and does not function. It is one of the last major divisions of the brain to develop, reaching its maximum growth rate at about six months of age. This point of maximum growth rate occurs fully three months after the maximum growth rate of the cortex.

Cortical Activity

Cortical activity is reflected in the pattern of electrical discharge recorded in an *electroencephalogram (EEG)*. Distinctive features of these discharge patterns have been labeled in the EEGs of adults and serve as reference points for describing the cortical activity of the newborn. The discharge patterns are classified according to the frequency of discharge in a given period of time. Delta waves exhibit a frequency of less than 4 cps (cycles per second); theta waves, 4 to 7 cps; alpha waves, 8 to 13 cps; and beta waves, over 13 cps. (See Fig. 4.2.)

Waking-State EEG Patterns

A distinction can be made between the EEG patterns during the waking and sleeping states as early as the eighth prenatal month. The waking-state EEG pattern of the one-month-old newborn does not differ significantly from that observed in the eighth prenatal month. It is characterized by activity from all areas of the cortex, with a predominance of theta waves and some evidence of delta and alpha waves.

A note concerning alpha waves is in order at this point. The alpha waves described previously designate only a range of wave frequencies, and should not be confused with alpha rhythms. The term "alpha rhythms" describes alpha waves occurring in

Beta

Alpha

Theta

Delta

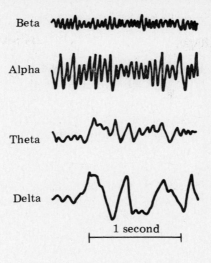

1 second

Fig. 4.2

the occipital and parietal areas of the brain when an individual is in a highly relaxed state. These alpha rhythms disappear upon the presentation of alerting stimuli. Although alpha waves, the precursor of alpha rhythms, are found in the newborn EEG, the full alpha rhythm is not characteristic of the newborn.

Sleeping-State EEG Patterns

Two patterns of sleep are discernible as early as the eighth prenatal month and continue to be differentiated in the newborn's EEG records.

Trance Alternate. The first sleeping-state EEG pattern, which is present in quiet sleep, is called the trance alternate. The EEG pattern in trance alternate is characterized by alternations between comparative silence in cortical activity and bursts of irregular slow activity mixed with more rhythmic theta waves. This sleep state is also characterized by regular, slow respiration and heart rate, muscle tone in the neck, and few body movements.

Rapid Eye Movement. The contrasting sleep pattern observed in the newborn is referred to as *REM* (rapid eye movement) sleep. REM sleep is characterized by fast, low-voltage, desynchronized EEG activity. It is accompanied by rapid eye movements that can be observed through the closed eyelids, irregular heartbeats and respiratory activity, and a lack of neck and muscle tone.

In adults, REM sleep is also associated with dreaming, but because confirmation of dreams depends upon the verbal reports of an individual, it is not possible to assess whether a similar phenomenon occurs in the newborn. The REM sleep of the neonate has been of interest to developmental psychologists because it characterizes over 50 percent of the newborn's sleeping time, a proportion that diminishes rapidly as the total amount of sleeping time for the child decreases.

Bodily Functions and Homeostasis

Until birth, the maintenance of the child is totally dependent upon the functioning of the mother. At birth, however, the newborn is thrust into a cold new world in which it must survive independently. It must circulate its own blood, provide its own oxygen, digest its own food, and maintain its own biochemical and thermal balance activities.

The *autostimulation* theory proposes that REM sleep allows the higher cortical centers of the newborn's nervous system to receive the stimulation needed for their development during a time when the child is unable to effectively process externally generated stimulation.

Circulatory System

The anatomy of the heart and circulatory system of the newborn is in a state of transition between that of the fetus and that of the older infant. To understand this transition state and its developmental implications, it is helpful to understand both the heart anatomy and the circulatory system of the fetus and that of the older child and the adult.

The Mature Heart and Circulatory System

In the circulatory system of the adult, the unoxygenated blood enters the right atrium (auricle) from the superior and inferior vena cava. From the right atrium, blood is pumped to the right ventricle and then through the pulmonary artery to the lungs, where the blood is saturated with oxygen and cleansed of its carbon dioxide (CO_2) waste. From the lungs, the freshly oxygenated blood returns to the left atrium of the heart, where it is pumped to the left ventricle and finally out through the aorta to the periphery of the body. (See Fig. 4.3.)

Fetal Circulation

Prenatal circulation differs from postnatal circulation in one significant way. In the fetus, oxygenation and cleansing of the blood occur at the placenta, and not in the lungs. To allow for this functional difference, the fetal circulatory system includes three important structures not included in the mature circulatory system—the umbilical cord, the valve of foramen ovale, and the ductus arteriosus. (See Fig. 4.4.)

1. The *umbilical cord* carries blood from the lower limbs and trunk to the placenta for oxygenation and cleansing. The same cord carries the oxygenated blood back to the fetal circulatory system. That oxygenated blood moves through the inferior venae cavae to the heart.

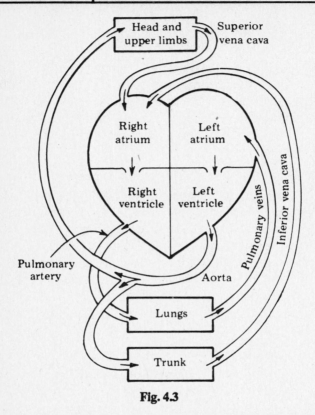

Fig. 4.3

2. The *valve of foramen ovale* allows blood from the inferior vena cava to move directly to the left atrium, rather than first flowing to the right side of the heart and through the lung, as occurs in the postnatal system.

3. The *ductus arteriosus* reduces the amount of blood flowing from the right ventricle to the immature and nonfunctioning fetal lungs. Instead, much of the blood flowing from the right ventricle of the fetus moves through the ductus arteriosus directly into the aorta and on to the umbilical arteries.

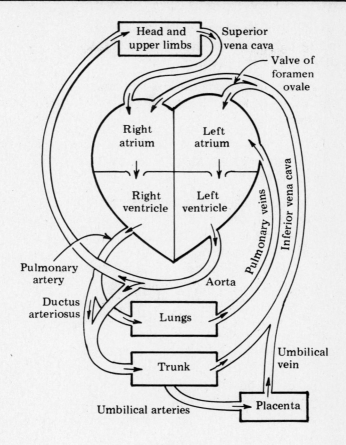

Fig. 4.4

The Newborn's Circulatory System

Shortly after birth, the umbilical cord spontaneously ceases to circulate blood to the placenta, and the respiratory system automatically begins to function. These changes increase the flow of blood to the lungs. As a result the changing pressure patterns within the component parts of the circulatory system cause two significant alterations in the pattern of blood flow observed in the newborn, and also in the anatomy of the newborn's circulatory system.

1. The *valve of foramen ovale* is mechanically closed, thus forcing the blood from the inferior vena cava to flow into the right atrium, as it does in the mature circulatory system.

2. The *ductus arteriosus* constricts and forces all blood from the right ventricle to enter the lung, where it can be oxygenated and cleansed.

While functional changes in these two structures take place within moments after birth, permanent anatomical closure of these fetal channels is quite slow and progresses through the period of early postnatal development.

On some occasions, complete anatomical closure of the ductus arteriosus does not occur. This incomplete closure is a major cause of congenital heart problems. In a child with this heart problem, some of the blood circulates directly from the right ventricle to the aorta and the periphery of the body, instead of being oxygenated in the lungs. Depending upon the severity of the defect, the result of patent ductus arteriosus can be labored breathing, susceptibility to fatigue, growth failure, respiratory infections, heart murmurs, congestive heart failure, or even death. For children suffering *patent ductus arteriosus*, corrective surgery in early life is called for.

The Heart

At birth the heart constitutes a greater portion of total body weight than it does at any other time in the life of the child or the adult: approximately 0.75 percent of the total body weight. At the end of one year, the heart weight is reduced to 0.50 percent of the total body weight. While the heart doubles its weight in the first year, the total body weight increases threefold. At maturity, the heart constitutes only 0.33 percent of the adult body weight.

The need for a large heart at birth may be dictated by the large size of the arteries in the neonate relative to their size later in life. Even with the neonate's relatively large heart, the newborn's blood pressure is significantly lower than the blood pressure recorded for older children and adults.

A fast heartbeat is also needed by the neonate to maintain adequate blood pressure in light of the large size of its arteries. In the first month of life, the heart rate of the alert neonate averages 150 pulses per minute. Compare that rate with the average of 70 pulses per minute found among adults. The speed of the heartbeat declines with age, but it does not reach the slower adult levels until after adolescence.

Blood

The blood of the newborn is lacking in vitamin K, an element that encourages blood clotting. One consequence of this deficiency is that injuries sustained during the first few weeks of life can cause severe hemorrhaging.

It is speculated that normally there is an excess of red blood cells in fetal blood, and that these should be destroyed at birth. In many newborns, bilirubin, a by-product of red blood cell destruction, cannot be adequately metabolized by the immature liver. This metabolic deficiency results in excesses of bilirubin in the blood of the neonate, a condition known as jaundice. The symptoms of jaundice are a yellowing of the skin and the whites of the eyes.

All neonates experience jaundice to some degree. In most cases, the presence of jaundice is of little concern. However, severe jaundice may be a symptom of inadequate liver function that can ultimately produce liver damage. Because exposure to direct sunlight increases the rate of bilirubin metabolism in cases of mild jaundice, it may be recommended that the newborn be placed nude in direct sunlight for short periods of time each day. In more severe cases, the newborn is placed under bilirubin lights, which provide synthetic sunlight.

Respiratory System

The respiratory system of the newborn is not functional until birth. During prenatal development, the oxygenation of blood occurs at the placenta. At present, the stimulants that activate the functioning of the respiratory system at birth are not fully understood. One major stimulant thought to activate respiration is the reduced levels of oxygen and increased levels of CO_2 in the blood that result from the spontaneous elimination of the umbilical cord from the circulatory system.

The muscles of the newborn's respiratory system are still immature, and breathing is characteristically shallow, irregular, and noisy. This grunting and gasping is often a source of concern to parents. With increased development of the muscles that control breathing, this respiration pattern is eliminated.

The rapid rate of respiration also contributes to parental concern. The respiration rate of the newborn is 40 to 45 breaths per minute, in contrast to the slow and steady 18 breaths per minute of the adult. By the end of the first week, the newborn's respiration rate drops to approximately 35 breaths per minute, but it still is twice that of the adult.

Gastrointestinal System

In contrast to the beliefs of some people, the neonate is capable of eating and digesting food. Enzymes are available to the newborn for the digestion of all basic foods except certain starches. The typical newborn will eat seven to eight times a day and ingest 18 to 25 ounces of food. By the end of the first month, the number of feedings desired by the newborn is usually reduced to five or six per day. This feeding schedule is not surprising if one remembers that the stomach of the newborn empties approximately four to five hours after eating, and that the contractions accompanying an empty stomach are experienced by the newborn as painful.

Temperature Control

For warm-blooded animals, humans among them, the maintenance of a constant internal temperature is critical for survival. One concern of most parents—and almost a compulsion among hospital personnel—is the maintenance of a constantly warm temperature in the neonate's room. The reason for this concern is the neonate's limited ability to maintain a constant body temperature in the wake of fluctuating air temperatures. For the newborn, the average rectal temperature is a little less than 99° F (37°C). This temperature is slightly higher than the average adult temperature. (Note: Rectal temperatures are usually slightly higher than oral temperatures.)

The newborn's poorly functioning temperature control system is not the product of an immature nervous system or a poorly developed metabolic system. Instead, the problem faced by the newborn stems from two factors: its large body surface area relative to its body volume, and its poor body insulation.

Much of one's body heat is lost through radiation at the skin surface. The more skin surface one has, the more potential there is for radiant heat loss to take place. Although the total skin surface area of the newborn is smaller than that of the older infant, the amount of skin surface area in relation to the total volume of the body is much greater for the newborn than for the older infant. Thus, relative to the volume of the body containing the heat, there is a greater potential for the newborn than for the older infant to lose heat through skin-surface radiation.

The body functions much like a house. Heat movement from inside the house to the outside is retarded by placing insulation in the walls and ceiling. In the body, fat can be thought of as insulation. In the newborn, the fatty insulation has not matured; thus, there is an overabundance of heat movement from the interior of the body to the skin surface, and a consequent loss of body heat to the surrounding environment.

Behavioral Activities of the Newborn

For purposes of discussing the behavioral activities of the newborn, it is valuable to be aware of the states of neonatal alertness in which those activities take place.

States of Activity

The newborn sleeps approximately 67 percent of the time. During nonsleeping hours, four states of activity have been described: (1) *drowsiness,* in which the eyes open and close intermittently and the newborn appears dull and unresponsive to its environment; (2) *alert activity,* in which the newborn is relaxed, relatively inactive, with open eyes that can—and do— follow objects as they move about; (3) *waking activity,* in which the newborn's eyes are open, but he or she is only semialert and frequently engages in diffuse motor activity involving the whole body; and (4) *crying,* in which the crying vocalizations are often accompanied by mass motor activity.

As one might expect, the alert waking state is the one most preferred by caretakers, while the crying state is the least preferred. Crying, however, may occur for different reasons in the newborn. Parents attest to this fact, and more systematic observations have differentiated three patterns of crying: a hunger cry, a mad or angry cry, and a pain cry.

Motor Activities

The motor activities engaged in by the neonate during its

periods of wakefulness can be divided into two categories: Reflexes, which constitute the newborn's predetermined systematic responses to particular sources of stimulation, and non-reflex movements, which will ultimately evolve into the child's instrumental responses to the environment.

Reflexes

Reflexes are important for two reasons. The first is that observation of some reflexes provides information concerning the neurological integrity of the newborn. Second, some reflexes provide the newborn its first systematic encounter with objects in the environment. Modifications of those reflexes are the newborn's first attempt to accommodate to the environment.

The following are examples of the more significant reflexes present in the newborn. For each reflex, the stimulus that elicits it is presented, the response associated with the stimulant is described, and the significance of that reflex response is indicated.

1. *Babinski Response.* Stimulant: Stroke the middle of the sole of the foot. Response: Toes fan out. Significance: Absence is indicative of deficits in the lower spinal chord.

2. *Plantar Reflex.* Stimulant: Press on the ball of the foot. Response: Toes grasp. Significance: Absence is indicative of a deficit in the lower spinal cord.

3. *Withdrawal Reflex.* Stimulant: Prick the sole of the foot with a pin. Response: The newborn withdraws the foot. Significance: Absence is indicative of sciatic nerve damage.

4. *Patellar Reflex (Knee Jerk).* Stimulant: Tap the patellar tendon immediately below the knee. Response: The lower leg kicks out. Significance: Absence suggests muscular disease, and exaggeration is present in hyperexcitable children.

5. *Moro Reflex.* Stimulant: Any surprising event, for ex-

ample, dropping the newborn's head, a loud noise, and so on. Response: The newborn stretches arms and legs, appears to reach out with the arms to grab self. Significance: Absence is indicative of general neurological dysfunction.

6. *Stepping Reflex.* Stimulant: Hold the newborn vertically with his or her toes brushing against the floor. Response: The newborn will make steplike movements. Significance: Unknown, but fun to watch.

7. *Swimming Reflex.* Stimulant: Hold the newborn horizontally in the air. Response: The newborn will reach out his or her arms and legs in swimming-like motion. Significance: Unknown, but also fun to watch.

8. *Palmer Reflex (Grasping Reflex).* Stimulant: Put pressure on the palm of the hand. Response: The hand will close and grasp. The grasp is strong enough to allow the newborn to be lifted and to support its own weight. Significance: The grasping reflex provides the basis for manipulatory exploration of objects in the newborn's world. With use, the reflex will be modified to allow for the differential handling and manipulation of varied objects in the world of the infant, thus facilitating the child's cognitive growth.

9. *Rooting Reflex.* Stimulant: Stroke the side of the cheek or lips. Response: The newborn turns his or her head to the side being stroked and prepares to suck. Significance: Facilitates feeding.

10. *Sucking Reflex.* Stimulant: The presence of any object in the mouth. Response: Sucking. Significance: Facilitates feeding and provides a basis for exploring objects in the newborn's environment. Much of the infant's exploration will be done through sucking objects as well as looking at and feeling them.

11. *Eye Movement Reflex.* Stimulant: The presence of a

sharp contour or a slow-moving object in the field of vison. Response: Fixation on the object or contour, and following the object's movement with the eyes. Significance: This reflex provides the newborn with a mechanism for exploring the environment; thus, it enhances cognitive and social development.

Gross Motor Activity

In addition to reflex activity, gross motor activity in the newborn. Gross motor activity differs from fine motor activity in that it involves activation of the larger muscles and increments in motor responses that are somewhat larger than those involved in fine motor activity. For example, reaching out to touch a ball is an example of gross motor activity, while grasping a pencil to write is indicative of fine motor coordination.

In response to many sources of both internal and external stimulation, the arms and legs of the newborn move spontaneously and the head moves from side to side. This gross motor activity is characterized by mass action; that is, the movement of one limb seems to spontaneously activate motion in the other limbs of the body.

Clearly, the newborn has not yet differentiated the various elements that make up his or her body and has no coordination over their activity. This lack of coordinated activity is not surprising if one reexamines the discussion of the cortical and cerebral development of the newborn. (See the section in this chapter entitled "The Cortex of the Newborn.") While the primary motor cortex is one of the first brain centers to evolve after birth, it is not well developed in the newborn.

CHAPTER 5

Perceptual, Cognitive, and Social Capacities of the Newborn

Learning begins with sensation and perception. We "take in" the world through our senses, and we process the information through our perceptions. There is an important difference between sensation and perception: sensation is an objective process, uncolored by the peculiarities of the individual's mind. Perception, on the other hand, introduces a reconstructive effort, often involving a process of censoring and coloring the sensed experience. We might say that sensation is transformed into meaning by perception. Although this is an oversimplification, it is accurate and can help us better understand why perceptual problems arise, what they mean in terms of the individual's development, and how they can be handled.

At one time, people thought that newborns were severely limited in their abilities to sense and perceive the world around them and to interact in any systematic way with it. Evidence suggests, however, that this is not true. Newborns can detect differences in light intensity and color, and discriminate among the primary sounds that make up human speech. They respond to sharp odors and prefer sweet tastes to salty or neutral ones. The earliest learning takes place through conditioning. Emotional responses in the first month of life center around the two extremes, distress and satisfaction. Social smiling may be observed.

Perceptual Capacities in the Newborn

The incorrect belief that newborns lack virtually all sensory and perceptual capacities may be an outgrowth of observations of some other familiar organisms at birth, such as cats. Because the eyelids of newborn kittens are not fully separated at birth, their visual capacities do not manifest themselves until they are nine to ten days old.

The aroused expectations of new parents may also account for the fact that just after birth the infant may seem unresponsive. Parents often become concerned that their newborn is deaf because the child makes few, if any, gross responses to sound. A pediatrician, however, soothes the parents' concerns by saying that gross responses to sound are not common in newborns, but that subtle responses to sound, often considered unimportant by the parents, have been observed by the physician.

Assessing Sensory and Perceptual Capacities in the Newborn

In assessing the sensory and perceptual capacities of the individual, one is concerned with whether or not an individual can detect the presence of a stimulus in the environment, and the extent to which an individual can distinguish between two physically different sources of stimulation.

The following questions might interest a developmental psychologist: Are neonates as capable as adults of detecting a white light—whose brightness is equivalent to the light of a star—reflected from a white piece of paper? Can neonates detect the difference between a white light and a red light of equal brightness? Can they perceive differences in color?

To answer these questions, psychologists must develop some method of allowing the individual to answer questions necessitating only the following types of responses. "Yes, I see the stimulus;" "Yes, I see they are different;" "I don't know if I saw the stimulus;" "I don't know if they are different."

With children or adults who are capable of understanding language and of speaking, it is not difficult either to ask those questions or to obtain answers. With the nonverbal neonate and infant, however, methods other than talking must be used both to ask the questions and to allow for the communication of an answer. In general, in order to study the responses of nonverbal subjects, researchers choose a particular behavior in which the subject can engage, and they observe whether the behavioral response to one stimulus situation is different from that to another. What follows is a description of some of the most common behaviors used to accomplish that task.

Reflexes

Some forms of stimulation, when detected, produce a reflex response in the newborn. When the reflex is elicited by a stimulus, the newborn is in effect saying, "Yes, I detect the presence of the stimulus." When no reflex is elicited, the psychologist does not know if the stimulus has not been detected or if some other factor has interfered with a detected stimulus eliciting a measurable reflex.

For example, a light shone in the eye of a newborn can produce a constriction of the pupil. If the reflex occurs, the newborn has signaled that it can detect the presence of the light

Habituation of the Orienting Responses

If a novel stimulus is presented to an individual, even a newborn, it will often elicit an orienting response. Heart rate will change, attention will be directed toward the stimulus, and other activities, such as sucking or body movements, will slow down. You can see these phenomena for yourself by banging a book on the table when a friend isn't expecting it and observing the responses.

If within a short time the stimulus is presented again, the orienting response will cease to be elicited. This cessation of response with repeated presentations of the same stimulus is called habituation. If a person has been habituated to one stimulus, but a new stimulus, detectably different from the first, is presented, the orienting response will be observed again. If the new stimulus is not discriminated from the habituated stimulus, it would seem to the individual to be no more than another repetition of the habituated stimulus, and no orienting response will be observed. Thus, one can assess when a newborn detects the difference between two stimuli by observing whether, after one stimulus has been habituated, the presentation of a second stimulus elicits an orienting response.

A special apparatus is connected to the chest of an infant to record its heart rate (one component of the orienting response). A tone is presented repeatedly until no change in heart rate occurs upon its presentation. A tone with a different frequency (pitch) is presented. If the heart rate changes when the new tone is presented, it implies that the infant can detect a difference between the two tones.

Body Movements and Facial Expressions

Many parents observe that increased gross body movement and/or smiles accompany the presentation of some stimuli and not others. If these different behavioral patterns are systematically associated with sources of stimulation, it can be inferred that the individual detects differences among stimuli. At 28 weeks of age, for example, infants smile and vocalize more often when shown female faces than when shown male faces. This differential response pattern implies that infants can discriminate between male and female faces.

Eye Fixations

If, using appropriate experimental controls, two stimuli are presented to an individual and one is fixated upon more than the other, it can be inferred that the respondent can detect a difference between the two stimuli. If no differential fixation time is observed, one cannot determine whether the differences in the pictures have gone undetected or whether the respondent simply has no preference for one picture over another. This principle has been used repeatedly to assess the visual capacities and preferences of very young infants.

Researcher Robert Fantz found that infants look longer at patterns of black and white stripes than at a homogeneous gray surface. This result is interpreted as proof that infants as young as eight to ten weeks can discriminate the presence of contours.

Visual Capacities

In assessing the visual capacities of the newborn, anatomical characteristics will be examined first. Then the newborn's abilities to detect and discriminate sources of visual stimulation will be assessed. Finally, the newborn's visual preferences will be examined.

Anatomical Characteristics of the Visual System

The visual system is one of the most fully developed systems possessed by the neonate. Still, it is not anatomically identical to that of the adult, and those anatomical differences account for some of the developmental changes that occur in visual perception.

Size of the Eye. The eyeball is smaller in the newborn than in the adult,which anatomical may account for reduced visual acuity in the neonate. (See the section on "Visual Acuity.")

The Retina. The retina is highly developed in the newborn. The *rods* and *cones,* which are sensitive to achromatic (noncolor) and chromatic (color) stimulation respectively, are nearly identical to their adult counterparts. Only the macula region of the retina is immature. The *macula* is that portion of the retina at which images are acutely focused. In that region there are fewer receptor cells in the neonate than in the adult, a fact that may also account for the newborn's reduced visual acuity.

Optic Nerve. While somewhat smaller than the adult optic nerve, the optic nerve of the newborn is functional at birth and within a very few months is fully covered by a myelin coating that facilitates functioning.

Visual Cortex. The cells of the visual cortex are all present at birth but have not become organized and differentiated to the extent that they will be in the more mature individual.

Muscle Control

The aspect of the neonate's visual system that most hinders its functioning is the limited ability of the neonate to control the muscles of the eye. While the lens of the eye can change shape to accommodate itself to objects at different distances, it responds slowly. The eye lens of the newborn functions best when objects are within a radius of 2 feet. The newborn's ideal focal point for visual stimuli is eight inches from the eye.

While newborns can fixate on an object, following a moving object with their eyes is difficult because of the poorly developed neural feedback system to the muscles controlling eye movements. That control, and the accompanying ability to track visual stimuli develops four to six weeks after birth. Even then, however, horizontal eye movements are more easily controlled than vertical movements.

Light Detection

The adult human is sensitive to light within the range of approximately 400 millimicrons to 760 millimicrons. Observations of the pupillary reflex of newborns suggest that they too can detect the presence of light and discriminate among lights of differing brightness. However, the sensitivity of newborns seems less acute than that of adults. By the end of the first month of life, the dimmest light that can be detected (the absolute threshold) is approximately two logarithmic units brighter than that detectable by adults.

One can infer that newborns can discriminate differences in light intensity by their differential levels of activity under different levels of illumination. Behavioral activity appears to be reduced as the intensity of light increases. Some people use this principle in helping newborns sleep. Paradoxically, a dark room tends to increase an agitated infant's activity, while a lighted room tends to decrease activity levels.

Color Detection

Evidence exists that even newborns can detect differences in color. Specifically, it has been observed that infants' responses to red light are different from their responses to blue light.

Visual Acuity

Visual acuity is a measure of how wide a line must be before it can be detected, or how much separation is required between two contours before they can be seen as being separated. The Snellen notation, which is commonly used to denote visual acuity, relates an observer's detection capacity to a standard detection capacity in terms of distance.

A Snellen notation of 20/20, which represents normal visual acuity, means that one's detection capacities for objects 20 feet away are the same as a standard detection capacity at 20 feet. Vision of 20/30 means that one's detection capacity at 20 feet is comparable to the standard capacity at 30 feet. The individual in this case is nearsighted. Newborns can see and detect differences among sources of stimulation; however, they are quite nearsighted.

While the determination of a newborn's acuity depends in part on the sensitivity of the measurement procedure used, recent data suggest an acuity for one-day-old infants of 20/150. The reason newborns are so nearsighted may be found in the anatomical characteristics of the optic systems. (See the previous section entitled "Anatomical Characteristics of the Visual System.")

Visual Preference

If newborns can see, at what do they prefer to gaze? Evidence from a variety of sources suggests that infants are attracted by movement, fixate on contours (the edge of a form), and given two figures to look at, prefer to fixate on the figure with the greater amount of contour.

When confronted with the two forms depicted in Fig. 5.1, newborns will look longer at Form I than at Form II because Form I has more contour. It appears that the outermost portion of the contour is focused upon. It has been found that neonates born to mothers who received large quantities of medication during labor and delivery exhibit less differential behavior to forms having different amounts of contour.

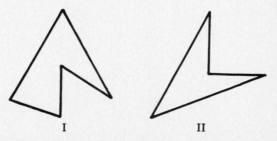

I   II

Fig. 5.1

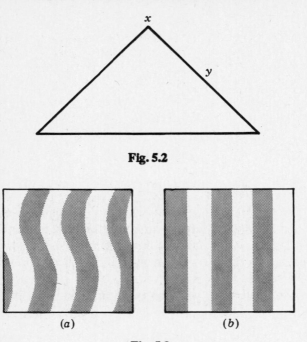

Fig. 5.2

(a)   (b)

Fig. 5.3

In Fig. 5.2, a newborn would be more likely to focus on the contour marked *x* than on the one marked *y*. Recent reports suggest that other things being equal, newborns prefer to look at curved contours rather than straight contours or angles.

In Fig. 5.3, newborns would be more likely to look at the form labeled *a* than at the form labeled *b*.

Auditory Capacities

For years it was thought that the auditory capacity of the newborn human was severely limited. Two factors probably stimulated that belief: the limited number of observable responses by the newborn to auditory stimulation, and the observation that the middle ear of the newborn is filled with a liquid that distorts sound transmission. While the sensitivity of the newborn to auditory stimulation is not as great as that of the adult, the deficiencies are not as large as was once thought.

Anatomy of the Auditory System

The peripheral mechanisms for hearing—the outer, the middle, and the inner ear—are well developed before birth, while the auditory cortex of the brain lags behind in development. However, even before birth, the auditory system is anatomically and neurologically capable of rudimentary functioning.

Although the auditory system functions at birth, its capabilities of detecting and discriminating sound are reduced because of the presence of a heavy liquid in the middle ear. This liquid hinders the movement of the small bones that mechanically transmit sound-wave patterns from the eardrum to the inner portion of the auditory receptive system. The presence of that liquid accounts for a reduction of approximately 10 decibels in the loudness of sounds that can be heard by the newborn. However, within a few days after birth, the liquid is absorbed and subsequently plays no detrimental role in hearing.

Threshold of Sensitivity

The majority of research concerned with the auditory sensitivity of the newborn has asked what kinds of sounds the newborn can hear. In that research, a variety of sound stimulation sources has been used, from tuning forks to whistles and gongs. Little research has systematically examined the sensitivity of the newborn to pure tones. Those systematic studies that have been undertaken reveal somewhat different results depending upon the behavioral measures used to assess auditory threshold and the frequency of the tones used.

By using the palpebral (eye-blink) reflex as a measure of response to pure tones of 500 and 1,000 cycles per second, it was reported that newborns could hear that tones at the loudest intensities were 105 decibels. In contrast, the same tones created changes in respiration when presented at intensities under 90 decibels. In the most recent research undertaken, it has been found that newborns can respond to tones presented at a volume as low as 45 to 50 decibels. In the adult, the threshold for those same tones is between 0 and 35 decibels.

One can summarize the research on newborns' auditory sensitivity by saying that (1) newborns can hear, (2) their thresholds of sensitivity are somewhat higher than those of adults, and (3) their responses to sound stimulations are subtle and not often observed by parents.

Frequency Discrimination

Given that newborns can detect the presence of sound, can they discriminate among different tones (sound waves having different frequencies)? It has been reported that newborns one to five days old can discriminate between tones of 200 and 250 cycles per second. However, the research methods used do not rule out the possibility that the differential responses made to the tones result from discriminations of loudness rather than pitch.

In many studies of frequency discrimination, the newborn is repeatedly presented with one tone until habituation to the tone occurs. (See the section entitled "Habituation to the Orienting Response.") A second tone is then presented to determine if an orienting response is elicited. In the case of auditory stimulation, however, repeated presentations of a pure tone reduce the sensitivity of the receptor organs for that tone and in so doing reduce its loudness. Because the new tone stimulates a second set of receptors whose sensitivity has not been reduced, the new tone appears louder than the first. Thus, when the new tone is presented, it is not possible to determine whether the change in the newborn's response results from perceived differences in the frequency of the tones or perceived differences in their loudness.

Recent observations also indicate that newborns as young as

one month are able to make fine discriminations among the primary sounds that make up human speech (phonemes). Specifically, it has been reported that discriminations are made between the phonemes /ba/ and /pa/, whose physical sound-wave patterns differ very little.

Sound Localization

Sound localization refers to an individual's ability to discriminate the location from which a sound emanates. Sound localization is usually detected by observing an individual turning toward a sound. The capacity to localize sound is not highly developed in the newborn, due to the fact that it requires the coordination of auditory information coming simultaneously from both ears. In contrast to the detection and discrimination functions of a single ear, sound localization involves the functioning of higher level cortical systems that may not be developed at birth.

Olfactory Perception (Smell)

The receptors for smell are located in a small area at the top of each nasal cavity. The effectiveness of those receptors at birth is difficult to assess, because responses to olfactory stimulation may reflect direct irritation of a surface nerve (the tegmental nerve) rather than stimulation of the smell receptors. It is known, however, that the threshold for responding to olfactory stimulation decreases rapidly and systematically during the first few days of life. Also, shortly after birth the newborn responds in some way to stimulation from ammonia and acetic acid, among other things.

Gustatory Perception (Taste)

Psychologists have studied the capacity of newborns to discriminate among the different taste qualities of sour, salt, bitter, and sweet. Newborns are observed to respond differently to salt solutions and milk.   This leads researchers to believe that neonates can discriminate taste and may prefer a sweetened substance to one that is neutral or salty.

In fact, preference for sweetened flavors is evident in the feeding of newborns. When increased liquid intake is required, a newborn may accept a bottle of sweetened water, while totally rejecting a bottle of unsweetened water.

Learning in the Newborn

Learning is typically inferred when one observes a change in behavior that does not result from the physical maturation or deterioration of the organism, states of fatigue or arousal, or other transient physical states of the organism.   An understanding of the newborn's capacity to change his or her behavior in response to environmental influences is critical to our understanding of child development.

Classical Conditioning

As we saw in Chapter 1, classical conditioning refers to learning that occurs when a previously neutral stimulus (the *conditioned stimulus,* CS) is associated with a stimulus that spontaneously elicits a response (the *unconditioned stimulus,* UCS); subsequently, the CS elicits a response of its own, namely, a *conditioned response* (CR).

Research has produced reports of classical conditioning in neonates as young as one day old. Infants a few days old hear a tone (CS) while they are sucking on a pacifier (UCS). After 15 presentations of these simultaneously presented stimuli, the neonate hears the tone alone. It is observed that the rate of sucking during the presentation of the tone is greater for these neonates than for other neonates who have heard the tone and sucked the pacifier but have never had the two stimuli associated with each other.

The most successful demonstrations of classical conditioning in the neonate have used stimuli and responses that are intimately involved in the feeding process. A rubber tube is put in the mouth of a neonate (CS). After ten seconds a dextrose solution (sugar water) is delivered through the tube for five seconds (UCS). After ten pairings of the tube and the dextrose solution, the neonate begins to suck the tube before any dextrose is delivered (CR). The conditioned response (sucking the empty tube) is observed more frequently in neonates who have frequently experienced the association between the tube and the dextrose solution than in neonates who have had an equivalent amount of experience with a tube and dextrose but did not have the two stimuli associated with each other.

Extinction

When a conditioned stimulus is repeatedly presented without an unconditioned stimulus, it loses its power to elicit the conditioned response. This phenomenon is referred to as extinction. Extinction may be observed in the neonate.

In the experiment reported above, the neonate began to suck (CR) the tube (CS) when no dextrose (UCS) was delivered. However, after presenting the tube five consecutive times but delivering no dextrose, the sucking was reduced significantly. Extinction had occurred.

Aversive Conditioning

When the UCS in classical conditioning is noxious, the conditioning is called aversive. Aversive conditioning has not been demonstrated successfully in infants.

In one experiment, neonates are given a shock on the foot (UCS) and retract their legs (response). Soon after, a tone is sounded (CS) and the legs do not retract. The tone is then sounded and at the same time the shock is administered. The neonates retract their legs. This association is repeated many of times and then the tone is sounded by itself. The conditioned stimulus (the tone) does not elicit a response, even after many pairings with the UCS (shock).

Temporal Conditioning

When an unconditioned stimulus such as food is continuously presented at the end of a particular time interval, the end of the time interval acts as a conditioned stimulus, and it alone begins to elicit responses that theretofore had been elicited only by the unconditioned stimulus. This phenomenon is called temporal conditioning and may be observed in the newborn.

For example, a newborn child is put on a three-hour feeding schedule. After a week on this feeding schedule, the parents are late for a feeding; however, at the appointed three-hour interval the child becomes agitated and irritable. Physical examinations of infants suggest that the biochemistry of the digestive system changes spontaneously at the end of regular feeding intervals. Because these changes are dictated by the previous experiences of the infant and are not inherent, they exemplify temporal conditioning.

Operant (Instrumental) Conditioning

In operant (instrumental) conditioning, an *instrumental response* (IR) is followed by a consequence. The characteristics of that consequence influence the future occurrence of the IR. If the consequence is rewarding to the individual, it is more likely that the instrumental response will recur. If the consequence is not rewarding to the individual, it is less likely that the IR will recur.

For example, each time a child cries loudly in his crib at night (IR), the parents quickly take him from the crib to the family room and play with him (reward). The parents are amazed when the child's crying fits increase in frequency and intensity after their extensive efforts to quiet him.

When an older child bangs a spoon and knife on the table and spits food out at mealtime (IR), the parents firmly remove her to an isolated room where she cannot receive a reward (nonrewarding consequence). After a few days, the child ceases table banging and food spitting.

Operant (instrumental) conditioning occurs in the neonate when consequences are contingent upon specific behavior occurring. If the receipt of milk from a special nipple depends on sucking that nipple in a novel yet physically possible way, a newborn will quickly adapt its sucking behavior (IR) to produce the positive consequence of receiving milk (reward).

In one experiment, one cheek of newborns was touched; when the children turned their head toward the touch, milk was delivered to them through a nipple. After 20 to 30 such experiences, it was found that newborns were more apt to turn their head to the side of the cheek touched than before the training began. No change in head turning was observed for control neonates who had not received milk contingent upon the head-turning response.

Partial Schedules of Reinforcement

If contingent consequences do not follow each instrumental response but instead occur after only some instrumental responses, an individual is said to receive partial reinforcement. When partial reinforcement is administered to a neonate, changes in the pattern of instrumental response are more difficult to extinguish than when rewards are presented continuously.

In one experiment, newborns were rewarded with dextrose when they turned their heads appropriately. One group of neonates received the reward of dextrose solution each time they turned their heads. Another group received an equal number of rewards, but the reward was given only after every third head turn. Subsequently, rewards for both groups were terminated altogether (extinction procedure). The first group (continuous reward) quickly reduced their head turning. The second group (partial reward) continued much longer with their head-turning responses than the continuously rewarded neonates.

Discrimination Learning

When an individual discriminates differences between two stimuli and produces appropriately different responses to each, discrimination learning has been exhibited. Discrimination learning is critical for enabling individuals to adapt effectively to the many different situations in which they find themselves and the many different responses those situations require.

Each of us responds differently to different people. While it may be appropriate to rush up and embrace a friend or acquaintance, to exhibit the same attention toward a total stranger would be inappropriate. We have learned to discriminate between friends and strangers and have learned a different response to each of those stimuli.

Although research efforts have been limited by the complexity of tasks required to demonstrate discrimination learning in the neonate, discrimination learning has nonetheless been systematically observed to occur in the newborn.

Either a buzzer or a tone was sounded when the right cheek of a child less than a week old was stroked. When right turns of the head occurred after the sounding of the buzzer, the child was rewarded, but no reward followed head turning when the tone was sounded. Soon the frequency of head turning increased when the buzzer was sounded. No similar changes in head turning were observed when the tone was presented. The child was able to discriminate between two stimuli, the buzzer and the tone, and exhibited different response patterns in the two situations.

Memory

Controversy exists as to whether the infant less than one month of age exhibits memory capacities. Some researchers argue that because neonates systematically repeat responses to particular stimulus situations, they must have the capacity to remember. Other evidence used to support the position that memory capacities exist during the first days of life comes from observing that repeated presentations of a visual stimulus habituate the orienting response, and that the introduction of a new stimulus reinstates it. If the repeated stimulus were not remembered during the interval between presentations, it would be a new stimulus each time it appeared and would elicit an orienting response.

A picture was presented to a neonate less than one week old. On initial presentation, a change in heart rate was observed (the orienting response). With repeated presentations, the neonate recognized the picture as the same one presented previously, and the orienting response dissipated. However, the introduction of a new picture reinstated the orienting response. The neonate could distinguish between the old and new pictures.

While observations similar to these have been reported, researchers have found it extremely difficult to reproduce those findings. At present, it is best to say that tentative evidence exists for the presence of memory capacities in the newborn; the most widely accepted view is that memory capacities develop toward the end of the first month of life.

Social Responsiveness in the Newborn

Emotions and social interactions are fundamental to personality development. How early can these be detected? Can we deduce whether the newborn is exhibiting these characteristics?

Emotional Expression

The term "emotion" typically conjures up images of internal joy or sorrow that may be known only to the person experiencing the emotion. Behavioral correlates of these internal states are not always viable indicators of the emotional experience. For example, a person may cry from sorrow or from joy. While the fact that behavioral correlates are not always useful indicators of emotional experiences makes it difficult to identify and categorize a variety of specific emotions in the newborn, two classes of emotional behavior are clearly exhibited by the newborn: distress, a negative emotion, and satisfaction, a positive emotion. Although we can observe in the newborn behaviors characteristic of these two emotional states, these observations do not allow us to infer the occurrence of internal experiences of emotion similar to those of the adult.

Distress

The most common emotion observed in the newborn is distress. Its behavioral correlates are agitation, grimaces, and crying. The exhibition of distress probably has survival value for the infant, for it signals to the caretaker that something is wrong. Distress is elicited by a variety of situations, including the presence of noxious stimuli, hunger, and general overstimulation.

A newborn child is brought home and confronted with loud talking, touching, and overly admiring relatives and friends. The child becomes agitated, cries, and feeds poorly. The infant is exhibiting signs of distress brought about by overstimulation.

Satisfaction

The positive emotional state of satisfaction is typically inferred from the newborn being soothed, alert, and tension-free. States of satisfaction are achieved from sucking, gentle movement, and low levels of repetitious sound. Those soothing techniques have been used for years by parents to pacify distressed infants.

Tape recordings of a steady heartbeat are used in some neonate care centers in hopes of producing a soothing environment. Speculations have been made that this constant sound is associated with the warm security of life in the uterus. However, there is no way to examine scientifically the adequacy of this speculation.

Social Interactions

We have seen that newborns can exhibit behaviors characteristic of positive and negative emotional states. Can they engage in social interactions as well? To many people, the child less than one month old is asocial. The child eats, sleeps, cries, lies passively, and evacuates wastes. Smiles and other responses associated with social interactions have often been identified as spontaneous reactions to physiological states. Closer observation of infants less than a month old reveals that, under some circumstances, smiling in response to social stimulation does take place.

Social Smiling

In what is now a classic piece of research, Peter Wolf provided photographic evidence of social smiling responses in three-week-old infants. Dr. Wolf reports, however, that the neonates employed in the study received far more social stimulation from the parents and the experimenter than is typically provided to a newborn. Apparently social responses can be made by newborns, but the responses are greatly dependent upon the social stimulation the infants receive and the consequences of their smiling.

Newborn smiling responses occur in the first weeks of life and appear to be elicited by particular types of stimulation. The human voice elicits smiling in neonates, but bells and other equally loud sources of auditory stimulation do not. The presence of a person does not itself enhance a smiling response to a voice. A tape-recorded voice is as effective in eliciting a smile as a real person standing over a crib and talking.

Response to Cuddling

While smiling is not readily observed in children under one month of age, cuddling behavior or tense rejecting postures are clearly evident. Consistent individual differences among newborns can be seen in their tendency to respond positively or negatively to cuddling.

Systematic observations of newborns confirm that some newborns are tense and rejecting, while others are cuddlers. Furthermore, two children may respond very differently to the same parents. This suggests that the behavior is inherent to the child and is not a result of parental attitudes or behavior.

Responses to the social advances of caretakers have a dramatic impact on the social relationship between the caretaker and child. Compared to the parents of a cuddling newborn, the parents of a tense, noncuddling newborn have greater difficulty relaxing and enjoying their child and have greater difficulty forming positive attitudes about him or her.

The social responsiveness of a newborn can set in motion a circular interchange between the parents and the child. A child who responds with affection when cuddled encourages the parents to cuddle and accept him or her. Thus, an environment that encourages positive social interchange between the parents and the child is established. Tense, noncuddling newborns tend to receive less positive attention, are more likely to be rejected, and may set in motion a pattern of interaction that encourages continued tension and rejection.

PART III:
The First Two Years of Life

In the human organism, the first two years of life represent a period of rapid growth and change, marked by the development of two key characteristics that differentiate human beings from many other animals. First, children increase their mobility during this time. In so doing, they increase the scope of the surrounding environment in which they live, explore, and develop. That increased mobility is highlighted by walking upright on two legs. Second, in the first two years of life children begin to utilize language, both as a tool for communication with the people around them and as a tool to facilitate thinking.

The following five chapters will explore the physical and motor development of the child between the ages of one month and two years, the perceptual and cognitive changes in that child, the acquisition of the rudiments of language, and finally, the emergence of social behavior and personality.

CHAPTER 6

Physical and Motor Development in the First Two Years

The first two years of life is a period of rapid physical growth. During the first six months, growth is most rapid. The growth rate tapers off slightly in the next six months, progressing toward the steady growth pattern of later childhood during the second year.

Surprisingly, growth does not take place consistently during all months of the year. Rather, it appears to be cyclical. Weight gain, for example, is maximal in the months of October, November, and December; it reaches a minimum level from April through June. Reverse patterns exist for gains in height, with maximum height gain occurring in April through June.

During this early period of physical and motor development, body proportions change, bone ossifies, and teeth emerge. The child stands, crawls, then walks, and literally reaches out and grasps the objects in his or her world. Toward the end of this period, some degree of bowel and bladder control is attained.

Physical Gains in the First Two Years

The first two years of life are marked by significant physical growth, unlike any other periods of development. These gains are in weight, height, changes in body proportion, and increasing motor dexterity.

Weight

In the first four months of life, the weight of the child doubles from birth weight and averages about 14 or 15 pounds (6,220–6,720 g). By the end of the first year, the weight has tripled to an average of 20 pounds (8,960 g). During the second year, weight gains diminish. The gain during the entire second year is only about 5 pounds (2,240 g),less than the weight gained during the first four months of the first year. This diminished weight gain has been attributed to the increased activity and accompanying energy use of the one-year-old child, who, unlike the younger child, is walking and running. Increased energy use burns more calories, and in so doing reduces weight gain.

Height

During the first four months of life, the child grows approximately 3 to 4 inches (8–10 cm). This 20 percent increase in length contrasts to the 100 percent increase in body weight that occurs during the same time period. By the end of the first year, the child has grown an additional 6 inches (15 cm), to an average length of 29–31 inches (73–78 cm). In the second year, the child's gain in length is only about 4 inches (10 cm), which brings the height of the average two-year-old to 33–35 inches (83–88 cm).

An interesting sidelight concerns the relationship of the height of a two-year-old to that same child's adult height. The correlation between the height of a two-year-old and his or her predicted adult height is about 0.70. Research suggests that the height of a child at the age of two is approximately one-half the child's adult height.

Body Proportions

At birth the infant's head seems disproportionately large. In the first two years, physical growth amounts to having the rest of the body "catch up with" the head. While the head of the child grows little during the first two years, the trunk increases in length by over 50 percent, and the arms increase in length by 60 to 75 percent.

The impact of these changes in body proportion extend beyond a simple change in the way a child looks. The shift in the weight distribution of the body (a shift in its center of gravity) from the head to a lower point makes the child less top-heavy, and thus better able eventually to walk upright.

Bone Development

At birth, the bones of a child are immature and consist almost totally of cartilage. Ossification, the replacement of that cartilage with bone, is ongoing during the first two years but is not complete until puberty.

Ossification in the first year results in the development of three wrist bones. With continued ossification, 28 wrist bones will ultimately develop. In the second year, the fontanels of the skull (the soft spots on the head) will close. By eighteen months, 50 percent of all children have closed fontanels; by two years of age, the fontanels of almost all children are closed.

Teeth

The emergence of teeth signifies a dramatic change in the child. The first teeth to erupt through the gum are the central incisors, upper front teeth. This initial teething usually takes place between the ages of six and eight months. Other teeth erupt quickly, and by the age of one year, the child will typically display four to six teeth. By the age of two, a child will possess approximately 16 of the 20 baby, or milk, teeth.

As a means of pacification for children experiencing teething pain, many parents allow their one-year-olds to suck on a bottle of milk or juice. This practice concerns dentists, who recognize that the children engaged in that activity are literally soaking their newly acquired teeth in a bath of sugar. In some cases, this practice has caused such severe tooth decay that by the age of three, all the child's baby teeth have required extraction.

Factors Affecting Physical Growth

Various factors, including genetics, nutrition, emotional states, and hormone balances, affect physical growth.

Genetic Factors

Four observations attest to the importance of genetic factors in physiological development.

1. *Consistent sex differences exist in physical growth.* Although girls mature more quickly than boys, boys weigh more and are taller, on the average, than girls. Interestingly, girls as a group are more homogeneous in their development than boys. The weight of 20 girls and 20 boys—all one year of age—was measured. On the average, the girls weighed less than the boys. For girls, however, the range of weights was small, with the heaviest girl weighing only 3 pounds more than the lightest. On the other hand, a great deal of variation existed in the weight of the boys. Some boys weighed as much as 6 pounds more than others.

2. *In spite of wide variations in children's home environments, the patterns of growth are similar for all children.* Ap-

parently, something inherent in the child is more powerful in directing growth than environmental forces.

3. *Environmental forces such as illness and malnutrition have a limited effect on physical development.* Either of these conditions will interfere with growth, but their negative impact will be overcome if the illness or malnourishment is not too severe or prolonged.

A child who is malnourished will not gain weight or grow in height as quickly as an adequately nourished child. If the malnutrition is not too severe or extended, however, the child will exhibit a growth spurt as soon as adequate nutrition is provided, but may never attain his or her normal level of physical development.

4. *The greater the genetic similarity of two people, the more similar their pattern of physical development is likely to be.* One measure of physical growth is the appearance of the physical ossification centers, locations in the young child's skeleton where some of the cartilage becomes bone as the child matures. (The wrist and ankle, for example, show this kind of development.) For identical twins, the correlation between the age at which these centers appear is 0.71. For siblings other than identical twins, the corresponding correlation is only 0.28.

Nutrition

One factor that has attracted much attention on the part of developmental psychologists is the effect that early (prenatal and early childhood) nutrition has on development, particularly on the development of intelligence. This is a clear example of how the early environment, often beyond the control of parents for social or economic reasons, can affect the entire course of an individual's development.

Evidence is now abundant that severe nutritional deprivation during the early years of life does retard—either temporarily or permanently—many areas of physical development, including the structure of the brain and nervous system. Nutritional deficiencies are also viewed as possible factors in the development of intelligence and the concomitant development of related skills, such as language, perception, and social abilities. While there are some questions about how permanent are the conditions caused by nutritional deprivation, it is clear that good nutrition during infancy and early childhood is helpful in the proper development of the child.

Poor nutrition is also an inhibitor of physical growth. Children who are not provided appropriate nutrition tend to be shorter and weigh less than their well-nourished peers. The impact of nutrition on physical growth has been used to explain the fact that persons reared in higher socioeconomic classes tend to be taller and to weigh more than those reared in lower socioeconomic classes. In addition, there is a tendency for recent generations of American children to be taller than their relatives of nearly a century ago.

American white males fifteen years of age in 1960 were reported to be approximately 5.5 inches (14 cm) taller and 33 pounds (15 kg) heavier than fifteen-year-old boys in 1880. It has also been observed that there are differences of as much as 5 to 6 inches in the average height of two-year-old children born in different countries. These differences may be in part attributable to dietary differences and in part may reflect genetic differences in the natives of the two countries.

Health

Prolonged illness, like malnutrition, can stunt growth. Like the growth-stunting that results from malnutrition, stunted growth that results from illness may be quickly overcome if the illness does no permanent damage to the body.

A boy nine months of age contracted an intestinal disorder that resulted in prolonged diarrhea lasting two months. Although the diarrhea was not so severe as to endanger the life of the infant, it was noted that in the two-month period of illness, he had lost 2 ounces of weight rather than gaining the expected 16 to 24 ounces. Furthermore, the height of the boy was less than expected at 11 months of age, as was his level of motor development. Within one month after the intestinal difficulty was cured, however, the boy had regained his normal weight and height, and had manifested a dramatic spurt in motor development as well. By the age of 11 months, his developmental progress could not be distinguished from that of his peers.

Emotional States

An environment filled with tension can also inhibit physical growth. While a child raised in a tension-filled home may appear to eat compulsively in an effort to relieve his or her tension, the overeating will not always result in an overweight condition. Instead, the child may suffer from deprivational dwarfism, a condition of stunted growth that is the result of emotional stress.

Children living under the extreme stress of a family completely broken down in its relationships were studied by Powell, Brasel, and Blizzard. The children, who ate and drank compulsively, gained weight but exhibited retarded physical growth. The stunted growth apparently resulted from the diminished production or release of growth hormones. This hormonal problem disappeared once the children were removed from the home, and shortly thereafter, they resumed what was considered a normal growth pattern.

Hormone Balances

Hormone imbalances resulting from a dysfunction of the pituitary or thyroid glands can cause permanent growth difficulties. For example, the hormone thyroxin, secreted by the thyroid gland, controls the metabolism of the organism. An underactive thyroid gland produces a state called *hypothyroidism*. When severe hypothyroidism exists at birth, a condition known as *cretinism* is produced. Children afflicted with cretinism fail to develop normally both physically and mentally, exhibiting dwarf stature and mental deficiencies. Currently, the availability of thyroxin as a medication that can be administered from birth onward has nearly eliminated cretinism as a significant cause of developmental dysfunctions.

Motor Development

In addition to rapid physical growth in the period from age one month to two years, the immobile newborn first evolves into a creeper who moves around the world on all fours and later into an individual who darts from place to place on two legs, leaving the hands free to manipulate and explore the objects in the surrounding world. The child's contact with objects in the world evolves from that of an essentially passive being whose responses are governed by the objects in the world to an active individual who can explore and manipulate those objects at will.

Learning vs. Maturation

In discussing motor development, it is important to distinguish between two classes of motor skills: specific motor skills and phylogenetic motor skills.

Specific Motor Skills

Specific motor skills are those whose development is dependent upon learning. Learning refers to changes in behavior that result from practice and are primarily dependent upon the characteristics of the environment in which the practice takes place. A skill that develops through learning greatly depends upon the amount and the quality of practice a person is given in that skill. For a girl who wants to become a great ice skater, development of this ability depends to a great extent on how much she is willing and able to practice skating and how effective her instructor is at teaching the art of skating. The motor skill that this girl develops is a specific skill whose acquisition is dependent upon learning.

Phylogenetic Motor Skills

Phylogenetic motor skills are skills that depend primarily upon maturation for their development. Maturation refers to those developmental changes that occur spontaneously in normal individuals as long as the environment allows the individuals to mature.

In one classic study, McGraw trained one fraternal twin in a variety of motor skills from the age of 21 days until the age of 22 months. This child's motor skills were observed periodically. The second twin was not provided with training in motor skills. While McGraw did observe enhanced development of specific motor skills (such as skating) in the trained twin, she observed no effect of the training on the development of such phylogenetic motor skills as walking, talking, bowel and bladder control, grasping, and hand control.

Organization Patterns of Phylogenetic Motor Development

Motor development is characterized by three organizational patterns:

Mass Action to Specific Action

Initially, the child's movements utilize only the large muscles of the body and involve the entire body rather than specific parts. When one arm moves, the other arm and legs move as well. Reaching for an object involves a swinging movement of the whole arm or even the whole body. As the child matures, motor actions become more specific; that is, smaller sets of muscles are used to undertake an action. For example, one arm can move without other parts of the body moving, and the child's fingers can grasp an object delicately rather than swiping the hand and arm at the object. These changes in muscle use and motor activity represent a change from mass action to specific action.

It is fascinating to observe the reactions of an infant to everything in the environment. When the infant becomes excited, it is like watching the classic Santa Claus whose body bounces like a bowl of jelly when he laughs. By the time the child reaches one year of age, however, this mass motor involvement no longer occurs during exciting events. Instead, the child will simply smile and laugh. The child's reaction becomes more specific with age and involves finer motor coordination.

Cephalo-Caudal Organization

The development of muscles begins with the muscles nearest the head and progresses to muscles in the lower limbs. This pattern of development is called *cephalo-* (head) *caudal* (tail). The infant first develops control over eye muscles and shortly thereafter may lift its head (age one month). But it is not until around one year of age that the muscles of the legs have developed to a point where walking can be accomplished.

Proximo-Distal Organization

The development of motor coordination begins with the muscles nearest the body trunk and progresses to the extremities of the body. This pattern of development is called *proximo-* (near) *distal* (far).

Children will develop the ability to swing the whole arm from the shoulder long before they learn to manipulate the wrist or fingers. The consequence of this developmental pattern is easily seen in children's manipulation of objects. Children a few months old will confront a pile of blocks by swinging their whole arm at the pile and knocking it down. Later, the children's movements will be coordinated at the elbow, but still a sweeping movement will knock down the tower. It will be nearly a year before children can carefully destroy the pile of blocks with hand and finger manipulations.

Progress Toward Walking

The ability to move around in the world is important to the normal development of the child. It allows the child to learn about the world in which he or she lives and to progress toward physical independence from the parents. The development of walking in a child is one of the most exciting changes in the first two years of life. Not only does it provide a new degree of mobility, but it signals a transition in the child from a horizontally oriented being (not dissimilar to nonprimates) to a vertically oriented individual who more closely approximates the human being.

Walking, however, does not emerge overnight. Although there is variability in the times at which children begin to become mobile and to later walk, all children normally progress through similar stages of mobility development during the first year. Some of these stages may be bypassed by a particular child, but the sequence of stages is universal.

The Early Months

At first, the newborn is totally dependent upon others to change the position of his or her body. The acts of lifting the head or rolling over are not observed in the young infant. However, the infant can roll from side to back by about two months of age, can roll from back to side by about four months, and by six months, can roll over completely. At the age of three months, an infant began to roll from back to front by reaching up, grabbing the ring on a toy suspended in his crib, and pulling himself over. At first, the movement surprised both the baby and his parents, but soon it appeared that the child had discovered a new skill that would allow him to obtain toys and other objects theretofore out of his reach.

Sitting

By the age of three or four months, the infant can sit. The muscles of his or her body, however, are not strong enough to allow the three-month-old to sit without external support. By seven to eight months, the child no longer requires external support to remain in an upright, sitting position. It is important to be aware of the stages at which development occurs in the infant, and understand the relationship between physical growth and behavioral change. The physiology of the body must develop to a particular capacity level before behaviors can emerge.

Most children can sit in a high chair at about six to seven months of age, shortly before the age at which they begin to have the muscle power to sit without external support. Parents who initiate highchair use before that time are often frustrated by the fact that the child tends to slide out of the chair and becomes tired and irritable. These parents may be expecting behaviors that the child is not developmentally prepared to perform.

Crawling

At about the same time children begin to sit up alone, they may be observed thrusting one knee forward as they lie on their stomach. This typical 28-week-old behavior is the initial step in learning to crawl. By 34 weeks of age, the average child has acquired the ability to coordinate those thrusting movements and propel the body along the floor. This active movement is called crawling; it is distinguished from later patterns of movement by the fact that in crawling the child's legs and arms are not yet strong enough to hold the abdomen off the ground.

Creeping

By 40 weeks of age, the average child's muscles have

developed the strength to hold his or her own body weight. The child can now move on all fours while at the same time lifting the body from the ground. This pattern of movement is called creeping.

Supported Walking

The first sign that a child is developing into more than a four-legged creeper typically emerges at about 49 weeks. Shortly before the first birthday, children will push themselves to a standing position and delicately balance on their legs as they grasp the furniture, the leg of a parent, or some other source of stability. After discovering this new skill, children will use supporting objects to maintain their balance as they walk from place to place.

With the emergence of supported standing behavior, it is useful for parents to purchase or construct a walker, which is nothing more than a mobile (wheeled) support for the child. When placed in the walker, a child is able to push the support around wherever he or she chooses to go.

Independent Walking

Shortly after the first birthday, children typically take their first shaky but unsupported steps. Progress in the development of coordination and versatility in walking progresses rapidly from that point. Between the ages of 14 months and two years, children begin to run as well as walk and to play with wagons and kiddy cars that can be moved by pulling, pushing, or straddling. However, even the two-year-old child has not yet acquired the coordinated movements needed to pedal tricycles or other mobile toys.

Factors That Influence Walking Progress

Three factors influence the rapidity with which children learn to walk: muscle development, neurological development, and experience.

Muscle Development. The skills associated with the stages of walking development each require the use of new and stronger sets of muscles. Creeping requires stronger muscles than crawling, and walking requires stronger muscles than those needed for creeping.

Neurological Development. Neurological development is necessary for the coordination of muscle groups. Until children can coordinate the thrusting of their knees, they cannot crawl. Balance is also dependent upon neurological development. It requires that children coordinate their muscle movements with feedback from sensory systems that indicate their orientation in space.

Experience. Experience or practice play a complex role in acquiring the skill of walking. While the development of phylogenetic skills such as walking may be speeded up slightly by systematic practice, the ultimate level of phylogenetic motor skill ability of a child does not appear to depend on training. Furthermore, while experience may accelerate the development of walking, that acceleration can occur only after the muscular and neurological systems have matured.

Children learn to walk a little earlier when parents help them practice walking by holding them in an upright position, by moving their legs in a steplike fashion, and by encouraging them to take their first steps. However, the walking skills of those children are indistinguishable from those of their peers once their peers learn to walk.

Extreme environmental restrictions can inhibit the development of walking and prewalking skills. However, if the restrictions are removed, accelerated development will occur, and within a short period of time, the child will reach a level of performance equal to that of his or her peers.

Two identical twins were studied by a psychologist. One twin was restricted in his movements for 37 weeks, while the other had the ability to move about. At the end of this time, the first infant could not sit upright or engage in other motor responses that were well developed in his brother. However, once the first twin was no longer restricted, he developed rapidly, and within a short time, the two were equivalent in their skill levels.

For children with problems that may result in extreme motor activity deprivation, special training may allow normal motor development to occur.

For many years it was reported that children with Down's syndrome (see Chapter 3) developed their motor skills at half the rate observed in normal children. This is true as long as the child is given no special training. However, if Down's syndrome children are given very careful training from an early age, the retardation of their motor development is not as great as was once observed. It should be noted, however, that this improved motor development has not been found to be generalizable to the intellectual development of children suffering from Down's syndrome.

Object Manipulation

A second significant motoric change in the development of infants is their ability to manipulate objects. Of course, to manipulate an object effectively requires that one first reaches for it and then grasps it. Thus, child psychologists have found it interesting to examine the development of infants' abilities to coordinate reaching and grasping activities.

Some psychologists have characterized infants in their first months of life as stimulus-controlled. Their interactions with objects in the environment appear to be responses to the presence of stimulation. Their actions are directed by the source of that stimulation rather than by self-control. It is not until children are approximately five months old that one can begin to observe them engaging in activities that reflect and attempt to control the environment. This change identifies the division between the first and second phases of object manipulation.

Phase I

Although various stages of object manipulation development can be observed in Phase I, the different skills representing those stages share the following characteristics:

1. Reaching and grasping are not differentiated as separate acts. The fingers, hands, and arms work as a single unit. This is an example of mass action and also exemplifies the principle of proximo-distal patterns of development.

2. The actions of the infant in Phase I involve a single hand and arm. The simultaneous coordination of two arms has not yet emerged.

3. The child is unable to stop a reaching movement once it is initiated; or, having initiated a movement, the child is unable to correct the movement if it is off target.

4. The grasping of an object is governed by the visual presence of the object and its visual relationship to the hand rather than governed by the feel of the object.

Prereaching Period. In the first month of life, newborns do not reach for objects in their world. Instead, they simply stare at objects that come into view. At one month of age, infants are particularly attracted to objects that are located off to one side of their visual field, and they will turn to look at those objects. Other object characteristics that elicit attentional responses in the infant are discussed in Chapter 7.

Early Reaching Period. At about two and one-half months of age, children begin to reach for the objects that they see. This reaching, however, is poorly controlled and often misses the target. Children at this age appear to be swiping blindly at an object rather than trying to reach, grasp, and manipulate something.

Visual Tracking. Infants three and one-half months old begin to follow moving objects with their eyes. This visual tracking may be thought of as a form of visual reaching. Unfortunately, at this point the visual reaching is not coordinated with hand and arm reaching.

Coordinated Reaching. By the age of four months, visual reaching and hand reaching become coordinated. One can observe children visually following their hand and arm as they reach for an object, and their attention alternates between the object to be grasped and the grasping hand itself.

Terminus of Phase I Behavior

By five months of age, the child ends the obvious switching of attention back and forth between the grasping hand and the object to be grasped, and moves his or her hand directly to the object. Though the movements of the child are smoothly coordinated, they represent Phase I reaching and grasping because the reach and grasp are controlled by the visual presence of the object sought and are a unitary action rather than two separate actions. The reach response is initiated by the visual presence of an object; even if the hand does not come into contact with the object, once the reach starts, a grasping response will take place when the hand is thrust forward.

Newly developed technical equipment allows scientists to persuade people that they are seeing three-dimensional objects even when such objects are not physically present. When these visual images are presented to infants a few months old, they will reach and actually grasp for the objects. The child's grasp is governed by the visual presence of the object, not by the physical touch of it. Older children and adults will reach for visual images but will not grasp at them, because physical contact is not actually made with the object.

Phase II

The age of five months marks the division between the first and second phases of object manipulation. Children in the Phase II stage of development share the following characteristics:

1. They reach and grasp with two hands rather than one.

2. They correct errors in reaching when such errors are detected.

3. They engage in reaching and grasping responses that are independent of one another.

4. They exhibit a grasping response that is controlled by actual contact with the stimulus rather than by its visual presence.

These changes represent an increase in the ability of the child to engage in coordinated motor activity.

Hand Preference. At about five to eight months of age, the child begins to evolve a preferred hand with which he or she will manipulate objects. A four-month-old will sometimes reach and grasp for objects with her left hand and at other times do so with her right. At six months of age, however, the girl will hold objects in her left hand as she manipulates them with her right hand.

Object Exploration. With the development of more sophisticated motor coordination, the child is able to reach for and grasp smaller objects. It has been reported that the child between eight months and two years of age will spend 20 percent of his or her waking time exploring and manipulating small objects. The child's fascination with and manipulation of small objects develops when he or she is about eight to nine months of age.

Most parents are plagued with an eight-month-old's fascination for the knobs on heaters, radios, and particularly television sets. One parent reports that it became necessary for him to "blockade" the television set to prevent his son spending most of the day turning the set on and off or from changing the color and volume at a crucial point in a sports program.

Although children before the age of one can reach for and grasp objects, their manipulation of those objects is limited to visual exploration—turning the objects in their hands, banging them on the floor, and so on. At about one year of age, however, children begin to engage in more coordinated activities. The one-year-old can pile one block on another and put a ring on a peg. Since they are more coordinated, children older than one year can enjoy a great many more types of toys than they could when they were younger.

Of particular curiosity to children eight months to one year of age are their own genitals. Because of the physical characteristics of the male penis, that organ is manipulated and explored by boys more than the female genitals are by girls. In either case, it is development of the ability to motorically explore and manipulate small objects in the world that leads the young child to this personal exploration.

Effect of Experience on the Development of Visually Directed Reaching

As is true with the development of walking, the development of reaching and grasping is dependent to a great extent on the maturation of the child. However, once the child has matured, his or her life experiences can accelerate or retard the development of these skills.

In some classic studies, Sheldon White has shown that visually directed reaching developed earlier in children who had mobiles and other visually and motorically stimulating toys in their crib than in children confined to nonstimulating institutional surroundings. However, it proved important that the toys with which the child interacted were compatible with the child's level of motor development. If objects were too stimulating, the infant tended to ignore them. Apparently, there is an optimal level of stimulation that enhances development; levels of stimulation above or below the optimal level may inhibit development.

Toilet Training

The motor control of the bowel and bladder has been, and continues to be, a developmental phenomenon surrounded by controversy. When and how should a child be toilet trained? What effect does this have on the child's personality? There are no correct answers to these questions, for there is great variability as to when individual children acquire the ability to control the bowel and bladder.

In part this variability is a result of individual differences in children's levels of physiological maturity, and in part it reflects differences in parental tolerances for diaper changing and cultural pressures to have toilet-trained children. Some rules of thumb are helpful for parents making the decision of whether or not to toilet train a child at a particular point in time.

1. Toilet training is not an easy skill to learn. It involves three tasks, each of which poses its own difficulties and challenges:

(a) The child must learn to pay attention to a sensory experience that is unimportant to his or her functioning until the time of toilet training.

(b) The child must control a muscle whose movements cannot be seen or even felt clearly.

(c) The child must know what to do when he or she senses the need to go to the bathroom, and must stop doing something enjoyable in order to accomplish that goal. For an adult, an analogous task would be learning to control the rate of heartbeat. While that skill can be learned, it is difficult and requires much effort.

2. Bowel and bladder control cannot occur until the child is capable of controlling his or her sphincter muscle.

3. Night training typically occurs after children are trained to stay dry during the day. The reason is obvious: During the day, children can feel the muscle sensations associated with the need to urinate and defecate, whereas when they are asleep, they cannot.

4. Bowel control typically precedes bladder control. The reason for this sequential development is that bowel movements occur less frequently than urination and at more regular times; thus, they are better anticipated by both the parents and the child. Anticipation of those events facilitates the development of an effective training program.

5. Although bowel and bladder control can be established early, it is typical to begin establishing bowel control at approximately eighteen months and to postpone attempts at bladder control until after a child has acquired language skills (approximately two years of age).

Nathan Azren and Richard Fox have developed, tested, and taught a widely used method of toilet training. They stress emphatically, however, the importance of establishing the child's toilet training readiness before their training technique is begun. Those readiness characteristics include an awareness of bladder sensations, the development of muscular dexterity, and the ability to understand and follow instructions. Given those prerequisite skills, Azren and Fox emphasize the use of imitation and extensive positive reinforcements such as verbal praise and physical affection to teach the child bowel and bladder control. Using this method of instruction, the authors claim that without exception they have been able to train all children who were twenty months of age or older.

Individual Differences in Motor Development

In previous sections, it has been noted that once appropriate maturation levels have been reached, children's experiences can have a great impact on their motor development. In addition, there are some individual differences in motor development. For example, boys appear to develop motor skills more quickly than girls; black children exhibit somewhat more rapid motor development than white children; and first-born children tend to develop motor skills at an earlier age than later-born children. In some countries, children may learn to walk at a younger age than children reared in other countries. Children with sensory handicaps may not develop for many years some motor skills that have already been developed by their normal peers.

Although the development of independent locomotion is retarded in blind children, they will advance through many stages of motor development that can be observed in sighted children. Even though blind children cannot see, they have been observed to follow their moving hand with unseeing eyes.

Motor Imitation

Imitation requires that a child modify his or her own behavior to fit the behavior of the imitated person, the model. Jean Piaget describes this as a pure form of accommodation. In this section, a description will be provided of the forms of imitation that are observed in children of different ages. Remember that while the stages through which imitative skills progress may be similar for all children, the ages at which those stages emerge differ greatly from child to child. The ages reported are only approximations.

Imitative Repetition (Imitations of Imitations)

At approximately one month of age, infants are able to exhibit rudimentary forms of motor imitation. From about one to four months of age, infants will repeat an action more readily if they observe another person simultaneously engaged in the same act. Imitation occurs only for responses the children can see themselves making and responses the children initiate.

A two-month-old, for example, opens and closes her hand. If a nearby adult opens and closes his hand at the same time, the child will be more likely to repeat the response than if no one else is observed making the response.

Formal Imitation

Between four and eight months of age, formal imitation can be observed. Children can now imitate responses in which they are not currently engaged. However, children's imitation is restricted to actions that are already in their behavioral repertoire; thus, no novel responses can be imitated. Furthermore, the imitated actions are still restricted to those the children can observe or hear themselves make.

Envision a child not engaged in any action. She observes an adult raising and lowering a hand, a response the child has made before. The child begins to raise and lower her hand as the adult is doing. This formal imitation is the basis by which children begin to wave good-bye or hello to parting and arriving visitors.

Novel Response Imitation

At approximately eight months, children add new responses to their response repertoire through imitation and imitate actions they cannot observe themselves make. At this age, children can begin to imitate novel speech sounds and facial expressions. Also at about this age, a child will imitate the hand-clapping responses in the game patty-cake. Games that include imitative responses of this type are extremely popular with children between the ages of eight months and one year.

Trial-and-Error Imitation

For six months following a child's first birthday, imitation improves to the point that the child, through trial and error, can more and more closely replicate responses he or she observes others make, regardless of whether or not the child can see his or her own imitative response. However, even at 18 months, the child must see the action of the model as he or she attempts to replicate it.

Delayed Imitation

After the age of 18 months it is possible for the child to delay his or her imitative response until after the action to be imitated has ended. Before reaching the stage of delayed imitation, a child may see another child throw at a tantrum and join in the act with an imitated tantrum. However, the child will not imitate the tantrum at a later time. After reaching the stage of delayed imitation, the same child can quietly observe another child's tantrum and then have a tantrum spontaneously, at a later time, even though he or she has never thrown a tantrum in the past.

CHAPTER 7

Perceptual Capacities During the First Two Years

Because of the infant's lack of verbal abilities, it is extremely difficult to assess perceptual and cognitive capacities in the child under two years of age. How can we know what a child is perceiving, how he or she is processing the perceived information, and what thoughts are instigated by these perceptions? Since the young child cannot yet communicate effectively through language, research in this area requires an abundance of patience and innovative observational techniques. Consequently, our understanding of those capacities has progressed more slowly than our understanding of the child's physical and motor development.

For many years, our limited observations of the infant's perceptual and cognitive abilities led to the speculation that those capacities were minimal. Observations in the past fifteen years, however, reveal that the foundation of basic perceptual and cognitive capacities are present early in the life of the infant. This chapter will trace their development.

Visual Perception

As noted in Chapter 5, the visual system of the newborn is more highly developed than was once believed.

Secondary Visual System

The infant can see with some clarity and can discriminate colors and brightness, as well as patterned and nonpatterned visual displays. Furthermore, within the first month after birth, the infant's attention is directed to certain visual displays more than others.

Psychologists refer to these capacities as a primitive, or secondary, visual system. The purpose of this system is to detect the presence of visual stimulation, orient the eye toward important parts of the visual display, and maintain those important parts of the display in the child's field of vision. The secondary visual system is well developed at birth, and improvements in its effectiveness result for the most part from improved motor control over the visual system.

Because of an immature motor control system, the newborn has difficulty adjusting eye focus to accommodate objects viewed at different distances. This deficiency reduces the visual acuity of the newborn. However, by the age of four months, the visual motor system has developed, and the infant is capable of fully utilizing the secondary visual system.

Primary Visual System

The primary visual system, which is distinct from the secondary visual system, provides the individual with the ability to make finer and more complex discriminations among visual displays. While the secondary system tells us that something is visually present, the primary system tells us what that something is. The development of this primary system may be reflected most in the changing visual capacities of the child.

Depth Perception

The ability to perceive depth is a skill that is central to perceptual development. The empiricist philosophy maintained that the acquisition of depth perception resulted from the experiences a child had in reaching for or in moving toward objects at different distances from himself or herself. It was assumed that this learning process took some time to accomplish; consequently, depth perception was not well developed in the infant.

Evidence for Depth Perception. Research using a "visual cliff" (see Fig. 7.1) demonstrates that shortly after beginning to crawl (six months), infants can perceive depth.

The visual cliff is an apparatus consisting of a center board, a glass-covered drop-off or cliff on one side, and a piece of glass covering a platform that is level with the center board (having no drop-off or cliff) on the other side. Lighting is arranged so that a child crawling on the center board cannot tell that the protective glass is present.

Infants who had recently learned to crawl were placed on the center board of the visual cliff and were coaxed to crawl across the noncliff side of the apparatus. They all performed well. No amount of coaxing, however, could induce an infant to crawl over the cliff side of the center board. One can conclude from this observation that the infant who has just begun to crawl can perceive depth, and attempts to avoid falling over edges.

Research studies using more sensitive observation techniques have demonstrated that depth can be perceived by infants only a few weeks old. One study, for example, found that infants

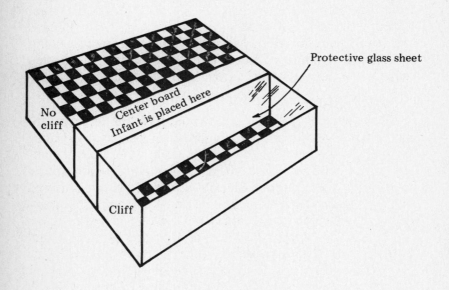

Fig. 7.1

a little less than two months old show heart-rate deceleration
when placed on the glass overlooking the deep side of a visual
cliff. Similar heart-rate deceleration does not occur when the
same child is placed on the glass overlooking the shallow side
of the cliff. This differential response pattern suggests that the
infant can perceive the differences in depth of the two sides of
the apparatus. Interestingly, in contrast to the response of the
two-month-old, the heart rate of a nine-month-old infant ac-
celerates when the child is placed on the deep side of the visual
cliff. This response pattern suggests that the younger infant
detects some difference in the two sides of the apparatus but does
not have a fear of the depth. The older infant, however, both
perceives the depth and responds emotionally to it—with fear.

In another study, it was found that infants under ten weeks of age spend equal time looking at three-dimensional spheres and two-dimensional discs of the same size. After the age of ten weeks, however, three-dimensional objects are looked at longer. This differential looking time implies that the ten-week-old can distinguish two-dimensional from three-dimensional objects.

Cues for Perceiving Depth. If infants as young as two months of age can perceive depth, what cues in the visual display allow them to do so? We know that adults may use a variety of cues to tell them that one object is closer to them than another is. They may attend to various cues that can be reproduced in a picture (*pictorial cues*). For example, nearby objects tend to cover up parts of objects that are behind them (*occlusion cues*). Fine details of nearby objects are more easily seen than those in objects far away (*texture cue*). The fact that the two eyes each see a scene from a slightly different angle provides another cue for the perception of depth (*binocular cue*). The brain combines the pictures from both eyes to form a single three- dimensional perception. The design of a stereoscope is based on this principle. In a stereoscope, two slightly different pictures are shown to a person, one to each eye. The perceived scene is a single, three-dimensional picture. Depth perception is significantly reduced when one eye is covered.

Objects close to the moving eye appear to move across a greater expanse of the field of vision than objects far away. Furthermore, objects close to a person appear to move in the opposite direction from the head or eye movement, while objects far away move with head movements. These cues of *motion parallax* can be used to perceive depth.

In human infants, as well as in newborns of other species, *motion cues* are used to perceive depth. Motion cues require the use of only one eye, which is neurologically a simpler task than coordinating the information received from two eyes. Controversy exists as to whether binocular cues can be used by the newborn in the perception of depth. It may be that the use of binocular cues requires further development of the nervous system to allow information from the two eyes to be coordinated by the brain. Apparently, the value of pictorial cues must be learned, as they are not used by the newborn.

These issues were investigated in a study by psychologist T. G. R. Bower. Under three viewing conditions, Bower trained 50- to 60-day-old infants to respond with a head turn when shown a 30-cm cube placed one meter in front of them. In one viewing condition, infants saw the cube with two eyes and could use binocular and monocular cues, as well as pictorial cues, for depth perception. Infants in a second viewing condition wore patches over one eye and could only use motion and pictorial cues to perceive depth. The third group was shown a picture of the cube that was rich in pictorial depth cues but eliminated the potential for using either binocular or motion cues for depth.

Following the training, Bower varied the size and position of the cube shown to the infants in order to assess whether they perceived depth. No depth perception was noted when only pictorial cues were available. Under both of the other viewing conditions, however, depth was perceived. Bower concluded that monocular motion cues are sufficient for depth perception in the infant less than two months old. The presence of binocular cues for depth did not improve that perception.

Visual Constancies

Constancy refers to the fact that changes in the image of an object on the retina of the eye do not result in changed perception of the object itself.

Although the size of the retinal image of a block becomes smaller as the cube is moved farther away from the viewer, the perceived size of the block, and thus its reported size, does not change. (See Fig. 7.2.) This is called size constancy. Similarly, a head-on examination of a plate has a circular image on the

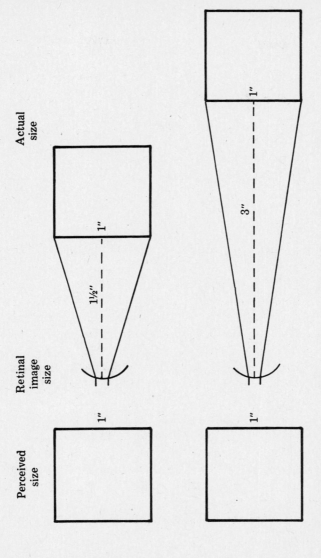

Fig. 7.2

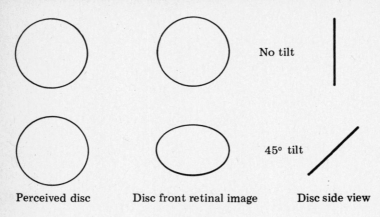

No tilt

45° tilt

Perceived disc   Disc front retinal image   Disc side view

Fig. 7.3

retina, while the same plate viewed in a tilted position projects the image of an ellipse on the retina. In spite of these different retinal images, the plate in both cases is reported to be a round disc. (See Fig. 7.3.) This is an example of shape constancy.

Size Constancy. Infants as young as six to eight weeks old do not respond to the size of a retinal image, but instead demonstrate size constancy when there are motion cues available for them to use in their perception of depth. T. G. R. Bower developed a unique method to explore an infant's visual world. He conditioned infants to respond with a head turn whenever a particular object was viewed. Having achieved this conditioning, Bower changed the object viewed by the infant. If the infant's response rate was unchanged, Bower concluded that the training and test objects were perceived as equivalent; changes in the rate of response were interpreted to mean that the infant perceived the two objects as different.

In one study, Bower worked with infants six to eight weeks old. He trained the infants to turn their heads when a 30-cm cube was presented one at a distance of one meter from the child. Bower found that when the same cube was shown at a different

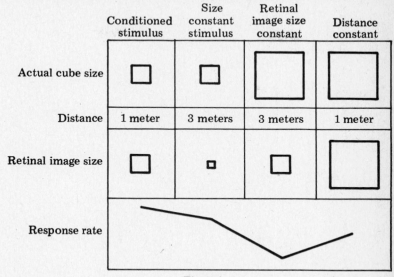

Fig. 7.4

distance (3 meters) from the infant, the response rate of the head turning remained the same as before, in spite of the fact that the size of the retinal image projected by the cube had changed.

In contrast, when both the size of the cube and the distance from the infant were changed so that the retinal image size remained constant, the head-turning response rate diminished. This result demonstrated that infants as young as six weeks old exhibit size constancy and do not respond simply to the size of the object's image projected on the retina. (See Fig. 7.4.)

Shape Constancy. Using a procedure similar to that described above, it has been observed that infants as young as six weeks of age exhibit shape constancy.

An infant is trained to respond to a rectangular geometric form presented at an angle such that its projected image on the retina is itself a rectangle. (See Fig. 7.5.) When that same form is rotated, its image on the retina becomes a trapezoid. Despite

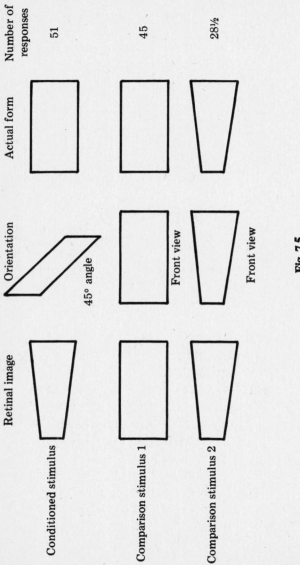

Fig. 7.5

this change in retinal image shape, there is no change in the infant's response rate.

By contrast, when a second geometric form, a trapezoid, is presented to the infant at an angle that results in its retinal image being rectangular, the response rate of the infant changes from the response rate initially observed. Apparently, the infant's perception is governed by the actual shape of the object and not by the shape of the projected retinal image.

Gestalt Principles in Infant Perception

Gestalt psychology emphasizes, among other things, that perceptions are based on certain organizational principles. Among those principles are the following:

1. *Good Continuation.* If part of an object is obscured, the obscured portion is perceived to exist and to be a simple continuation of the observable parts of the object. (See Fig. 7.6.)

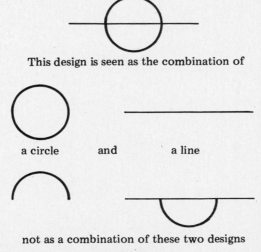

Fig. 7.6

Four circles equally spaced in a row will be viewed as two pairs if two of them move off in one direction and two move off in another direction.

Fig. 7.7

The dots are seen as forming three clusters of four dots each, not two lines of six dots.

Fig. 7.8

2. *CommonMotion.* Objects that move together are perceived to be a unit. (See Fig. 7.7.)

3. *Proximity.* Objects physically close together are perceived as a unit. (See Fig. 7.8.)

4. *Summation.* The whole is greater than the sum of its parts. What one perceives is different from what one would perceive by adding together the perceptions formed by the individual elements making up an object. (See Fig. 7.9.)

Are these principles evident in the perceptions of infants? Recent studies suggest that the principles of good continuation and common motion are evident in the perception of infants as young as six weeks of age. The principle of proximity, however,

This picture is viewed as more than
thirteen circles and one arc.

Fig. 7.9

has not been observed to function in infants that young. The
principle of summation develops at about ten weeks of age. Prior
to that age, an infant's response rate to a visual display can be
predicted by summing up the response rates to each of the
elements making up the display. After that age, the response rate
to the whole is greater than the sum of all the response rates to
the individual elements.

Auditory Perception

Less research has been done to examine auditory perception
than has been done to examine visual perception. This neglect
may have occurred because the capacities for auditory perception appear to exist at the time of birth or to emerge within the
first month after birth. There is also evidence that hearing is
present during prenatal development, although its extent and
discriminative potential still are not known.

Sound Localization

One auditory phenomenon that does emerge between the end
of the first month and the end of the second year is the ability to
relate an auditory stimulus to its spatial location and visual

source. It has been consistently observed that an infant four months old will turn his or her head toward the position from which a sound emanates, while a one-month-old infant will be considerably less accurate in the localization of sound. However, it has also been reported that when a mother's voice is distorted so that its location of origin is different from the location of the mother's head, an infant as young as one month old will respond with distress. This observation suggests that the infant can localize sound, and knows that it is not coming from its normal source.

Speech Perception

A second important auditory perceptual process that evolves early in the infant's development is discrimination of speech sounds. Infants as young as four weeks old can discriminate the sounds /ba/ and /pa/.

This perceptual discrimination is particularly interesting in light of the fact that the physical differences in the acoustical signals defining those two speech sounds are minute. It is hard to believe that the infant learns this discrimination in a short four weeks. More likely, there are inherent neurological centers in the brain that analyze the sounds of speech.

Discrimination of speech sounds will be discussed further in Chapter 9.

Factors Affecting the Distribution of Attention

During the first two months of life, infants are attracted to stimuli that provide stimulation to their nervous system. That stimulation is heightened by increases in the intensity of stimulus, by motion in the stimulus, or by the presence of contours in the stimulus array.

By the age of four months, the infant begins to pay attention to stimuli that are similar to objects with which they are familiar. For example, a four-month-old will attend to a picture containing the elements of a face far more readily than a similar picture with identical physical characteristics not associated with a face. For the child over the age of one year, attention appears to be directed primarily at those object that generate numerous hypotheses about their identity. Thus, the infant is attracted to pictures that may take on many meanings.

Because the perceptual and cognitive abilities of an infant change with age, the stimulus characteristics that attract and maintain the infant's attention also change. Thus, the patterns of attention exhibited by an infant reflect the child's increasing levels of higher cognitive and perceptual functioning. Generally speaking, four factors affect the stimuli toward which an infant's attention will be directed: amount of contour, movement, and intesity; complexity; stimulus familiarity (the schema); and hypothesis generation.

Amount of Contour, Movement, and Intensity

Up to the age of two months an infant's attention is attracted by the intensity of a stimulus—for example, how bright it is—and, more important, by the amount of contour it possesses and the presence of movement in the object. Given a large square with six inches of perimeter (contour) and a square with only three inches of perimeter, the two-month-old will attend longer to the larger square. In this example, the amount of contour is confounded with the area of the figure; however, the amount of contour appears to be the factor determining attention levels.

In another experiment, a stationary geometric is attached to the crib of a one-month-old infant, while at the same time an identical form swings freely from a string nearby. Observations of the infant's eye fixations reveal that more time is spent attending to the moving object than to the stationary form.

If one considers the neurological system of the infant, it is

Fig. 7.10

not surprising that motion and the amount of contour initially affect attention. That system responds to changes in stimulation, and contour is a change in brightness, while movement is a change in position. Apparently, infants respond to stimuli that provide stimulation to their nervous system.

The infant younger than two months of age spends more time looking at a picture of a human face than at any other visual displays. However, this fact is probably a result of the amount of contour contained in the face—including the eyes, hairline, and mouth boundaries. If that infant is confronted by a face whose parts have been rearranged, or another display with an equal amount of contour, he or she will look at it for as long a time as at the face picture. (See Fig. 7.10.)

Complexity

Complexity refers to the pattern of the elements in a stimulus array. If there are many objects in a display, it is said to be more complex than a display with few objects. The number as well as the variability of the elements also contribute the complexity of a display. If all objects in a display are alike, the display is not as complex as one with a variety of objects. Finally, the arrangement of elements in a display contributes to its complexity. If the elements are arranged in a systematic and easy-to-identify pattern, the display will not be as complex as a display with less obvious patterns.

Whether stimulus complexity affects patterns of infant attention is a controversial issue. One hypothesis espoused by Daniel Berlyne, among others, states that other stimulus characteristics being equal, individuals seek out and attend to stimuli of moderate complexity. They do not attend to very simple or to very complex stimuli. Others, such as Bernard Karmel, argue that in typical studies that manipulate the complexity of stimuli, the more complex stimuli also possess greater amounts of contour or other physical characteristics known to affect attention. Therefore, it might be argued that the attention of infants is influenced by those physical characteristics and not by the complexity of the stimuli.

Stimulus Familiarity—The Schema

At about four months of age, the physical characteristics of a stimulus alone no longer dictate the amount of direct attention. At this age, infants begin to pay attention to stimuli that are similar to objects with which they are familiar.

To examine the influence of familiarity on attention, one must first define the meaning of familiar. The commonplace definition is that familiar objects are those with which a person has had experience. However, psychologists say that during those experiences, the infant has formed a schema for an object. This schema is a nonpictorial representation of an object or event. It contains the distinctive features that define the object. The closer the characteristics of a newly presented object are to those of a schema, the more familiar that object is.

At about four months of age, attention directed toward a stimulus is determined in part by the extent to which the stimulus has the same characteristics as a schema already possessed by the infant; that is, the extent to which the stimulus is recognized as familiar. Most attention is paid to stimuli whose features are slightly different from those of the schema.

In one experiment, a picture of a face is rearranged but contains all the distinctive elements of a face—nose, mouth, and

Fig. 7.11

eyes. A second facial outline is constructed with the same amount of contour and complexity but no facelike elements. An infant of four months will attend longer to the first face than to the second. The first face is discrepant from the face schema, but is still familiar because it contains facelike features. (See Fig. 7.11.)

The same response is demonstrated in a second experiment. A four- month-old infant is regularly shown a mobile in his crib every day for two weeks. During those two weeks, a schema of the mobile is formed. After two weeks, the infant is shown (1) the original mobile, (2) a mobile similar but not identical to the original, and (3) a totally new mobile. (See Fig. 7.12.) The infant tends to look longest at the second mobile, which is moderately discrepant from the schema.

Standard   Slightly discrepant   Totally discrepant

Fig. 7.12

Hypothesis Generation

Forming a hypothesis is a cognitive act, the purpose of which is to understand how a familiar stimulus has been transformed into an unusual one. When you see your friend Susan with a cast on her leg, you quickly recognize her as your friend; that is, you match her to the schema of Susan. However, you may generate many hypotheses to account for the fact that your friend has a cast on her leg, that is, to account for the discrepancy between the unusual condition in which you find your friend and her usual condition.

For infants over one year of age, cognitive development results in the distribution of attention being determined, in part, by the number of hypotheses they can generate about an event or object. Other things being equal, objects or events that can generate many hypotheses are attended to longer than those that generate few hypotheses.

For infants over one year of age, attention increases toward pictures or models of faces that are moderately discrepant from the face schema. This increased attention results from the fact that the infant is now able to generate hypotheses about how and why the face models are distorted.

The Chemical Senses: Smell and Taste

Smell (olfaction) and taste (gustation) are sensory processes that receive stimulus energy in the form of chemical substances. In a manner comparable to that of the other senses, receptors transduce these energies into action potentials, which are relayed to specialized areas of the brain to be recorded as odors or tastes. There is some evidence that the developing fetus can respond to smell and taste sensations, and it is clearly evident that the newborn is able to perceive and respond to varying smells and tastes. For example, a neonate will respond differently to a solution of sugar (which it accepts and sucks) than it will to a quinine solution (which it rejects).

The Skin Senses

The skin (touch) senses are the most highly developed in the newborn, especially on the forehead, lips, tongue, and ear. The skin senses provide sensory experiences from receptors found in the skin. Four varieties are identified—heat, cold, pressure, and pain. These receptors are distributed unevenly throughout the body. Certain areas, such as the face and hands, have many more receptors than do other areas, such as the back.

The receptors consist of free nerve endings, corpuscles, and hair follicles. All appear to receive the various types of stimuli, with registration of the event occurring in the brain. The stimuli may be provided by either mechanical or radiant energy, although the latter does not create pressure stimuli. Neonates respond to all four types of skin sensation.

CHAPTER 8

Cognitive Development in the First Two Years

Cognition refers to the process of acquiring and using knowledge. During their first two years of life, infants acquire a wealth of knowledge about themselves and the world in which they live. However, the acquisition of that knowledge is not determined by verbal exchanges with other people, as it is with older children, nor is the knowledge reflected in verbal utterances. Instead, knowledge is acquired through children's sensory and motor interactions with sources of stimulation in the environment, and is reflected in the changing way in which infants react to the world around them. For this reason, Jean Piaget called infancy the sensorimotor stage of cognitive development. Of course, changes take place even within this two-year period of sensorimotor cognition. In this section, we will explore some of those changes.

Because Piaget's account of cognitive development forms the foundation for much of our current knowledge about the cogni-

tion of infants, we will utilize his observations as a structure within which to describe cognitive development during the sensorimotor stage of development. However, where new information about the infant's capacity has been revealed, that information will be reported and compared with Piaget's observations and accounts.

The fundamental assumptions that underlie Piaget's theory of cognitive development, as well as some of the fundamental vocabulary associated with that theory, were discussed in Chapter 1. The discussion in this chapter will focus on Piaget's description of cognitive development during the first two years of life.

The Sensorimotor Stage

Piaget saw infants' knowledge or cognitive process reflected in their organized sensory and motor actions. The term Piaget used to refer to such an organized pattern of actions is *schema*. He described six substages of sensorimotor development through which children progress during their first two years. Initially, children exhibit only reflex actions in response to their world. This earliest substage of development (Stage One, 0-1 month) has been described in Chapter 4 and will not be discussed further here. (Note: For convenience, these substages of sensorimotor development will be referred to as stages throughout the chapter.)

In order for infants to respond more effectively to the objects in their world, new organized action patterns (*schemata*) are formed, and both reflexes and those schemata are modified. The process of schema modification is called *accommodation*. These modifications are the basis of cognitive development for infants. Of particular interest to the child psychologist has been the recognition of those changes in the following cognitive functions:

1. *Discrimination and Classification.* Children's increasing awareness of properties that differentiate one object or event from another and their ultimate development of the ability to respond differentially to classes of objects and events.

2. *Cause-Effect Relations.* Children's coordination of their different sensorimotor actions and their ultimate development of an understanding that actions can cause effects to occur.

3. *Object Permanence.* Children's understanding of the concept of an object, and particularly their awareness that objects have some permanence, that they exist even when they cannot be seen, heard, or felt.

Stage One (0-1 Month)—Reflexes

Stage One covers the first month of life. During this time, the newborn's reactions to environmental stimulation are natural reflexes. It is through the modification of those reflexes that the infant evolves to the second stage of sensorimotor cognitive development.

Stage Two (1-4 Months)—Primary Circular Reactions

The infant in Stage Two continues to be a reactive individual rather than one who interacts with the environment. Stimulation from the outside world elicits sensory and motor actions on the infant's part. However, infants in Stage Two have advanced over their Stage One counterparts in several ways.

Primary Circular Reactions

The defining characteristic of Stage Two infants is their tendency to stumble upon new experiences through their actions and then to repeat those actions. Apparently, Stage Two infants achieve pleasure simply by engaging in the actions they are able to perform.

This pattern of repetitious responding is called a primary circular reaction. Primary circular reactions epitomize two characteristics of the Stage Two infant:

1. Infants are occupied by their own activity and not by the effects of those activities on the objects with which they interact. It is this Stage Two emphasis on the individual's own activities that gives rise to the term "primary."

2. Without any apparent external motivation, the infants repeatedly engage in the same action, as if practicing it. The term "circular reaction" refers to the repetitive character of the action. The internal motivation to practice those skills the infant has just acquired is an important factor in cognitive development that will be observed throughout the developmental process. Piaget referred to such practice as *functional assimilation*.

Discrimination and Classification

A reflex act observed in Stage One is performed in a similar way regardless of the stimulation eliciting it. In Stage Two, a reflex act is changed according to the source of stimulation that triggers it. These modifications allow the infant to interact more effectively with sources of environmental stimulation and to exhibit a primitive form of discrimination among objects.

John at age two weeks sucked nipples and all other objects in the same way. At two months, however, records of his muscle movements revealed that he sucked nipples differently from the way he sucked on a block or on his hand.

Coordination of Sensorimotor Acts

Teachers often say that the best way to understand an object or event is to look at it from more than one perspective. Infants in Stage Two exhibit behavior that suggests they have accepted that advice and, in so doing, are preparing themselves to better understand the world around them. In Stage Two infants no longer respond to a source of stimulation with a single sensory or motor response. Infants look for what they hear and inspect what they grasp. Although it is far too early to speak of cause-effect relationships, this coordination of sensorimotor schemata represents an initial step toward understanding the the association of causes with their effects.

During the first month of life (Stage One), John would grasp objects placed in his hand or look at moving objects in his line of sight, but he did not look at the objects he was grasping. At three months of age, however, his behavior was quite different. When an object was placed in his hand, he would grasp it, and at the same time, he would turn his eyes to look at it. The two sensory experiences became coordinated. Similarly, when John heard a sound, he would turn his head to see its source.

Object Permanence

Piaget observed that when he covered an object with which an infant in Stage Two was playing, the infant would not search for the missing object. The principle that best describes the Stage Two infant's concept of the object is "out of sight, out of existence." The object exists in the mind of the child only while the child is in direct sensory or motor contact with it.

Observations made more recently have confirmed Piaget's initial account of the infant's response to hidden objects. When three-month-olds are playing with and grasping a small toy in their hands, the grasping immediately stops if the toy is covered by a cloth. In another demonstration of the importance of visual contact in determining the infant's motor responses to an object, an experimenter will cover a Stage Two infant's hand while he or she is reaching for a toy. Although the arm continues to reach and the hand comes in contact with the toy, the hand will not grasp the toy when contact is made.

Despite the confirmation of Piaget's observations, some phenomena are incongruent with his description of the infant's lack of an object concept. For example, infants as young as two or three months old will cry when their parents leave them. This crying suggests that the infant is responding to the absence of an object. The fact that a parent is out of sight does not mean the parent is out of mind. Furthermore, it has been shown that when infants only six to eight weeks of age are given extended exposures to an object, they can remember that object for as long as 24 hours.

As we shall see in later stages of infant cognitive development, children's responses to missing objects may depend upon their memory capacities rather than on their understanding of the properties possessed by objects. In Stage Two, objects such as parents, with whom the infant has had a great deal of contact, may be remembered for a few hours; thus, these objects may be responded to as if they were permanent. Objects with which the infant has had little experience, such as those one might employ in a psychological experiment, may be forgotten quickly; thus, the experiments produce behavior that could be interpreted by Piaget and others as evidence for the infant's lack of the concept of object permanence.

Stage Three (4-8 Months)—Secondary Circular Reactions

Stage Three is characterized by a shift on the part of infants from exclusive interest in their own bodies and the body's actions to an interest in the characteristics and actions of objects other than themselves. Infants six months of age will fling out their feet and kick a large doll attached to their crib. The doll makes a noise, and the infants appear attentive to the sound and movement of the doll. As long as this behavior is accompanied by interesting events, the kicking action is repeated over and over again.

Secondary Circular Reactions

The repetitive action described above is called a secondary circular reaction. It is secondary because it describes not only the infant's action (as is the case for the primary circular reaction), but also the action of the doll (its movement and sound). However, in spite of infants' interest in the actions of objects around them, there is no evidence that infants recognizes a cause-effect relationship between their own actions and the interesting events that are observed.

While Piaget maintained that secondary circular reactions do not occur until the third stage of sensorimotor development, the principle that underlies those reactions is quite similar to that of operant conditioning: a response (kicking the doll) followed by a pleasant outcome (seeing the doll move and hearing a sound) results in the repetition of the response. The recent observation that infants younger than four months of age may be operantly conditioned by using interesting visual displays as a reinforcement draws into question whether or not this form of behavior is first observable in the Stage Three infant.

Object Discrimination and Classification

Although Piaget did not discuss the continued development of object discrimination and classification in his accounts of Stage Three sensorimotor development, it is interesting to note some of the social behavior that implies such changes in discrimination. For example, at the age of six to eight months, infants will react strongly to the presence of a stranger in the room. For such a reaction to take place, clearly the infant must discriminate between familiar caretakers and strangers.

Parents are sometimes disturbed by their child's development of discrimination among people. Although children less than six months old often respond favorably to a familiar baby sitter, after six months of age they might cry when the baby sitter enters the room. Apparently, they are discriminating between family members and other people. While parents often fear that they can no longer leave their child with a baby sitter, fortunately this fear of strangers quickly passes. (For a further discussion of discrimination development in Stage Three, see Chapter 10.)

Cause-Effect Relations

Despite the infant's coordination of sensory and motor actions and the repetition of actions that cause interesting results, there is little evidence that the Stage Three infant understands the relationship between actions and their outcomes. An infant may observe two related events—the kicking action and the interesting movements and noise made by a toy. However, the child does not experiment to determine if changes in the action affect the outcome, and there is no other evidence that the infant engages in the response with the intention of causing the outcome.

Object Permanence

Piaget observed that infants in Stage Three begin to develop a rudimentary concept of object permanence even when they do not have direct sensory or motor contact with the object. At this stage, infants will search briefly for objects they themselves have caused to disappear or will search for the missing part of a familiar object if only part of it is visible.

In Stage Two, infants may ignore a half-covered bottle, but in Stage Three, infants will pull the cover off half-covered familiar items to obtain the whole object. Apparently, infants expect the covered part of the bottle to be under the cloth even though they cannot see it.

The observation that the infant will search for objects that are not fully visible is evident only when the infant is confronted with very familiar objects. Confrontation with unfamiliar objects tends to result in behavior characteristic of Stage Two. If infants in Stage Three have observed a model train traveling through a tunnel on a number of occasions, they will begin to direct their attention toward the end of the tunnel out of which they anticipate the train to come, even though they cannot see the train. Thus, the infants are responding to an object that is not present. However, unless infants have considerable experience with the train traveling through the tunnel, no anticipation will be observed.

Memory

In spite of the amount of exposure apparently required before infants in Stage Three will search for and anticipate objects, by the age of four to six months the infant does remember—for up to two weeks— objects that have been seen for only a few minutes.

Although numerous trials are required before an infant will respond to the unobservable train described above, a short experience with a doctor who administers a shot may result in that infant recognizing the doctor and exhibiting fear on the next visit to the office. Clearly, infants are able to remember their experiences for some time. Apparently, the infant in Stage Three has some knowledge of the missing object, such as the doctor, that is not reflected by the experimental tasks typically used to demonstrate an awareness of object permanence.

Recognition vs. Recall Memory

We are confronted with two pieces of conflicting information. Infants require extended periods of familiarization in order to demonstrate the concept of object permanence, yet at the same time, they appear to remember some events and objects after a number of weeks even with only limited exposure to those objects or events—for example, the doctor giving an injection. The resolution of these conflicting observations requires that psychologists distinguish between two kinds of memory.

Recognition Memory

Recognition memory is revealed when an individual is confronted with a stimulus and recognizes that he or she has been confronted by that stimulus before. Recognition memory is exemplified in infants when they habituate to a stimulus or look longer at a novel object than they do at a familiar one.

Recall Memory

Recall memory requires that the individual construct a mental representation of the missing object when it is not present. Research that describes the early development of memory capacities typically uses tasks that measure recognition memory. Studies demonstrating the habituation phenomenon suggest that some primitive form of recognition memory develops at a very early age. However, the demonstration of Piaget's concept of object permanence requires the use of recall memory, which probably requires more time to develop than does recognition memory.

Recall memory is exhibited in the Stage Two infant only for objects that are highly familiar, such as parents. In the Stage Three infant, recall occurs for objects or events that are less familiar than those recalled in Stage Two; however, the interval between the exposure to an object or event and the attempts to recall it must be short for memory to be exhibited. In the earlier example of the train, object permanence will only be exhibited if the train is out of sight for a second or two. If the train is removed from sight for longer periods, recall of it will quickly wane.

Stage Four (8-12 Months)–Coordination of Secondary Schemes

The fourth stage of sensorimotor cognition is characterized by the emergence of behavior that reflects the infant's awareness of the relationship between means and ends. Before Stage Four, the infant's actions are directed toward the immediate achievement of goals and objectives, such as gaining access to or maintaining contact with food, a toy, or an interesting event. The infant will not combine two separate actions in order to achieve a single objective. During Stage Four, however, the infant will engage in a pattern of action that does not result directly in attaining or achieving the sought-after object or event but does make possible a second action that will bring about the desired objective.

For example, an infant of six months who wants to play with the knobs on a television set is easily deterred from this activity by a chair placed in front of the set as a barricade. At ten months of age, however, the infant quickly pushes the chair aside and proceeds to play with the knobs. The infant has engaged in one secondary action pattern (chair moving) in order to allow himself an opportunity to engage in another secondary action pattern (knob turning).

The ability to coordinate one's own action patterns in a temporal sequence is also reflected in the infant's ability to anticipate the actions of others in ways that he or she has experienced sequenced actions on their part before. Parents frequently observe that their eight- to ten-month-old child begins to raise a fuss before he or she is sent to bed. Even infants hate to go to bed, but before this age the infant cannot anticipate bedtime. The running of bath water or the initiation of prebedtime games can serve as a cue to the Stage Four infant for an impending event, and can result in protests of anticipation.

Discrimination and Classification

Although Piaget did not discuss refinements in the Stage Four infant's ability to discriminate objects from one another or to place objects into common classes, research suggests that such refinements occur. Toward the end of this developmental stage, infants tend to classify objects into groups on the basis of physical characteristics and respond in a common way to objects that possess characteristics common to the class.

For example, a group of one-year-old infants are each presented a tray containing four red cubes and four blue balls. Nearly 50 percent of the infants will touch all the objects from one class, for example, the red cubes, before touching any of the objects in the second class, the blue balls. Although subtle, this response pattern reflects the infant's ability to form simple classes.

Cause-Effect Relations

Stage Two of the sensorimotor period of cognitive development was characterized by the coordination of simple reflexes. In Stage Four we see a similar coordination activity—the coordination of secondary action patterns that form the foundation for the infant's first true recognition of cause-effect relationships.

These cause-effect relationships are reflected in infants' attempts to engage in one activity in order to allow themselves the opportunity to engage in a second, and in their ability to anticipate parental actions by watching parents' current behavior. In addition, one can observe infants engaging in activities that are intended to result in others doing something for them.

The play activities of infants are directly affected by their awareness of cause-effect relationships. A favorite game of Stage Four infants is to drop objects out of their playpen or crib, or to drop food from their highchair. The children expect that someone will pick up the object or food and that they will be able to repeat the act. This is a great game for infants and they often laugh with glee, although parents often fail to see the humor in these games and, unfortunately, often fail to see the significance of such games in relation to the cognitive development of their child.

Object Permanence

In Stage Four, the child will consistently search for objects that are hidden. They must, however, see the object as it is hidden. Apparently, this searching response reflects the development of a behavioral rule rather than the ability to reconstruct a representation of the missing object. This conclusion stems from the observation that even when children witness the object being hidden in a new place, they may search for it where it had been hidden in the past.

Stage Five (12-18 Months)—Tertiary Circular Reactions

The fifth stage of sensorimotor cognitive development is characterized by the emergence of true trial-and-error exploration.

Tertiary Circular Reactions

Infants in Stage Five are no longer content with using old action patterns in combination to achieve objectives. Instead, they repeatedly try variations of those old action patterns to discover the ends they may achieve. This repetitive behavior is called a tertiary circular reaction. An act is repeated with systematic variations so that new cause-effect relations can be discovered.

Jason, at fourteen months old, delights in throwing food from his highchair. At ten months of age, the activity was a game he played with his parents. He would drop the food, and one of his parents would pick it up. This game was constantly repeated with little variation. Now the game has changed. Jason first drops the food and explores its landing place. Next the food is thrown with force and its landing place is again noted. On a third act, the force of the throw is moderate and the food lands in a third location. In contrast to his behavior at ten months of age, Jason is no longer repeating the same act. Instead, he is changing his actions (the force of his throw) and is exploring the impact of these changes on the outcome of those acts (the place the food falls).

Classification

While the classification ability of Stage Four infants was inferred from their touching objects having one characteristic before touching objects possessing a second characteristic, Stage Five infants can be observed to gather together all objects of a given color while leaving objects of another color in a separate pile. This is a clear example of classification.

A fifteen-month-old is given a set of blocks for her birthday. Some of the blocks are cubes of various colors, and some are triangles of various colors. She is observed to play only with the cubed blocks and to leave all the triangular blocks in the toy box. The girl discriminates between the two classes of objects.

Cause-Effect Relationships

An understanding that particular actions cause particular results to occur is the defining characteristic of the Stage Five infant. Furthermore, the infant is actively trying to discover new cause-and-effect relationships.

Object Permanence

The Stage Five infant can think about objects and events that are not present. This capacity derives from the newly acquired capacity to create a representation for an object or event. That capacity is reflected in the child's improved recall memory and improved ability to search for missing objects.

Suppose a man hides a favorite children's toy under a red pillow and then moves the toy to a hiding place beneath a blue cushion while his daughter and niece are watching. His daughter, who is ten months old, will still search intently for the toy under the red cushion. This behavior is characteristic of the Stage Four infant.

However, even though his sixteen-month-old niece has seen, searched for, and found the toy hidden under the red cushion on many previous occasions, she will search immediately under the blue cushion. Since the niece has a Stage Five representation of the missing object, her search for the toy is not dependent upon the learning of specific behavior patterns.

Despite having a representation for the missing object, infants in Stage Five still lack some skills in understanding missing objects. Although they can represent the missing object mentally, they cannot represent changes occurring to the object while it is missing; if a change occurs in the object while it is hidden, that change shocks the infants.

Stage Six (18-24 Months)–Mental Combinations

The characteristic that differentiates the infant in the sixth stage of sensorimotor cognitive development from infants in earlier stages is the child's ability to use symbols that are distinct from the objects and events they represent. Of specific importance is the development of words as symbols. This development has ramifications for almost all the infant's cognitive functioning and represents the transition from the sensorimotor to the preoperational period of cognitive development.

Classification

As was true of the play behavior of Stage Five counterparts, the play behavior of Stage Six children exhibits their ability to respond to objects as if they belong to classes. However, Stage Six children have the ability to use words as symbolic representations of those objects and events, and exhibit behavior that suggests they can also respond to those symbols as if they too belong to classes.

If a two-year-old is asked to remember and repeat a list of words such as *dog*, *car*, *cat*, and *bye-bye*, the child may repeat only those words in the list that have some association with one another—*dog* and *cat*, for example—or the child will rearrange the list so that the words associated with one another are recalled together: *dog* and *cat*; *bye-bye* and *car*. This phenomenon is called associative clustering.

Cause-Effect Relations

The characteristic most evident in Stage Six children is their ability to discover means to an end without actually engaging in the activities that result in reaching the objective, or observing the means-end relationship exhibited. Instead, infants in Stage Six engage symbolically in trial-and-error activity. This added cognitive capacity results in the children appearing to display insight into the solution of problems confronting them.

Twenty-month-old Lisa sat in front of her play pen attempting to retrieve a favorite toy that would not fit through the bars unless it was in a particular orientation. Lisa unsuccessfully tried to retrieve the toy and then paused. Unlike the infant in Stage Five, who would try a variety of ways to retrieve the toy before discovering a method that worked, Lisa looked at the situation as if she was contemplating it in her mind, and then immediately turned the toy sideways.

The ability to represent potential activities symbolically results in another characteristic possessed by Stage Six infants. Children in Stage Five tend to modify already-possessed action patterns to discover new means to achieve ends. For Stage Six infants to achieve new means-end relationships, however, may involve totally new patterns of behavior. These infants do not appear to be restricted to modification of old action patterns.

Justin's parents reported that they were always able to keep their son out of the top drawers of cabinets because he could not reach them and did not seem to grasp the idea that he could pull a stool over to use as a tool in extending his reach. However, although Justin had never before used objects as a means of climbing higher, when he was twenty months old he eyed the drawers one morning and with little hesitation pulled over a nearby stool, climbed upon it, and discovered a totally new means to his objective.

Object Concepts

The concept of the object is fully developed in Stage Six. As in Stage Five, infants can symbolize an object when it is missing. They can also symbolize changes that can potentially affect the object when it is out of sight.

One exciting game for a child is the Easter Egg hunt. For

Stage Six children, this game can be played effectively because they have an object concept that allows them to consider eggs as present although they are unseen and the children have not observed exactly where they have been hidden. In devising an Easter Egg hunt for an eighteen-month-old child, take an egg and show it to the infant, then move from place to place in the room pretending to hide the egg at each stop. Then return without the egg. With glee, the child will begin to retrace your steps looking for the lost egg. Clearly, the infant in Stage Six can symbolically follow the potential patterns of change in the egg's location.

Measuring Infant Intelligence

In an effort to diagnose potential neurological and emotional disabilities as well as to predict intellectual performance at later ages, attempts have been made to develop measures of infant intelligence.   Typical of these instruments are the Gesell Developmental Schedules and the Bayley Scales of Gesell Infant Development.

When administering these tests of infant intelligence, the examiner makes systematic observations and notices whether the infant exhibits behaviors characteristic of his or her age. When observing four-month-old infants, the examiner notes whether or not the children recover a rattle that has been removed from their hand but is still within reach. Fifty percent of infants 4.9 months old pass this test. Fifty percent of 9.7-month-old infants can be expected to imitate another person stirring with a spoon, while the same percentage of 13.8-month-olds can build a tower of two cubes.

Though measures of intelligence can be useful in detecting neurological impairments and developmental delays in infancy, controversy exists about the ability of these tests to predict performance on intelligence tests given at later ages.   Based primarily on results from a longitudinal study undertaken in Berkeley, California, most textbooks report little or no relationship between performance on intelligence tests given prior to age two and those administered after that age.

In that classic study, the IQs of a group of infants were measured regularly during the first two years of their life and again when they were 17 and 18 years old. The correlation between IQ performance at those separated times was: 1–3 months and 17–18 years (0.05); 4–6 months and 17–18 years (–0.01); 7–9 months and 17–18 years (0.20); 10–12 months and 17–18 years (0.41); 13–15 months and 17–18 years (0.23); 18–24 months and 17–18 years (0.55). In contrast, correlations between IQ test performance at ages over 5 years and IQ test performance at 17 to 18 years consistently exceed 0.85.[1]

This lack of relationship between measures of infant intelligence and later intellectual performance is attributed to two factors:

1. Infant intelligence tests tend to measure perceptual and motor skills, while intelligence tests for older children and adults tend to emphasize verbal skills, reasoning, and abstract thinking. Because the tests measure different skills, they cannot be expected to correlate well with one another.

2. A significant qualitative change takes place in the development of intellectual ability at about the age of two. The form of intelligence possessed by the infant is nonverbal, nonsymbolic, and based primarily on sensorimotor activity, while that of the older child is founded on verbal symbolism. This argument is compatible with Piaget's view that a qualitative change in intellectual functioning occurs at about two years of age,

---

1. N. Bayley, "Consistency and Variability in the Growth of Intelligence from Birth to Eighteen Years," *Journal of Genetic Psychology*, 75:165-196 (1949).

when the child moves from the sensorimotor to the preoperational period of cognitive development.

Some evidence exists to support a correlation between infant IQ performance and IQ test performance at later ages. When specific tasks from tests of infant intelligence, particularly those concerned with verbal skills, are used to assess total intellectual performance, high correlations do exist between these infant intelligence scores and intelligence test performance at later ages. These correlations have been observed for girls, but not for boys. For example, data from the Berkeley Growth Study indicates that a correlation of O.74 existed between the age at which girls first passed items related to verbal skills and verbal IQ test performance at age.

Recent attempts have been made to develop tests of infant cognition based on a Piagetian analysis of sensorimotor cognitive development. These tests measure such conceptual attainments as object permanence. Correlations between performance on these tests and more traditional tests of infant intelligence are moderately high.

CHAPTER 9

Language and Communication in the First Two Years

Developmental and learning psychologists, as well as psycholinguists, have studied extensively the way in which children learn to understand and use language to communicate with the outside world.

The infant's motor abilities—especially those involved in controlling the mouth, lips, and tongue, the vocal cords, the throat, and the windpipe—contribute to his or her ability to make more complex sounds. The child's developing language competencies are also tied in with increased neurological development. Only as the brain and nervous system mature is the child able to master more complex language skills, such as the production of meaningful words and word combinations. Finally, the influence of the child's immediate environment—the parents, siblings, mass media—contribute not only to the specific sounds the child can generate but to the development of complex language abilities as well.

The development of language skills in the first two years of life can be seen as occurring in four phases: the prebabbling phase, the babbling phase, the phase when single words are used to communicate, and the phase in which words are combined into two-word utterances.

Prebabbling Phase (1–6 Months)

During the prebabbling phase the infant's communication may sound like crying to the uninitiated observer. Although a few of the sounds heard, such as /k/, /g/, /i/, and /w/, are similar to those used in later language, they are infrequently produced. To the parent or trained observer, however, the crying sounds of the first six months are not uniform. Different cries reflect different messages.

The Frequency Pattern of a Cry

Because the infant's cries are longer in duration than a single respiration, there is a tendency for the infant to run out of breath before the end of an utterance. The result of this phenomenon is that the infant's cry initially exhibits a rise and then a fall in the frequency of the sound waves. (See Fig. 9-1.)

A similar pattern is observed in later babbling and is characteristic of the frequency pattern in the declarative sentence used by older children and adults. Furthermore, while spectrographic analysis reveals that each infant's cry is unique to that infant, for a given infant the frequency pattern in the cry differs depending upon his or her state.

Infant Perception of Intonation

Although infants apparently produce cries that declare their state, evidence suggests that at four months they do not discriminate the intonational differences between a question and a

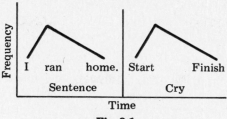

Fig. 9.1

declarative sentence. In one experiment, sound patterns characteristic of the intonation of a simple declarative sentence and a question were recorded on tape and played to a four-month-old infant. The sound pattern characteristic of one type of sentence—that is, a question—was repeated over and over again until its presentation produced no change in heart rate, respiration, or body movement. A second sound pattern, characteristic of a second type of sentence, was then played. If the infant discriminated a difference between the intonational patterns of the two sentences, it was hypothesized, a difference in heart rate, respiration, or motor activity should be observed. Upon measurement, however, it was as if the sound pattern characteristics of the original sentence were still being presented. The infant could not discriminate questions from declarations.

Babbling Phase (6–12 Months)

At about six months of age, the infant begins more systematically to make sounds, combine them, and repeat their production over and over again. At the same time, the infant begins to exhibit the ability to produce and perceive differences in the intonation of sentences.

The most dominant characteristic of the babbling phase is the extent to which infants practice their newly discovered skills. Infants six to eight months old will usually babble endlessly to themselves in bed or babble the same sound over and over as they crawl around the room.

First Sounds

The simplest sounds of a language are called *phonemes*. Interestingly, all the words used in all the languages throughout the world are made by combining sounds from a small set of phonemes. The first phonemes produced by infants are similar regardless of the language they ultimately speak. The "open" vowels /a/ and /e/ are the first to be heard. They are produced in the back of the mouth and require little motor control and tongue or lip manipulation.

The first consonants heard are usually /m/, /p/, /d/, /b/, and /t/. These consonants require less complex manipulation of the tongue and lips and are thus easier to produce than other consonants.

An important principle to remember is that the sounds initially produced by an infant are determined to a great extent by the infant's motor abilities. New sounds are made and new combinations of sounds are formed as the infant becomes more adept at controlling the lips, tongue, and air passages. To produce the sound /m/, for example, infants need only to close their mouth and let air vibrate in the nasal cavity. In contrast, the sound /r/ requires manipulation of the tongue and lips. Consequently, /r/ sounds are produced later in the child's development than are /m/ sounds.

First Sound Combinations

At about eight months of age the infant will combine sounds. Initially, the combined sounds are repetitions of the same sound, that is ma, ma, ma . . . During this same developmental phase, the variety of sounds produced by the infant will become restricted to those that commonly occur in the language he or she hears. It is at this point that children who are learning to speak Chinese or Hebrew develop different sound skills from children learning to speak English or African !Click! languages.

Intonation

At eight months of age, the infant is able to perceive differences in the intonation of questions and declarative sentences. This observation is documented using the experimental techniques described in the earlier section, "Infant Perception of Intonation." At ten months of age, the infant's babbling includes intonational characteristics of a declaration, which is slow to rise and then falls in frequency, and a command, which is quick to rise and then falls in frequency.

Many parents will tell you that their ten-month-old infant can be very demanding, even without words. What the parents are observing is a change in the child's ability to use the intonation of a command in his or her babbling. Even without words, the child's babbling sounds are perceived by the parents as commands.

First Words (12–15 Months)

In discussing language, we can consider three topics. The first is semantics, or the meaning of the individual words in an utterance. The second is syntax, or the structure and meaning of sentences in which the words are used. The third is intonation, or the tonal rising and falling of the utterance, which may also convey the intended meaning of the sentence. In addition, we must differentiate between the child's understanding or comprehension of words and sentences produced by others and the child's own spontaneous use of language.

Semantics

The first words used by infants are idiosyncratic, and typically they are not words that children have heard their parents or other adults use. This observation is important because it exemplifies the creative quality of language production and demonstrates that the infant's language is not a simple imitation of the language he or she hears. Initially, the words used by the infant tend to be names for general classes of objects or events, and the use of these early words is typically overgeneralized.

For example, a girl begins referring to the banana fed to her as *nana*. Although the girl has learned a word to identify that specific fruit, it is quickly apparent that she calls all foods nana. When she desires food, she calls "nana" and is pleased when any food is brought to her. The word *nana* for this child is a general nominal, that is, a label for a class of objects. The word is overgeneralized, since it refers to an extremely broad class of objects that may have few characteristics in common.

Vocabulary Size

The number of word meanings acquired by infants may reach as many as 250 to 300 by their second birthday. The acquisition of that vocabulary is not steady. Instead, one observes very limited increases in vocabulary until the child is 18 months of age, when a significant acceleration in vocabulary occurs. (See Fig. 9.2.) Furthermore, while Fig. 9.2 depicts the words that are understood by the infant at two years of age, this number far exceeds the number of words spontaneously used by the child, which may be only 40 to 50 words.

It is interesting to note that corresponding to the rapid increase in speech production and comprehension observed in the infant at about 18 months of age is the maturation (at approximately 17 months of age) of a brain structure called Brocca's area, which has been identified as an important neurological system in the production of speech. This concurrent

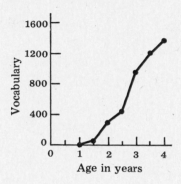

Fig. 9.2

development exemplifies the close relationship between neurological maturation and the acquisition of language.

Syntax

The single words initially used by a child are not labels but instead, convey whole thoughts. They are called *holophrases,* indicating that the words themselves carry as much meaning for the child as sentences would for the adult.

The conclusion that single words are used as more than just labels and carry more complex meaning stems from two related observations. First, a child may see a pair of shoes and say "dada." If the child were only labeling what he or she sees, one would expect to hear a word specifically meaning shoes. The use of the word *dada* instead suggests that the child is communicating that they are daddy's shoes.

Second, the intonation used in expressing the word reveals whether the word is being used as a declaration (for example, "food" means "That is food" or "I am hungry"); a command ("food" means "Give me some food!"); or a question ("food" means "Is that food?"). Analysis of sound spectrograms confirms that these distinctive intonations perceived by parents and psychologists are reflected in the physical properties of the sound pattern.

Theories of Holophrasic Speech

While psycholinguists agree that holophrases are used to express an idea, they differ about what the infant who uses holophrases really knows about language. The three most prominent positions are as follows:

The Assumed Linguistic Knowledge Viewpoint. The infant has knowledge of the structure of language but lacks certain skills in memory and attention that are needed to fully utilize that knowledge. The single word is used by the infant because it does not exceed the infant's memory and attentional capacities. As those capacities increase, so does the infant's ability to use the knowledge of language he or she possesses; consequently, more complex sentences are produced.

The Relational Understanding Viewpoint. The infant has an idea that he or she wishes to convey and understands the relationships among the parts of that idea. However, the child lacks the knowledge of language needed to express the idea in sentence form. Thus, to express the idea, the child uses the single word that identifies the most important concept in the idea he or she is attempting to express.

The Naive Egocentric Viewpoint. The infant has an idea that he or she wishes to express but is unaware of how to express it properly. The infant does not yet understand the relationship among the elements of the idea of how they are connected. Thus, the child simply says a word that identifies part of the idea and assumes that the listener understands the expressed meaning.

Unfortunately, to prove the validity of any of these positions requires reading the mind of the infant, a feat that is impossible for even the most skilled psychologist. Thus, a resolution of the controversy appears unlikely.

Intonation

Controversy exists about whether or not children employ intonation to differentiate the meanings they wish to convey when using a holophrase.   Conflicting research has been presented. One position maintains that single words are only inconsistently given two or more intonations to differentiate declarative, interrogative, and command meanings from one another. In contrast, another position reports that the intonation of the first single-word utterances is clearly expressive of particular meanings, including declarations, commands, and questions.

The following experiment supports the latter position. During a conversation, a child repeated a single word on a number of occasions. An experimenter recorded this series of repeated utterances, along with repetitions of other words and played them to two adult listeners. These adults were asked to classify each utterance of a specific word as either declarative, interrogative, or empathic in meaning. The listeners were able to make such classifications on the basis of intonational cues, and 81 percent of the time, they agreed on the class into which each utterance fell. Furthermore, spectrograms revealed distinctive characteristics for each class of utterance identified by the listeners, suggesting that the child does convey particular meanings through intonation.

Two-Word Utterances

One can begin to discuss a structure of language only when two words are put together to convey an idea. The first such utterances usually occur when an infant has a useful vocabulary of fifty words. That milestone may arise anytime from 10 to 28 months, but it typically occurs at about 18 months of age. The structure, if any, that is exhibited in those two-word utterances has been discussed under three labels: telegraph speech, pivot-open-class grammar, and semantics.

Telegraphic Speech

The term *telegraphic* speech reflects the potential analogy between the messages of the infant, whose limited capacity for memory and attention restricts his or her ability to use long sentences, and the output of the telegraph operator, who must convey a message using as few words as possible in order to conserve money. In each case, the individual's communication uses only those words that have the greatest amount of information about the idea being expressed, and eliminates the extra "fun" words that serve less important communication roles. The retained words are typically those that would receive the greatest intonational stress if a complete, nontelegraphic sentence were used to express the idea.

For example, a two-year-old says, "Daddy find hat. Put Justin head." An older child uttering this same message might say, "Daddy, will you find the hat? Will you put it on Justin's head?" The younger child's telegraphic speech excludes the use of some words that are not critical to the meaning of the message.

Pivot-Open-Class Grammar (Distributional Analysis)

Some psycholinguists emphasize the role played by syntax or grammatical structure in determining the sentence forms used by a child. They suggest that the two-word utterances of infants can be described using a simple structural grammar containing two classes of words and also rules that govern the way words from each class can be used.

Pivot Words

In this model, one class of words are called pivot words, and are defined by three characteristics: (1) They are a small group of words in a child's vocabulary that develop slowly and consist primarily of words that adults use as verbs; (2) a pivot word is used either in the first or last position of a two-word utterance, but not in both positions; and (3) two pivot words never appear in the same sentence.

Open Words

All words not used as pivot words are referred to as open-class, or X, words. Open-class words consist of a large class of words that can be used in either position of a two-word utterance. Two words from this class can be used in the same sentence.

Using the rules of pivot-open grammar, three types of word combinations can be formed: Pivot$_1$-Open, Open-Pivot$_2$, and Open-Open. Note, however, that many word combinations are unacceptable as sentences: Pivot$_2$-Open, Open-Pivot$_1$, Pivot$_1$-Pivot$_2$, or Pivot$_2$-Pivot$_1$. Thus, one can speak of a structural grammar that defines some utterances as sentences and others as nonsentences.

Assets and Criticisms of the Pivot-Open-Class Grammar

Because the two-word utterances of a few infants followed the patterns suggested by the pivot-open grammar, psychologists became excited by the evidence that the infant's language was not random and unpredictable, but rather appeared organized from the very beginning of its development. However, later observations demonstrated inadequacies in the pivot-open grammar as a complete description of the early structure of language. Those criticisms center on two facts:

1. It is hard to find a child whose vocabulary exhibits a set of pivot words that actually adheres to the definitional restrictions of the pivot class. For example, the word "bye-bye" is often defined as a pivot word in an infant's vocabulary. According to rule two, "bye-bye" should either appear as an initial pivot word ("Bye-bye Daddy"), or as a terminal pivot word ("shoe bye-

bye"), but for a given infant, both uses of the word should not be observed. However, for most infants, "bye- bye" is used in both the first and second positions, thus violating the principle of the pivot-word class. In fact, there are few, if any, words that do not violate one or more of the rules defining a pivot word.

2.   The pivot-open-class grammar is developed from an analysis of how words are distributed in utterances, that is, where they are used. The analysis does not take into account how the words are used in the utterance, that is the meaning of the utterance.

"Mommy shoe" is an example of an open-open utterance. The pivot-open-class grammar, with its emphasis on the class of words used in each position of the sentence, suggests that this sentence exemplifies a single sentence form. However, it has been noted that this single sentence may have a number of meanings: "That is mommy's shoe," or "Mommy is putting on her shoe," or "Mommy, get your shoe," or "Mommy, put on your shoe," or "Mommy, put on my shoe," and so on. The pivot-open-class grammar's emphasis on the distributional analysis does not account for those differences in meaning.

Semantic Emphasis

Emphasizing the role of syntax implies that a sentence consisting of a noun followed by a verb ("John ran") is a different type of sentence than one consisting of two nouns ("John's shoe"). However, two sentences, each consisting of a noun followed by a second noun, have the same form as each other.

Sentences with the same structure may express different relationships between the words in the sentence. For example "Mommy lunch" and "sweater chair" both have the same noun-noun structure. In the first sentence, however, one noun is the owner of the other, while in the second sentence, one noun describes the location of the other. Infants distinguish between these two kinds of sentences; thus, they must discriminate sentences on the basis of the relationship described by the sentence as well as the sentence's syntactic structure.

Table 9.1 is a list of eleven relationships commonly expressed in the two-word utterances of the two-year-old child. Note that the same structure may express more than one relationship.

Table 9.1

Expressed Relationship	Syntactic Structure	Example
Nomination (naming)	That + Noun	That book
Notice	Hi + Noun	Hi puppy
Recurrence	More + Noun	More banana
Nonexistence	All-gone + Noun	All-gone milk
Attribution	Adjective + Noun	Big Train
Possessive	Noun + Noun	Mommy shoe
Locative (1)	Noun + Noun	Sweater chair
Locative (2)	Verb + Noun	Sit bed
Agent-action	Noun + Verb	Mommy run
Agent-object	Noun + Noun	Bobby bike
Action-object	Verb + Noun	Fall puppy

Some psychologists, including Roger Brown and Lois Bloom, believe that the two-word utterances of infants do not reflect an understanding of a sentence's syntactic structure but reflect instead the child's discovery of a set of useful relationships that can be observed in the surrounding world, and a selection of words that describe these relationships. These psychologists are emphasizing the importance of semantics (how words are used) in the acquisition of language.

Factors Influencing Early Speech Development

The factors influencing early speech development can be divided into two categories: biological and environmental.

Biological Factors

Specific areas of the brain control language production and understanding. In adults, damage to those areas results in language impairment. Until the brain has developed adequately, infants do not develop language. Evidence for the importance of neurological development for the initiation of language acquisition stems from three sources.

1. Language develops in a similar sequence for all children, regardless of the environment in which they are reared.

2. The milestones in language development are correlated with milestones in motor development. (See Table 9.2.)

3. Infants who come from a variety of environments and who ultimately learn different languages all begin their speech with similar utterances.

Environmental Factors

The feedback given to infants when they make language sounds, as well as the kinds of language they hear, can influence their development of language. In one study, parents were divided into two groups based on the style of language they used with their children. Some parents (designated R) talked primarily about things, making statements such as "This is a ball" and "The ball is red." Other parents (designated E) talked primarily about themselves, the baby, and other people, saying things like "Baby is sad, Mommy is happy," and so on. The infants of R parents begin using two-word utterances at a slightly earlier age

Table 9.2 The Correlation between Language Skills and Motor Development*

At the completion of:	Motor Development	Vocalization and Language
12 weeks	Supports head when in prone position; weight is on elbows; hands mostly open; no grasp reflex.	Markedly less crying than at 8 weeks; when talked to and nodded at, smiles, followed by squealing-gurgling sounds usually called *cooing,* which is vowel-like in character and pitch-modulated; sustains cooing for 15–20 seconds.
16 weeks	Plays with rattle placed in hands (by shaking and staring at it); head self-supported.	Responds to human sounds more definitely; turns head; eyes seem to search for speaker; occasionally some chuckling sounds.
20 weeks	Sits when propped up.	The vowel-like cooing sounds begin to be interspersed with more consonantal sounds; acoustically, all vocalizations are very different from the sounds of the mature language of the environment.
6 months	Sitting: bends forward and uses hands for support; can bear weight when put into standing position, but cannot yet stand without holding on; reaching: unilateral; grasp: no thumb apposition yet; releases cube when given another.	Cooing changing into babbling resembling one-syllable utterances; neither vowels nor consonants have very fixed recurrences; most common utterances sound somewhat like /ma/, /mu/, /da/, or /di/.

Table 9.2 *(Continued)*

At the completion of:	Motor Development	Vocalization and Language
8 months	Stands holding on; grasps with thumb apposition: picks up pellet with thumb and fingertips.	Reduplication (or more continuous repetitions) becomes frequent; intonation patterns become distinct; utterances can signal emphasis and emotions.
10 months	Creeps efficiently; takes side steps, holding on; pulls to standing position.	Vocalizations are mixed with sound-play such as gurgling or bubble-blowing; appears to wish to imitate sounds, but the imitations are never quite successful; beginning to differentiate between words heard by making differential adjustment.
12 months	Walks when held by one hand; walks on feet and hands, knees in air; mouthing of objects almost stopped; seats self on floor.	Identical sound sequences are replicated with higher relative frequency of occurrence and words ("mama" or "dada") are emerging; definite signs of understanding some words and simple commands ("Show me your eyes.").
18 months	Grasp, prehension, and release fully developed; gait stiff, propulsive, and precipitated; sits on child's chair with only fair aim; creeps downstairs backward; has difficulty building tower of three cubes.	Has definite repertoire of words—more than three, but less than fifty; still much babbling but now of several syllables with intricate intonation pattern; no attempt at communicating information and no frustration for not being under-

Table 9.2 *(Continued)*

At the completion of:	Motor Development	Vocalization and Language
		stood; words may include items such as "thank you" or "come here," but there is little ability to join any of the lexical items into spontaneous two-item phrases; understanding is progressing rapidly.
24 months	Runs, but falls in sudden turns; can quickly alternate between sitting and stance; walks stairs up or down, one foot forward only.	Vocabulary of more than fifty items (some children seem to be able to name everything in environment); begins spontaneously to join vocabulary items into two-word phrases; all phrases appear to be own creations; definite increase in communicative behavior and interest in language.
30 months	Jumps up into air with both feet; stands on one foot for about two seconds; takes few steps on tiptoe; jumps from chair; good hand and finger coordination; can move digits independently; manipulation of objects much improved; builds tower of six cubes.	Fastest increase in vocabulary with many new additions every day; no babbling at all; utterances consist of at least two words, many have three or even five words; sentences and phrases have characteristic child grammar—that is, they are rarely verbatim repetitions of an adult utterance; intelligibility is not very good yet, though there is great variation among children; seems to

Table 9.2 *(Continued)*

At the completion of:	Motor Development	Vocalization and Language
		understand everything that is said to him or her.
3 years	Tiptoes three yards; runs smoothly with acceleration and deceleration; negotiates sharp and fast curves without difficulty; walks stairs by alternating feet; jumps 12 inches; can operate tricycle.	Vocabulary of some one thousand words; about 80 percent of utterances are intelligible even to strangers; grammatical complexity of utterances is roughly that of colloquial adult language, although mistakes still occur.
4 years	Jumps over rope; hops on right foot; catches ball in arms; walks line.	Language is well-established; deviations from the adult norm tend to be more in style than in grammar.

* Adapted from E. Lenneberg: *Biological Foundations of Language* (New York: John Wiley & Sons, 1967) pp. 128–130.

than those of E parents and at two years of age have slightly larger vocabularies.

If an infant is rewarded for making sounds, speaking words, and producing sentences, that infant will continue to do so. Infants raised in institutions, where little reinforcement is provided for making verbal utterances, make fewer language-like sounds and produce fewer verbal utterances than infants who are rewarded for their verbal activity. Research has indicated that by systematically rewarding children for making verbal utterances, the rate of producing those utterances increases. Note that in this example we are speaking of the impact of reward on the rate of speech production and are not implying that the nonrewarded children cannot understand language or do not have the potential to produce it.

The language infants hear also influences their development of language. Both deaf and hearing infants make prebabbling and early babbling sounds. Deaf infants, however, stop making those sounds at about nine months of age, while hearing infants continue to develop language skills. The deaf infant's inability to hear interferes with his or her development of language.

CHAPTER 10

Personality and Social Development in the Child Under Two

During the first two years of life, human infants undergo major transformations. From creatures who seem only minimally responsive to the people around them, they develop into "little people" with unique personality characteristics who are clearly interactive with the social environment.

As noted in Chapter 1, psychoanalytic theory views the first two years as especially significant in personality development. In Freudian theory, the infant passes through the oral and anal stages of development, while Erikson views this period as the time when children must initially form a bond of trust with those closest to them and then, later, develop a sense of autonomy— that is, a sense that they can do things for themselves.

Three observations concerning this early stage of personality and social development have been of particular interest to psychologists. First, psychologists are interested in the individual differences in infants' responsiveness to their environ-

ment and the potential influence of those response patterns on reactions of parents and others to the infant. Second, psychologists pay a good deal of attention to the emergence of social responses such as smiling, and they investigate the impact of these responses on interpersonal relations. And third, psychologists pay special attention to the infant's developing attachments to certain significant persons in his or her life, and the consequent appearance of anxiety associated with separation from those persons or with the appearance of strangers on the immediate scene. In this chapter, each of these issues will be discussed from the standpoint of the infant interacting with significant others and in the context of the different environmental factors that surround the infant.

Individual Differences in Personality

Clearly, the behavior and attitudes of parents, in addition to other environmental experiences of the infant, influence development. However, the personality of a child is not shaped solely by these factors. Recent evidence suggests that inherent in each infant are characteristic ways of interacting with the environment. Thus, in discussing development we must consider not only the impact of the environment but also the impact the child makes in determining the environment in which he or she will exist.

Characteristic Ways of Reacting to the Environment

Some of the specific characteristics that show up in the first few months of life are as follows:

1. *Activity Level.* Some infants are inherently more active than others.

2. *Regularity.* Some infants are more regular than others in their patterns of sleeping, eating, and waste elimination.

3. *Responsiveness to New Stimulation.* Some infants withdraw from or ignore new sources of stimulation, while others respond quickly to those new sources and adapt well to them.

4. *Attention, Persistence, and Distraction.* Some infants are easily distracted from their ongoing activity, have short attention spans, and in general do not persist at an activity after it is initiated. In contrast, other infants are difficult to distract and, once having established a set pattern of behavior, persist in that behavior.

5. *Irritability.* Some infants are more likely to cry and fuss than are others.

6. *Cuddliness.* Some infants are much more receptive than others to being held closely and cuddled. It is interesting to note that while cuddlers develop stronger attachments to their caretakers than do noncuddlers, noncuddlers are quicker to develop motor and perceptual skills.

7. *Quality of Mood.* Some infants are more friendly, pleasant, and joyful than others.

Classification of Children Based on How They Adjust

Researchers Stella Chess and Alexander Thomas postulate that infants can be placed in three categories based on their methods of responding to the world around them. The three categories are as follows:

1. *Easy Children.* These children approach situations positively and are regular in their biological functioning, including sleeping, eating, and bowel and bladder functioning. Because

they can adapt easily to the style of the parents, almost any kind of parenting technique will work effectively with them.

2. *Difficult Children*. These children find it difficult to adapt to new situations and exhibit a negative attitude as well as disruptive behavior when confronted with the need to adapt. However, this negative attitude toward new situations can be overcome, and once adaptation takes place, the children are comfortable in the new situation and can function well. Parents of a difficult child are most effective when they provide him or her with a highly structured environment that allows the child to avoid the discomforts of continually having to adapt to new situations.

3. *Slow-to-Warm-Up Children*. These children, like difficult children, do not adapt quickly to new situations. However, their difficulty in warming up to a new situation is not accompanied by negative attitudes and behavior. Instead, these children tend to withdraw from new situations. Effective parents for the slow-to-warm-up child provide a structured environment for the child so as to reduce the stress of adapting to new situations. The parents also draw the child slowly into new situations through encouragement and expressing their understanding of the child's feelings.

The inherent individual differences among infants are important because they determine, in part, how others will respond to the child, and thus play a significant role in determining the environment in which the child will live. Furthermore, frustration and anxiety may result from the child's confrontation with an environment not compatible with his or her constitutional character.

A highly active infant is born into a family with passive parents. The activity level of the infant is incompatible with the parents' own activity level. This incompatibility results in the parents becoming frustrated and tired. They consider the infant unmanageable and, in their own state of frustration, are continually punishing the child. The incompatibility of the infant's and parents' activity levels result in an unfavorable developmental environment filled with punishment and inhibition. If the same child had been born to parents who were themselves very active and accepting of high activity levels, the developmental environment confronting the infant might have been more favorable.

The Smile

The infant's smile is a significant response because it has the power to stimulate adults' responses toward the infant. Thus, individual differences in the amount of smiling in which infants engage can result in the establishment of different interpersonal environments within which they will develop.

The First Social Smile

The first smile directed toward a person can be observed between the third and the eighth week after birth. Although a variety of sources of stimulation will produce smiling, the sound of a human voice coupled with a moving face is the best elicitor of the social smile. By the age of four months, pictures or statues depicting faces will also elicit smiles.

Three explanations have been given for the development of smiling in the infant. It is worth noting that the three explanations are not totally incompatible with one another.

Genetic Hypothesis

Bowlby maintains that the needs of smiling infants are responded to more readily than the needs of nonsmiling infants. Thus, in the evolution of the species, infants who spontaneously responded to social stimuli with a smile survived, while those who lacked that spontaneity did not. This evolutionary process has resulted in the development of a species with the characteristic of smiling spontaneously in the presence of eliciting stimuli. Support for this genetic hypothesis comes from the observation that blind infants smile spontaneously in the same way as sighted infants. The age at which infants begin to smile is best determined by calculating their age from the date of conception rather than from the date of birth. Apparently, environmental stimulation has a minimum influence in the onset of this response.

Perceptual Recognition Hypothesis

Jerome Kagan has postulated that the smile is a natural response to any object or event that is represented by an emerging schema. The infant of three to eight weeks is just beginning to recognize the face and develop a mental characterization for it. Thus, at this age the infant smiles when his or her attention is drawn toward a face or voice.

Social Learning Theory

Smiling behavior can be modified by reinforcement. Infants who are reinforced for smiling do so more often than those who are not reinforced. Furthermore, as one would predict from reinforcement theory, smiling that is reinforced only occasionally is more difficult to extinguish than smiling reinforced all the time. Although these observations have been used to support the position that the smiling response is acquired through the learning process, it is more plausible to speculate that the smiling response is a natural response that, once observed, can be modified through the use of reinforcement.

Later Smiling

By the age of six months, the infant does more than just smile in response to social stimulation. Infants will actively laugh during play with other people.

One of the popular games of infancy is chase. A parent crawls after the child, and the child quickly crawls away. For an adult, the most exciting consequence of playing this game is to hear the child's shrills of laughter. This is clearly a response distinct from the social smile seen in the younger infant.

By the age of one year, the infant may exhibit a variety of smiles, each with its own distinct characteristics. Among the smiles observed in a single one-year-old infant are social smiles, smiles of appeasement, and smiles of triumph.

Attachment

Attachment refers to the tendency of a child to seek and attempt to maintain a close physical relationship with another person. Components of the attachment system comprise a number of behaviors that help the child make sense of the world, form a bond with another person, and navigate reality in an effective way. These include rooting and sucking (oral behaviors), looking and following (visual pursuit), listening, smiling, vocalizing, crying, grasping, and clinging.

The development of attachment requires certain prerequisite accomplishments, according to Leon Yarrow.

1. Infants must first establish that they are distinct from the environment around them. The fact that infants will respond to objects in their environment suggests that this conception is typically established within four weeks after birth.

2. Infants must learn to differentiate between the person or persons to whom they will become attached, and others. Infants have accomplished this task when they respond differently to the person to whom they are attached than to others. The fact that infants 14 weeks of age are reported to stare fixedly at

strangers rather than to smile, as they do to familiar faces, suggests that this task is accomplished at least by three and one-half months.

3. Infants must develop specific expectations for those to whom attachment will develop. The accomplishment of this task requires not only regularity of behavior on the part of those to whom the infants will become attached, but also that the infant have the cognitive ability to anticipate events based on past experiences.

4. Infants must develop trust and confidence in those with whom attachment will develop.

The accomplishment of the first two tasks described by Yarrow places some lower limitations on the emergence of attachment in the infant, while the third and fourth accomplishments place emphasis on the parental practices to which the child is exposed. Interestingly, during the first five or six months of life, infants exhibit the indiscriminate attachment one would predict from an individual who had not yet mastered those tasks.

Although two-month-old infants may cry when they are not held, they will cease crying upon being held, regardless of the person holding them. One person's presence is as good as another's. In contrast, only those persons to whom the infant is attached will relieve the crying of an older infant.

Around seven months of age, the infant begins to develop attachments to specific individuals, typically the mother. Note that at about this same age, the infant begins to understand that an object with which it is familiar—a parent, for example—has an existence even when the infant does not have sensory contact with it.

The intensity of attachment is often measured by the intensity of the protest exhibited by a child when the individual to whom it is attached leaves the child's view, or the extent to which the child will seek out the individual when a stranger is present. Comparing the amount of protest exhibited by infants of various ages when either the mother or another individual left the child's view, Schaffer and Emerson report a similar level of protest under both conditions for infants under eight months of age. By the age of ten months, there was no increase in protestation when nonmothers left the child's view, but a near- doubling of protest by the infants when the mother was removed from view.

The mother is typically the first individual to whom the infant becomes attached, and even though infants tend to be more strongly attached to their mothers, it has been noted that nearly one third of the infants studied by Schaffer and Emerson exhibited stronger attachment to their fathers than to their mothers.

Levels of Attachment

Three levels of attachment have been identified: secure, insecure, and unattached.

Secure Attachment

Secure attachment is characterized by infants who can leave the individual to whom they are attached in order to explore new experiences for a short time. These infants will protest somewhat when forced into a separation with the person to whom they are attached, but they will adapt to that situation and exhibit a calm contentment.

Insecure Attachment

Infants who are not securely attached to another person cry extensively, even when being held. Often these infants will cry to signal that they wish to be held, but when picked up, they will break away from the person holding them. Insecurely attached infants are demanding of the person to whom they are attached and exhibit extreme protests when separated from that person.

Unattached

Unattached infants exhibit no concerns for the presence of others. They ignore people when they are present and show no anxiety when people leave. Unattached infants do not develop interpersonal bonds.

Factors Influencing Attachment

Parent-Child Relations

Parents who respond quickly to the needs of their baby and who spend long periods of time interacting with the baby produce infants who are securely attached. Interestingly, parents who respond quickly to their child's cries produce infants who cry less than infants of parents who delay their responses, fearing the infant will learn that he or she can obtain attention by crying.

Even though they often spend more overall time with their baby than the quick-to-respond parents, parents who delay in attending to their offspring's needs and who have short, abrupt encounters with their baby tend to produce infants who are insecurely attached.

Almost all babies exhibit attachment of one sort or another. For an infant to be unattached, almost total neglect or some emotional dysfunction is indicated.

In most children, multiple attachment, or attachment to a number of people, emerges a few months after specific attachment. In some children, however, multiple attachments are evident from the outset of any attachment behavior.

Role of the Father

Clearly, the relationship with the mother is not the sole factor in the child's early socialization. Particularly important today—with the rapid changes of sex-role stereotyping—is the role of the father, who is being viewed more and more as a significant factor in a child's psychosocial development.

Although the mother traditionally and typically has taken care of the infant and so becomes the object of the infant's earliest attachment, the father is increasingly becoming a significant figure during this early developmental period. This is especially true if the father participates actively in the child's caretaking, including diapering, singing to the baby, bottle-feeding the baby when it is hungry, rocking the baby at night, and the like.

Still, the father's role is usually less significant than the mother's during early infancy, but increases in significance at about age two, when the child's verbal abilities allow a greater degree of interaction. In one study of children aged two through four, it was found that boys in this age group prefer to play with the father more than with the mother. Girls at two years also show a greater preference for playing with the father, but at three years old, their preference reverts to the mother, perhaps because of a beginning sense of gender identity and, consequently, an identification with her as a female.

Multiple Caretakers

A hotly contested issue is the impact of multiple caretakers on children. The presence of multiple caretakers is a standard feature of some societies, for example in the kibbutz in Israel. The practice is also becoming more common in the United States, with the increased use of infant-care centers by working parents.

Existing evidence suggests that multiple caretakers and the use of surrogate parents do not significantly interfere with the development of attachment when infants are provided the quality of interpersonal relationships that facilitate the development of attachment. Children raised in an Israeli kibbutz, for instance, are cared for by a group of caretakers and have limited contact with their parents except at night and on Saturdays. The time spent with the parents, however, is of a quality compatible with the development of secure attachment. It has been found that kibbutz children attach to their parents in the same way as nonkibbutz children do.

Jerome Kagan has undertaken an extensive study of children reared in child-care centers and has compared them to children reared at home. He found no differences in the attachment of these two groups of children to their mothers.

Outgrowths of Attachment

Two phenomena appear as outgrowths of attachment: stranger anxiety and separation anxiety.

Stranger Anxiety

Specific attachment emerges at about the age of seven months, and there often develops an accompanying fear of strangers. While the one-month-old child may respond equivalently to strangers and familiar people, or at worst, stare blankly at strangers while smiling and making positive overtures to familiar people, the six- to nine-month-old child may exhibit wild crying and agitation when a stranger enters a room. This response is called stranger anxiety.

At six months of age, a child may be left peacefully with a baby sitter. Many parents note, however, that the baby sitter who was once responded to pleasantly by the six-month-old elicits crying and screaming in the nine-month-old. This response often concerns both the conscientious parents, who wonder whether they should subject their child to a person who evidently seems distasteful, and the baby sitter, who often takes the tantrum as a sign of personal rejection. Yet the child is exhibiting a natural reaction referred to as stranger anxiety.

Separation Anxiety

Separation anxiety refers to the distress and accompanying crying and tantrums that occur when children are separated from or anticipate separation from an individual to whom they are attached. Separation anxiety often begins to emerge at about ten months of age, reaches a peak of intensity between 13 and 18 months, and diminishes naturally after the age of two.

Parents often complain that their child became a problem at about the time of his first birthday. Prior to that time, it was possible to leave him with a baby sitter with little or no difficulty. When a sitter would first arrive at the house, there were no problems. He would play pleasantly with her, glancing now and again at the parents to assure himself of their presence. However, as he matured, he learned the cues associated with the parents' leaving, and his behavior changed. Once he saw his mother put on her coat, his face would distort and he would start to cling to her. As the parents left the house, they could hear the crying begin. The boy was exhibiting separation anxiety. Fortunately, the crying did not last long, and the child did not appear to suffer any long-term negative effects from the separations.

Factors Influencing Stranger and Separation Anxiety

Children who are securely attached manifest less intense and prolonged stranger and separation anxiety than those who are insecurely attached. However, the intensity of stranger and separation anxiety can also be influenced by a number of situational factors.

1. Stranger anxiety is heightened when the infant confronts the stranger in unfamiliar surroundings and is not physically close to the mother or other individuals to whom he or she is attached. For example, infants aged six and one-half months old were either seated in a chair with their mother close by or held by their mother when approached by a stranger. When seated alone in the chair, the infants exhibited four times as much uneasiness and crying as when held.

2. Separation anxiety is increased whenever the infant is

confronted with unusual surroundings. A parent's leaving a room may elicit anxiety; when the parent leaves the room by an exit unfamiliar to the infant, separation anxiety is intensified. In like manner, the parent's leaving the infant in a familiar setting may arouse some separation anxiety, but greater anxiety is aroused if the infant is left in a strange place, and anxiety is intensified even more if the child is left with a strange person in a strange place.

3. Stranger anxiety can also be influenced by the way in which a stranger confronts an infant. A stranger who approaches an infant abruptly will elicit more anxiety than one who allows the infant time to adapt. Furthermore, observing a parent engage in a pleasant interchange with a stranger will alleviate the infant's anxiety.

Information regarding stranger and separation anxiety provides the basis for effective techniques of introducing infants to baby sitters. Wise parents often begin these introductions by sitting with their child while the baby sitter remains at a distance. The parents and baby sitter interact pleasantly, with little or no concern exhibited for the child. Soon after, the parents and baby sitter may play a short game of ball rolling or block building and invite the child to join in. Once having established the baby sitter as a familiar and acceptable part of the environment, the parents can leave the house with a limited amount of resistance.

Explanations of Attachment

Five explanations have been postulated for the development of attachment. They derive from an ethological theory, psychoanalytic theory, social learning theory, communication theory, and cognitive theory. These theories are distinct, but in many cases they are not mutually exclusive.

Ethological Theory

Ethological theory postulates that the development of attachment is a natural and spontaneous phenomenon that has survival value for the species and is triggered by a particular stimulus in the environment, such as separation or the presence of danger. The infant responds to those eliciting cues by clinging, crying, or smiling. The individuals to whom those responses are made are those to whom the infant will become attached. The key word in the description of the ethological theory is "triggered." Attachment is not learned; it is an inherent phenomenon triggered by appropriate conditions.

Imprinting is the term used to describe the process by which animals of some species become attached to objects associated with certain behavior-eliciting characteristics. The greylag gosling, for example, becomes attached to the first large moving object with which it has contact. Having become attached to the object, the gosling will follow it everywhere and exhibit anxiety when the object is absent. In the natural environment of the greylag gosling, the first large moving object with which it will come in contact is a parent goose. However, by altering the natural environment of the gosling and naturally introducing other large moving objects, experimenters have demonstrated that the gosling will attach itself to a variety of objects that are large and moving, such as a mechanical robot and even the experimenter himself.

Psychoanalytic Theory

In its explanation of attachment, psychoanalytic theory emphasizes the importance of the infant's investment of psychosexual energy (libido) in maintaining contact with objects that are associated with the satisfaction of instinctive biological needs.

During the first two years of life, the mouth is the source of this instinctive gratification, and the feeding of the infant by the mother serves to establish her as an object associated with need gratification. Thus, the infant becomes attached to the mother. The key concept in the psychoanalytic model is that attachment is a natural phenomenon triggered by an internally directed maturational process and mediated by need gratification.

An outgrowth of the psychoanalytic model of development has been the assignment of importance to the roles of feeding patterns and toilet training in the subsequent development of attachment. Although the quality of contact between a caretaker and an infant clearly does have an effect on the development of attachment, there is no evidence to suggest that breast feeding causes infants to develop more secure attachments than bottle feeding. Similarly, there is little in the way of empirical evidence to associate methods of toilet training or the age at which toilet training takes place with differences in the intensity or quality of attachment.

Social Learning Theory

Although there are a variety of social learning theories, all have one theme in common: the idea that infants attach themselves to a caretaker because that caretaker has been associated with the receipt of a primary reinforcer—that is, either food or tactile stimulation. Thus, according to this position, the caretaker becomes a secondary reinforcer.

When the caretaker is associated continuously with the infant's good feeling of having his or her needs satisfied, the infant begins to perceive a similar good feeling whenever the caretaker is near. The key principle in social learning theory is that attachment is a set of learned behaviors.

While social learning theory has had a significant influence on psychologists' views of attachment, research has indicated that primary needs, such as the need for food, may not be as important in the development of attachment as those creature contact needs whose satisfaction is derived from close physical and emotional contact between the caretaker and the infant.

Harry Harlow raised monkeys using a doll-like figure as a substitute for a real mother. One mother substitute was made of wire; and while this surrogate mother provided adequate food to the infant monkey, she was not emotionally responsive and the infant monkeys had difficulty clinging to her. A second surrogate mother did not provide food to the infant monkeys, but was covered with terry cloth, which made her warm and soft, and the infant monkeys could cling easily to her. Harlow observed that the monkeys developed a stronger attachment to the warm, clingable terry cloth monkey that did not provide food than to the cold wire monkey that was their source of food.

Communication Theory

T. G. R. Bower postulates that the ability to communicate with significant people around oneself is of critical importance to the security of any human. An infant's communication is nonlinguistic and probably idiosyncratic to each child and to the people with whom the child is in continual contact. Thus, the bond of security we refer to as attachment results from a shared nonverbal communication system.

Strangers may not understand the infant's nonverbal cues, and the infant may not understand the communications of the stranger. Thus, the presence of a stranger presents to the infant a threatening condition: the infant can neither communicate with the people in the room nor understand their communications. This model suggests that stranger anxiety emerges when infants are about seven months old, the age at which they develop an effective nonlanguage communication system to use with those familiar to them. Prior to that age, the infant's communication abilities are so poorly developed that he or she cannot distinguish between those that can and cannot be communicated with.

In order to understand the communication theory of stranger

anxiety, imagine yourself at a party at which you understand no one and no one understands you. Because communication with the other party-goers is impossible, you will probably become anxious. A similar type of tension exists in infants who are confronted with strangers unfamiliar with their personal communication systems.

Cognitive Theory

Unlike the four theories discussed previously, cognitive theory does not postulate a motivational basis for attachment. Rather, it postulates that certain cognitive or intellectual skills must be possessed by an infant in order to develop attachment. In that regard, cognitive theory attempts to account for the time frame within which attachment emerges.

Two cognitive capacities are of particular importance for the development of attachment.

1. *Ability to Differentiate People.* The ability to differentiate people in the environment is essential. Without this skill, it would not be possible to develop a specific attachment because all people would fall into the same class. The emergence of this skill is the basis for the perceptual discrepancy hypothesis of stranger anxiety.

The perceptual discrepancy hypothesis, postulated by Jerome Kagan, assumes that the infant develops mental characterizations, or schemata, for people, objects, and events with which he or she comes into contact. Sources of stimulation that are similar to those schemata tend to bore the infant, while sources of stimulation that are slightly different from the schemata are exciting and elicit exploration and smiling behavior. However, sources of stimulation that are extremely different from the schemata are frightening.

By the age of seven to nine months, specific schemata develop for the people with whom the child has regular contact. With the development of those schemata, the infant can dis-

criminate between familiar and strange individuals. Those individuals who are not characterized by the familiar person
schema are frightening, and stranger anxiety is manifested. As
the infant has expanded experiences with a variety of people, he
or she develops additional schemata that can assimilate strangers
who were once frightening.   With the expansion of those
schemata, stranger anxiety diminishes.

   2. *Understanding of Object Permanence.* Also critical in the
development of attachment is the infant's understanding that an
object has permanence even when he or she does not have
sensory contact with it. It would be difficult to exhibit concern
over the loss of a person to whom you were attached if you could
not even conceive that the person still existed when he or she
was gone. It is assumed that separation anxiety is particularly
dependent upon the development of this second cognitive
capacity.

   Sylvia Bell investigated the development of the concept of
object permanence. In doing so, she tested both the infant's
tendency to search for hidden inanimate objects and to search for
the mother. Bell found that a child's concept of person permanence tended to develop earlier than the concept of nonhuman
object permanence, and that infants who exhibited the best-
developed concept of person permanence were those who were
most strongly attached to their mothers.

PART IV:
The Young Child—Age Two
to Six

By the age of two, infants have been transformed from immobile, helpless, and noncommunicative newborns to young children who can walk and run, feed themselves and otherwise maintain many of their own bodily functions, satisfy many of their own needs, and use the rudiments of communication. However, children of two still have a long way to go before they become adults.

CHAPTER 11

Physical and Motor Development in the Young Child

Accelerated physical changes occur in the first two years of life and again at puberty. Between the age of two and the onset of adolescence, growth occurs at a slow but constant rate. This slow, constant growth is explained best by examining the activity of the thyroid gland, whose production of the growth-regulating hormone thyroxin diminishes at the age of two and remains at a constant low level until puberty, when it again increases.

Typically, the two-year-old can walk and run. Motor development from two to six years of age consists of perfecting those skills of mobility and enhancing finer motor skills, such as the finger dexterity needed to manipulate hand tools or a pencil.

Physical Growth

Height

The average height of the two-year-old is approximately 33 inches (85 cm), and the child will grow approximately 12 inches (30 cm) between his or her second and sixth birthday. It is interesting to note that persons who are taller than the average of their peers tend to perform better on standard tests of intelligence. No satisfactory explanation for this tendency has been found.

Weight

The average two-year-old weighs approximately 26 1/2 pounds (12 kg) and gains an additional 11 pounds (5 kg) by the age of six. A six-year-old child will weigh approximately five times his or her birth weight.

Body Proportions

Between the ages of two and six, the child's head becomes a less prominent portion of the total body size, and the legs become a more prominent factor in overall body length. At two years of age, the head constitutes 20 percent of the body length, while the legs constitute 34 percent of that length. By the age of five or six, the head's size is 16.5 percent of the total body length, and the legs constitute 44 percent of the body length. In contrast, the adult head is only about 10 percent of the body length, while an adult's legs usually constitute about 50 percent of his or her height.

Brain Development

The brain of the two-year-old is well developed and weighs 75 percent of its adult weight. By the age of five, the brain is 90 percent of its adult weight. The process of myelinization is nearly completed by the age of two. However, the amount of brain development that has already occurred by the age of two does not negate the significance of later brain development. The complexity of dendritic connections, for example, increases with little corresponding increase in brain weight. Furthermore, myelinization continues to occur through the period of adolescence.

Because of continued neural development, the speed with which a neural impulse is transmitted along a neuron increases steadily to the age of ten. This increased neural transmission speed explains the quicker reaction times of older children.

Strength

While the muscles of the body are established by the age of two, their strength increases significantly during the next four years. This increase in strength and endurance is identical for boys and girls, both in terms of the speed of change and in the absolute level of strength and endurance exhibited by the sexes.

Teething

Typically, by the age of two, the 20 baby teeth, or milk teeth, have erupted through the gums. At about six years of age, those baby teeth begin to dislodge and are replaced by permanent teeth. Baby teeth dislodge in the same order in which they initially erupt; the front incisors first, followed later by the molars.

Motor Development

Milestones in Gross Motor Development

Various psychologists have observed systematic developmental changes in gross motor skills. Although practice may account for some of these changes, much of this development is attributable to maturation. Table 11.1, on the next page, depicts some of the gross motor activities characteristics of children at different ages.

Tricycles and bicycles are favorite toys for parents to buy their children for birthdays and Christmas. Yet some parents feel disappointed when their three-year-old does not quickly learn to pedal the new tricycle. It does not cross the parents' minds that nearly two out of three children (66 percent) cannot ride a tricycle at age three. But by the age of four, most children are able to enjoy pedal toys fully.

While there is a trend to have children participate in little league baseball at earlier and earlier ages, maturational factors do put limits on the child's ability to participate in ball-throwing sports. Only three out of four children (75 percent) can throw a ball overhand by the age of five, while only one in five (20 percent) can do so at the age of four.

Bowel and Bladder Control

By the age of two, most children will exhibit bowel control. However, only 50 percent of these two-year-olds exhibit nocturnal bladder control; by the age of three, 75 percent of children can control their bladder, and 90 percent can do so by the age of five.

A frantic parent brought her three-year-old child to a psychologist complaining that the girl was still wetting her bed at night. To the parent's amazement, the doctor was not the least bit surprised. One in every 4 children (25 percent) three years of age experience the same problem. The parent's emotional response to the bed-wetting was of far greater concern to the psychologist than the child's bed-wetting itself.

Table 11.1 Motor Skills Typical of Children at Ages
Two to Six

Twenty-four months (Two years)
    Throws small ball 4 or 5 feet
    Jumps with two-foot takeoff
    Walks forward, sideward, and backward
    Walks upstairs alone
    Runs
Thirty-six months (Three years)
    Stands on one foot, hops two to three steps
    Jumps off ground with both feet
    Walks on balance beam for short distance
    Throws a small ball 10 feet
    Rides a tricycle (63 percent)
    Jumps well (42 percent)
    Walks up and down stairs with alternate footing
Forty-eight months (Four years)
    Walks down stairs one foot at a time with assistance
    Rides a tricycle (100 percent)
    Skips on one foot
    Jumps skillfully
    Climbs proficiently (60 percent)
Sixty months (Five years)
    Skips on alternate feet
    Hops on one foot for eight to ten hops
    Throws a ball overhand (74 percent)
    Broad jumps skillfully
    Catches a bounced ball
Seventy-two months (Six years)
    Rides a bicycle
    Climbs proficiently (92 percent)
    Throws a ball overhand proficiently (85 percent)

Fine Motor Coordination

Although changes in children's drawings may reflect changes in their conceptual and perceptual ability, the development of fine motor coordination is also reflected in them. A discussion of the stages through which children's drawing progress provides a basis for demonstrating changes in motor control.

2 years, 8 months   4 years, 1 month

5 years, 4 months   6 years, 2 months

Fig. 11.1

Scribbling

Scribbling emerges before the second birthday. Initially most scribbles are repeated horizontal or vertical lines. Not until midway through the second year do the scribbles begin to reflect the child's increasingly fine coordination. Fig. 11.1 exhibits in reduced scale the repetitive character of early scribbling and its development into more coordinated motions.

Enclosed Figures

By three years of age, the child begins to produce enclosed figures. Initially, the figure produced is usually a circle. With increased fine motor coordination, new figures are added to the child's collection and continue to be added even in the period from seven to nine years.

The circle is a design that requires a continuous motion and no abrupt directional changes. Not until the age of four do children adequately reproduce squares. Crosses and triangles are not drawn until six and one- half years of age. Note that the triangle requires a movement that differs from either the natural horizontal or vertical movement. Often children will reproduce triangles by turning the paper, an act that allows them to produce the design using only horizontal and vertical strokes. It is not until the age of seven or eight that diamonds are clearly reproduced.

Reproducing figures is one of the tasks used in the Stanford-Binet test of intelligence. On that test, reproduction of a circle is a task for a three-year-old child. Reproduction of a square represents a task appropriate for a five-year-old child, while the reproduction of a diamond is characterized as a task appropriate for a seven-year-old child.

Combinations and Aggregates

Combinations of two figures are produced shortly after the single figure can be produced (three years of age). However, while aggregates of three or more designs appear in the drawings of children shortly before four years of age, four- and five-year-olds have difficulty arranging the figures in appropriate spatial positions and may not overlap the designs in the reproduction of aggregates. These characteristics of the child's drawings probably represent cognitive and perceptual difficulties rather than simple deficiencies in motor control.

The Bender Motor Gestalt test is often used to assess the development of visual motor coordination and to detect neurological dysfunctions. The test involves the reproduction of designs, some of which are in combination with one another. Fig. 11.2 depicts in reduced scale the reproduction of a combination design by children of different ages.

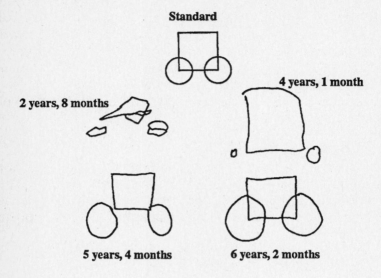

Fig. 11.2

Pictorial Representations

Representations of objects appear in the drawings of children shortly after their fourth birthday, that is, shortly after the emergence of design aggregates. The creation of representational drawings reflects changes in representational thought as much as it shows improvements in fine motor coordination.

The first artistic representations of objects are usually done of people. At four years of age, the child will draw a face consisting of a round circle with randomly placed spots used to represent facial features. By the time he or she reaches five years of age, buildings, airplanes, cars, and so on are drawn with some precision, as long as the representations require only the use of circles and squares. Triangles and diamonds are not yet employed in the five-year-old's pictorial drawings.

CHAPTER 12

Cognitive and Perceptual Development in the Young Child

The cognitive functioning of children from birth to age two is centered on their sensory and motor interactions with the objects and events in their world. At about the age of two, a new tool for thinking emerges that demarcates the child's entrance into the preoperational period of cognitive development. That tool is the child's ability to utilize symbolic representations of objects and events in his or her thinking, rather than depending upon actual sensorimotor contact with objects and events.

This capacity for representational thought allows preoperational children to think about objects and events that are not currently present, to engage mentally in some forms of problem solving, to create (eventually) symbolic representations that do not correspond to experienced objects or events, and to think about abstract ideas that may have no physical representation.

Modes of Representation

Jerome Bruner suggests that three modes of representation exist: enactive, iconic, and symbolic. Although all three modes of representation may function at the same time, the transition from sensorimotor cognition to preoperational cognition is marked by the rapid growth of the symbolic mode.

Enactive Representation

The beginnings of representational thought can be seen during the second part of the first two years of life. An infant may use a motor response to represent an object or event. This mode of representation is called enactive representation, which is the simplest of the three modes. It is not dissimilar to the representational mode used in the adult game of charades, in which people act out their representations of objects or events.

An infant may open and close her mouth to symbolize that she is hungry. The event of eating is represented by an action that often accompanies eating.

Iconic Representation

An iconic representation is a mental picture of an object or event. The availability of iconic representation to the infant is demonstrated when the infant searches for an object that is not present. The infant must have some internalized representation of the object to guide such a search.

While iconic representations are not tied to the motor activity of the infant, they are still restricted to representations of concrete objects and events. Furthermore, it is difficult to mentally manipulate iconic representations; thus, creative productivity is restricted for those whose sole modes of representation are enactive or iconic.

Symbolic Representation

The highest form of representation is symbolic. The symbol has no direct relationship to the object or event it symbolizes. Thus, in using the symbolic mode, one is not restricted to representing those objects and events with which one has had sensory or motor contact. It is possible to represent symbolically abstract as well as concrete concepts. Furthermore, symbols can be manipulated more easily than iconic or enactive representations; thus, thinking about symbols is more likely to result in the generation of new ideas or concepts.

The most common form of symbolic representation is language. Words and sentences represent objects and events that have no physical resemblance to them.

Characteristics of Preoperational Cognition

Although children from the age of two to six can symbolically represent objects and events, their thinking is not qualitatively comparable to that of an older child's or adult's. The cognition of the preoperational child is characterized by five main properties: concreteness, egocentrism, centration, attention to states rather than transformation, and irreversibility.

Concreteness

The most evident characteristic of preoperational thinking is its concreteness. While symbolic representational capacities may ultimately allow one to think about abstract concepts, such as love or justice, the preoperational child has not reached that stage of development.

Realism

For the child from the age of two to six, everything is real. This characteristic is closely associated with the concreteness of the child's thinking. It is hard for the child at this age to distinguish between a dream or a fantasy and reality.

Because it is difficult for children between the ages of two and six to distinguish dreams from reality, they often react to nightmares with emotional outbursts. The characteristic of realism is also manifested in the child's conception of God, religion, and morality: God is a real person, and to think of God differently is beyond the capacity of a child in the preoperational stage.

Egocentrism

Preoperational children see the world only through their own eyes. Their thinking reflects a self-centered position, and they are not able to see a situation from the viewpoint of another person.

A child between the ages of two and five does not understand that a person sitting in a different part of the room from the child sees the room in a different way. A child who looked at the room from the perspective shown in drawing *(a)* in Fig. 12.1 would imagine that a nearby adult saw the room in the same perspective; the child would not be able to imagine the adult's actual perspective, which is shown in drawing *(b)*.

Because of the egocentrism of children's thinking, they are unable to understand how their actions can affect the feelings of other people. Thus, attempting to control the behavior of young children by explaining the effect of their behavior on others may be useless. For example, saying "Don't call Fred names because it hurts his feelings" would be of little use. It is more likely that children's behavior will be controlled by the consequences of that behavior in their own situation. Thus, saying "If you call Fred, names you will not be able to play with him" would be an effective way to control preoperational children.

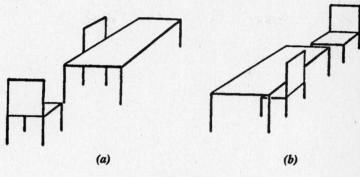

(a)   *(b)*

Fig. 12.1

Animism

Associated with the egocentric characteristic of preoperational thought is the child's tendency to endow all objects with the same animate qualities that he or she possesses. Thus, a tree, a rock, and the child's doll are all thought to see, have feelings, and think in the same way as the child.

If a child of three is confronted with a rock that has been moved from one location to another, the child may say that the rock was tired of its original home and decided to move to a new home.

The animate characteristics attributed to dolls are clearly evident in the child's demands to sleep with, bathe with, and never lose a doll. If a doll is mistakenly left at home when a family goes on a trip, it is not uncommon for the three- to five-year-old child to express strong concern that the doll will be lonesome or unable to take care of itself. Parents, who may forget that for the preoperational child all objects truly possess the characteristics of life, often reject the feelings of the child as bizarre and unrealistic.

Centration

The preoperational child typically concentrates on or responds only to a single aspect of a situation. This centration may be physical, such as paying attention to one physical aspect of an object or event, or it may be temporal, such as attending only to one point in time. This tendency simplifies the world with which the child must interact, but it also eliminates the ability to solve problems that require the simultaneous consideration of more than one aspect of a situation.

Suppose two identical glasses are filled with equal amounts of water (Fig. 12.2, Phase 1). Then the water in one glass is poured into a third glass that is taller and thinner than the first two (Phase 2). A four-year-old child who observes this proce-

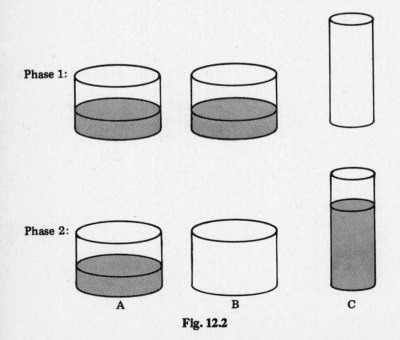

Fig. 12.2

dure is then asked if the amount of water in glass C is the same as the amount in glass A, more than the amount in glass A, or less than the amount in glass A. The child will respond that there is more water in glass C than in glass A. The child does not understand the principle of conservation; that a change in one property of an object (in this case the height of the water in the glasses) does not necessarily signify a change in another property (the amount of water in the glasses). By centrating attention on the height of the fluid in each vessel, the child reaches an incorrect conclusion.

Strong emotional expression may make an event salient, or highly attention-getting. Thus, when a mother is seen crying at a wedding, the child may centrate on that aspect of the event, assume incorrectly that the tears are indicative of sorrow, and develop a distorted perception of the marriage ceremony.

Perceptual Dominance

The centration of preoperational children is often directed by the physical properties of an object or situation. Their thinking is dominated by their perception of a situation, and they cannot mentally reflect on those perceptions. Piaget suggests that the effect of the Muller Lyer illusion, depicted in Fig. 12.3, stems from inappropriate attentional patterns. Centration makes line A appear longer than line B, although they are identical in length. Children four to six years old are more susceptible to this illusion than are adolescents or adults.

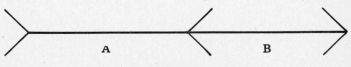

A   B

Fig. 12.3

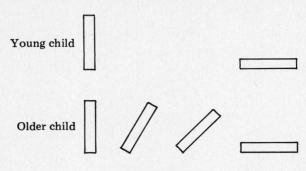

Fig. 12.4

Attention to States Rather Than Transformation

The child from two to six years of age thinks about the way things are now, and to some extent how they were or how they might be, but does not focus thoughts on how the transitions occur from one state to another.

A child of four or five is shown a stick standing on end, watches it fall over, and is then asked to draw what she saw. The child will draw the original stick and the stick lying on the ground, but even with coaxing will find it nearly impossible to draw the positions of the stick during its falling transition. (See Fig. 12.4.)

Irreversibility

Preoperational children can think about what is happening now and may think how they will get to the next goal, but they lack the ability to think about how they arrived at their present state. That is, they cannot retrace their steps in thinking. This deficiency is called irreversibility. Reversible thinking begins to emerge in the five- or six-year-old and signifies the transition to higher levels of cognitive functioning.

A young child is given a glass full of water and pours its contents into a second glass. When asked if the first glass had been full of water and to describe how the water was transferred from the first to the second glass, the child responds correctly. However, when asked whether the water would refill the original glass if it were poured back into that container, the child is unable to respond.

Characteristics of Reasoning

Transductive Reasoning

The adult typically engages in one of two forms of reasoning, deductive and inductive. *Deductive reasoning* refers to movements from the general to the specific. For example, if I know that all Labrador retrievers are black, and someone says that he has a Labrador retriever, I reason that it too is black. *Inductive reasoning* refers to movements from the specific to the general; thus, because I have seen fifty Labrador retrievers and all have been black, I reason that all Labrador retrievers are black.

Preoperational children engage in what Piaget has called *transductive reasoning,* moving from one particular to another without taking into account the general. The preoperational child reasons that if two concrete events have occurred together in the past, they must always occur together in the future.

A three-year-old child has observed that whenever her father goes to the closet for his coat, he shortly thereafter leaves the house. One morning when the father went to the closet on his way to work, the girl ran to the front door, opened it, and said, "Go to work, Dad." For the girl, one event (getting one's coat) went with a second event (going away).

Transductive reasoning may produce appropriate conclusions, as seen in the example above. However, because the direction of the cause-effect relations is ignored, incorrect conclusions may also occur.

On numerous occasions a young boy has seen his father put

on his coat before going to work. The boy sees the father put on his coat one Sunday (a specific event) and concludes that his father is going to work (another specific event). Furthermore, one hot summer day, when his father states that he is going to work the boy runs to the closet and brings his father's coat. Going to work and wearing the coat have become synonymous. To the child, wearing the coat is seen as causing his father to go to work.

Emotional Interference in Reasoning

A second characteristic of children's reasoning from the age of two to six is that it may be distorted by including, as one of the specific events in their reasoning process, a personal need or motive.

A four-year-old girl sees a doll she dearly wants in the window of a store. She asks her father for the doll, and they go to the store together only to find that the store is closed. The girl says, "I want the doll, the store is open. Open the door." While some might perceive this response as inappropriate and as exemplifying misbehavior, the child's conclusion about the store's closure is simply distorted by her own desire for the doll.

Concepts of the Preoperational Child

The concepts used by the preoperational child are characterized by five properties. These properties are more evident in the concepts of the three-year-old child who is just entering that stage of cognitive development than in those of the six-year-old child.

Simplistic

The concepts used by the preoperational child are defined in terms of one or, at best, a small number of characteristics. This concept characteristic is the result of the child's tendency to centrate and his or her inability to attend simultaneously to more than a few dimensions.

At a Thanksgiving dinner, a young child meets an adult male who is called "uncle." The concept she forms of uncle is defined in terms of this circumstance–uncles are those adult males who come to family gatherings. Clearly, the concept is too simple, and its simplicity results in overinclusiveness—that is, persons being called uncle who are not—and results also in restrictiveness—real uncles not being thought of as such because they do not come to family gatherings.

Idiosyncratic

The concepts of preoperational children are often unique to the child and are not easily understood by the social community.

At five years of age, Michael continually reported that he had focused on an object or that an object or person had been, or was focused. This report confused everyone because the concept of focusing was understood only by the child. Although we don't know what "focusing" meant to Michael, we believe that it had something to do with his attempts to stare at an object or person in order to understand it fully.

Unreliable

The concepts used by preoperational children may be poorly defined even by the children themselves. The defining characteristics of a concept may change quickly from time to time.

A four-year-old child is given a set of pictures of cars. Some cars are large and some are small, but all are black. The boy is asked to divide the pictures into two groups such that all the pictures in a group are alike in some way. The child puts large cars in one box and small cars in a second box. Then more pictures are given to the boy, one at a time. These, too, are pictures of large or small cars; however, the cars are white or black. The boy continues to separate the pictures on the basis of their size, ignoring their color.

Finally, in addition to more car pictures, pictures of large or small animals, either black or white, are introduced to the child. At this point the reliability of his classification system breaks down. He will sometimes place animal pictures in one box and car pictures in another, and at other times will assign a picture to a box on the basis of its size.

Absolute

The concepts used by the preoperational child are often absolutely defined. The child believes that an object or event either does or does not represent a concept. If an object or event represents one concept, it cannot represent another concept at the same time.

One result of this absoluteness in conceptual definition is the child's inability to understand relational terms, such as bigger and smaller or higher and lower. Things are either absolutely big or small, absolutely high or low.

A young child is given blocks of two sizes (one-inch and eight-inch cubes) and is told to put the large blocks in one box and the small blocks in a second box. The boxes are labelled "small" and "large." Subsequently, the child is given a one-inch block and a six-inch block and is asked in which box each block belongs. The child puts the one-inch block in the box labeled "small," but is confused about where to place the six-inch block. For this young child the concept of "large block" is absolutely defined as corresponding to eight-inch blocks.

Inaccessible

Although young children may spontaneously act as if their

actions are guided by a concept, it is often impossible for them to describe that concept or to use the concept on demand.

A girl of four begins to help her father sort nails—her first task being to separate the box nails from the finish nails. After observing her father for a while and receiving some constructive feedback on her initial attempts at the job, the girl performs this task well. However, when asked to tell an experimenter how she knew in which carton to place a particular nail, she could not respond.

The Ability to Classify

Single Attribute Classification—Age Two to Three

Between the ages of two and six, significant changes take place in the child's ability to classify objects. As noted in Chapter 8, infants demonstrate a rudimentary form of classification when they systematically touch objects possessing a given property, such as a common color. The two- to three-year-old child also exhibits a simple form of classification in which classes are defined by single attributes. The classification systems of children two to three are characterized by their *unreliability:* the defining property of a class of objects may change rapidly.

A child is given a set of blocks having different shapes and colors. Two round balls, one red and one blue, are put together, and the child says, "Balls." Then a blue cube is added to the group, and the child informs us that it has been added because it is blue, like the blue ball. In this example, the defining characteristic of the class is based on a single attribute, either form or color, but it is unreliable; first it is form (balls), then it switches to color (blue).

Underinclusive Classification—Age Four

By the age of four, a child can place objects into clearly defined classes. However, the classes formed by the child are often underinclusive; that is, they leave out members that should be included.

Given the task described above, a four-year-old child puts only balls into a group and includes no cubes. However, when given a ball larger than those previously grouped and asked if it also belongs to the group of balls, the child says, "No." The classification scheme is underinclusive because the child has centered on the absolute size characteristic of only certain members of the class.

Systematic Classification—Age Five to Six

Not until the age of five or six does the child begin to demonstrate the use of systematic classification, in which objects are defined by an attribute they share in common and irrelevant attributes are disregarded. A six-year-old child given the same problem described above states that the big balls and little balls all go together because they are all balls.

Limitations of Classifying Ability

In spite of developments in the child's use of classes, his or her classification abilities are limited. Two characteristic limitations are (1) defining on the basis of a single attribute (lack of skill in class multiplication) and (2) a lack of awareness that classes of objects may be combined to form higher level classes or that classes may be broken down into subclasses. In other words, the child has not mastered the superordination and subordination of class hierarchies.

A child of five is given a set of cards with either a circle or a square drawn on each one. Half the circles and squares are red

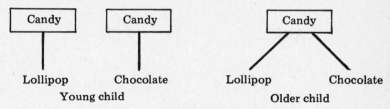

Fig. 12.5

and the other half are blue. The child is asked to put the cards into two piles so that all the cards in a pile are alike in some way. She does this by putting all the circles together and all the squares together. Next she is told to make two new piles in which the cards in each pile are alike in some way other than shape. She succeeds at this task by piling red cards together and blue cards together. However, when asked if there are any ways she can make more piles in which all the cards in the pile are alike in some way, she fails to perform adequately. To make piles of red squares, red circles, blue squares, and blue circles requires the development of a classification scheme that uses two defining attributes simultaneously.

A five-year-old child is shown a lollipop and a bar of chocolate and asked if the lollipop is candy. He responds that it is. He is then asked if the chocolate bar is candy. He responds that it is. Finally he is asked, "If I take away all your lollipops, will there be any candy left?" This question results in a tearful child saying, "I won't have any candy." The child does not appear to understand the properties of subordinate and superordinate classes. (See Fig. 12.5.)

Nonuse of Multidimensional Classification Schemes

Although the preoperational child has been accused of lacking the cognitive ability to form multidimensional classes, recent evidence suggests that the child's nonuse of those classification schemes is not the result of an incapacity to respond simul-

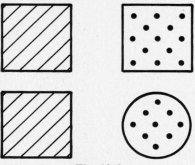

Fig. 12.6

taneously to two attributes of an object, but rather is due to the child's tendency to attend only to a single attribute. When procedures are used that increase the chances of a four-year-old child attending to more than one attribute of an object (decentering), the child exhibits the ability to understand the logic underlying multidimensional classification.

In one experiment, children were asked to rate the similarity of two objects that differed in only one way (for example, their pattern) or objects that differed in two ways (their pattern and shape). (See Fig. 12.6.) To consistently rate the first pair of objects as more similar than the second pair requires that a child use the cognitive ability needed to form multidimensional classes. Four-year-olds did not perform this task adequately under normal conditions. However, when the children's attention was directed toward all of the defining characteristics of the objects by having them label each object's range of attributes—having them say, for example, "It's a large red square"—the four-year-olds' performance did reflect the ability to form multidimensional classes.

Memory

As documented in Chapter 8, even two-year-olds have a

memory. In this section, we will examine how that memory capacity changes from age two to age six.

A premise often made is that the basic neurological capacities for memory storage are fully functioning by the age of two, and the changes that we see in the children's memory as they grow older are the result of their using those basic capacities in more efficient ways. However, some psychologists maintain that the improved memory exhibited by children as they grow older is the result of increase in actual memory storage capacity. Because the research needed to resolve this debate has not been completed and because the majority of the research explores the changing ways in which memory storage capacities are used, our discussion will focus on the first assumption.

Recall vs. Recognition Memory

As noted in Chapter 8, when one studies memory, one finds that a given child's performance in a task can vary, depending upon the task. How well or poorly the child does depends on whether the child is required to recall from memory previously presented information or is simply asked to recognize if something that is currently presented is the same as something that was presented before.

Recognition memory is always better than recall memory, and the difference between performance on the two types of tasks is more pronounced with younger children than with older ones.

The recall memory of four-year-old children is 75 percent poorer than their recognition memory. Thus, given a set of 16 pictures to remember, the four-year-olds may recall only 3 or 4 pictures but recognize 14 or 15 of them.

Sensory Memory

If you look at an object or hear a sound, a trace of the stimulation lingers even after the stimulus is terminated. That trace is sensory memory, a memory thought to last a little over one quarter of a second. Although there is no evidence that with increased age there is an increase in the length of time the sensory trace remains available, there is evidence that children five years of age cannot respond to as much of the information in sensory memory as older children and adults can.

A group of five-year-old children and a group of adults were shown a series of stimulus arrays flashed before them very briefly (150 milliseconds). Each array consisted of either one, two, three, or four familiar geometric drawings. After each presentation, each subject was asked to identify the drawings he or she had seen by pointing to them on a display that contained both the drawings actually seen and other drawings.

For adults, the number of geometric forms recognized increased as the number of drawings in the stimulus array increased. However, for children, there was no improvement in performance after arrays of more than two drawings were presented. Apparently, when two designs were presented, the children had reached the limit of information to which they could respond.

Short-Term Memory

Information in sensory memory is transferred initially to short-term memory, where it may be held in storage for approximately 30 seconds. It is then either lost or transferred to long-term memory.

Even though you hear a telephone number repeated and remember it long enough to dial it, when asked for the number an hour later, you can't remember it. The number was stored in short-term memory but was not transferred to long-term memory.

As is true for sensory memory, the basic capacities for short-term memory do not appear to change with development. However, the effectiveness with which the capacity for short-term memory can be used depends on the strategies employed by an individual.

Strategies for Short-Term Memory Enhancement

Rehearsing (repeating) information is an effective strategy for increasing short-term memory. To rehearse, however, one needs language. The two- to four-year-old child's language development precludes the effective use of a rehearsal strategy, thus reducing the child's short-term memory. This child is said to have a mediational deficiency.

Four- and five-year-olds may have the language skills needed to use rehearsal strategies, but they do not use the strategies spontaneously. They are said to have a spontaneous production deficiency. The short-term memory of children four to five is also deficient, but may be improved significantly if they are taught or forced to use a rehearsal strategy.

Thirty five-year-olds are divided randomly into two groups who are each shown a set of pictures to remember for 20 seconds. One group is instructed how to use a rehearsal strategy, repeating the names of the pictured objects while waiting to recall them, and the second group is given no instruction. The group instructed in the rehearsal strategy performs the memory task significantly better than the group not instructed in that strategy. However, identical procedures used with three-year-olds produce no differences in the performance of the two groups. Furthermore, in a test in which all the three-year-olds receives rehearsal instruction, they all perform as if they have been given no instruction.

Long-Term Memory

Information stored in short-term memory may be transferred to long-term memory for use at a much later time—minutes, hours, or even years from the time it is encountered. Unlike its role in short-term memory, continual rehearsal is not important for maintaining information in long-term memory. However, the effectiveness of long-term memory storage is determined in part by the way in which an individual organizes the encountered information in the long-term memory storage system.

Children from the age of two to four use poor organizational strategies, if they use any at all. By the age of four, children will organize the information to be remembered, typically using physical properties of the objects as a basis for organization rather than using conceptual properties symbolized by verbal labels.

A set of 16 pictures is shown to a child four years old. Four pictures are of mammals, four are of plants, four are of vehicles, and four are of birds. One picture in each of the categories is blue, one is red, one is green, and one is yellow. After viewing the 16 pictures in a random order, the child is asked to recall them. Although the pictures were shown in no particular order, the child's order of recall suggests that the pictures were stored in long-term memory in an organized way. First the child recalls the red pictures, then the blue, then the yellow, and finally the green. Note that the pictures were grouped together in memory based on their colors, not on the conceptual categories to which they belong.

Although they do not group objects on the basis of conceptual categories, children five and six years of age can use those organizational strategies to enhance memory if they are trained to do so. Earlier it was noted that children who are capable of using rehearsal strategies but do not do so spontaneously have a spontaneous production deficiency; similarly, five- and six-year-olds can have a production deficiency in the use of organizational strategies. A mediational deficiency in organizational strategies is shown if the child's memory is not improved even after he or she is taught an appropriate strategy.

Five- and six-year-old children are presented with 16 pictures to remember. The pictures can be grouped into four categories: things to wear, things to eat, and so on. Half the children are given no instructions on how to remember the pictures, while the other half are given elaborate training, during which they name the pictures, place them into groups, named the groups, and are instructed to use those groups to help them recall the pictures. The children in the second group exhibit better recall of the pictures than children in the first group, and in that recall, they display more clustering of pictures according to the conceptual category to which they belong.

Perception

The perceptual capacities of the child are well developed by the time he or she has reached two years of age. However, the young child's utilization of those capacities is influenced by some of the same factors that influence other cognitive processes: concreteness, centration, and so on.

Depth Perception

Although the child of two can perceive depth, there is evidence that the child's ability to use a multiplicity of cues in depth perception increases with age. There is no apparent difference in depth perception between young children and adults as long as both are presented with a viewing situation that is unobstructed and thus contains innumerable different cues for depth. However, if any obstruction to that total viewing field is established, the younger child does not perceive depth as accurately as the older child or adult.

Children are asked to look through a cardboard tube and estimate which of two objects is nearer to them. The four-year-olds will have more difficulty correctly responding to this task than will the older child or adult. When the tube is removed, however, the children and adults perform equally well.

Distance Perception

Although discriminating near objects from far objects under unobstructed conditions is equivalent for young and older children, estimation of distance improves with age.

A one-foot rule is placed at a child's feet, and he is asked to help an experimenter mark off a series of one-foot distances in a line away from him. Children and adults will usually make errors in this task by increasing the actual length of a perceived one-foot interval as the interval is farther and farther away from them. However, the errors of the four-year-old will be greater than those of the adult, and they will occur at a distance closer to the child. (See Fig. 12.7.)

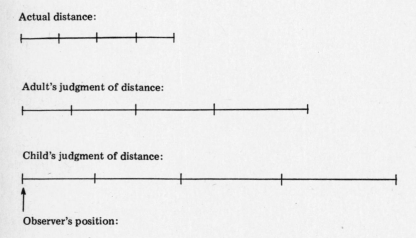

Fig. 12.7

Illusions

Younger children are more influenced by some illusions than are adults, and less influenced by other illusions. Illusions whose effects are minimal in young children are those in which invalid conclusions about reality result from what would appear to be normal cognitive functioning. The younger child thinks less, and thus perceptions of those illusions are not as distorted as are the perceptions made by the thoughtful adult.

The Delboeuf illusion depicted in Fig. 12.8 is more effective with young children than with older children or adults. In contrast, the Pronzo illusion, shown in Fig. 12.9, is more effective with older children and adults than with younger children.

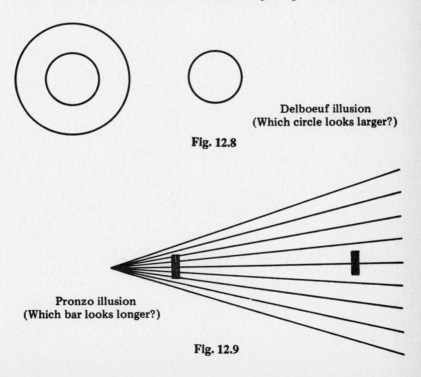

Delboeuf illusion
(Which circle looks larger?)

Fig. 12.8

Pronzo illusion
(Which bar looks longer?)

Fig. 12.9

Fig. 12.10

Object Recognition

One characteristic of young children is their inability to recognize objects when given only a few cues to the object's identity. As children become older, they seem better able to generate hypotheses about objects from minimal cues.

The drawings on the right-hand side of Fig. 12.10 were developed by removing parts of the lines used to depict the objects on the left-hand side of that figure. Children from two and one-half to six years of age have much more trouble identifying the objects in these incomplete drawing than do older children and adults.

Part-Whole Identification

Young children respond to whatever characteristic of a stimulus array—be it the parts of the array or the whole array—conforms best to the Gestalt properties of good form. With increasing age, however, the child is able to respond effectively either to the parts of an object or to the whole object.

Fig. 12.11

When children were asked to describe drawings such as those depicted in Fig. 12.11, 71 percent of the four-year-old children tended to describe the individual parts of the object, such as two giraffes, or a potato and two carrots, while only 21 percent of the children nine years of age did so. In contrast, only 11 percent of the four-year-olds described both the parts and the whole picture such as a heart and an airplane, while 79 percent of the nine-year-olds did so.

Attentional Strategies

The way we perceive a situation influences the way we will cope with that situation. Because perceptions are dictated by those aspects of a stimulus to which we attend, attentional strategies in perception play a major role in problem solving. Younger children have more difficulty than older children and adults ignoring information that is irrelevant to the solution of a problem.

A child of four hears a tape recording of two voices and is asked to repeat what was said by only one of the voices. The young child will attend to the irrelevant voice as much as to the relevant one; thus, he or she will have more difficulty than an older child in accomplishing this task.

In addition to difficulties restricting their attention to relevant parts of a stimulus, younger children are impulsive about attending to the information in a stimulus. A quick glance at only a part of the stimulus may result in the establishment of an invalid perception.

A young child is asked to look at a standard picture such as that depicted in Fig. 12.12 and select from six alternative pic-

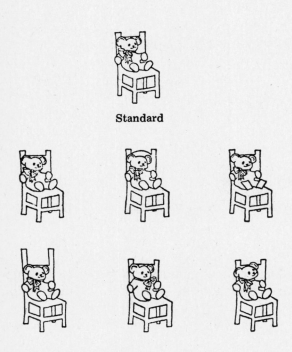

Standard

Circle the drawing that is the same as the standard.

Fig. 12.12

tures, also depicted in Fig. 12.12, a picture that is identical to the standard. A child may look at the teddy bear in the standard picture, see a teddy bear in the picture, and perceive that the two pictures are identical. The decision is based on a poor attentional strategy.

The outcome of impulsive attentional strategies is dependent, in part, on the characteristics of the stimulus to which a child attends. If a child attends only to the color of objects and not to their size or number, the resulting perceptions will be different from those of a person who attends to a different characteristic. Children under six years of age attend primarily to the color and shape of objects. These are called the salient dimensions for a preoperational child.

A child is shown the three pictures in Fig. 12.13. Pictures *a* and *b* both depict squares (same form), but differ in the number

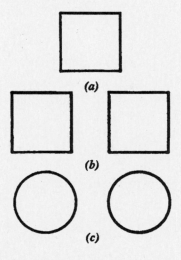

(a)

(b)

(c)

Fig. 12.13

of squares present. Pictures *b* and *c* display the same number of objects, but the objects have different forms. When asked which two pictures are most alike, the child of four will pick pictures *a* and *b*, because form is a more salient dimension than number for children of this age.

A similar test can be used to demonstrate the salience of color for young children. In contrast, older children are as likely to group the pictures on the basis of the number of elements present as they are to group the pictures on the basis of the form or color of the objects in each array.

When problems can be solved by the child within the framework of his or her salient dimension, the ability of that child to solve the problem is nearly the same as that of an older child or adult. The young child's performance at a task diminishes, however, when the dimension relevant to task performance is not salient to him or her. Richard Odom has suggested that many of the differences we observe between perceptual and cognitive abilities of children and adults are the result of differences in the stimulus dimensions to which persons of different ages attend.

A four-year-old child is given a memory task in which the information to be remembered is the color of an object. If color is a salient characteristic for this child, the child will perform as well on this memory task as an older child. However, when the size of the object becomes the information to be remembered, the younger child does less well than the older one. Size is not a salient stimulus characteristic for the younger child.

Because three-dimensionality is a salient characteristic for young children, learning to discriminate among three-dimensional objects or perspective drawings of those objects is easier for a child than learning to discriminate among two-dimensional objects or nonperspective drawings.

Orientation in space is not a salient characteristic for young children. When asked whether two pictures that differ only in their spatial orientation are the same or different, the five-year-olds will most often say they are the same. The lack of salience attributed to spatial orientation by children is not unusual if one considers the concept of object constancy. In most cases, an object remains the same regardless of its spatial orientation. Thus, to pay attention to spatial orientation is not useful. However, in some circumstances, spatial orientation is a relevant characteristic. The letter "d," for example, becomes the letter "b" simply by reversing its orientation. Because the dimension of spatial orientation is important to reading, teachers must reorient young children in order to make that dimension salient for them.

The Child's Concepts of Time, Space, and Number

The concepts of time, space, and number represent only three of the many properties of the universe that the child must come to understand if he or she is to progress toward adult levels of cognitive functioning. Children from age two to six possess a rudimentary understanding of each concept, which allows them to produce solutions to some problems that are superficially similar to the solutions produced by older children and adults.

However, the defining characteristics of the preoperational child's thinking (egocentrism, centration, and so on) result in imperfectly formed concepts. For each concept the child demonstrates the limitations of his or her knowledge when confronted with a problem that requires for its solution a fully developed conceptual scheme.

Number

Although many children can count by the time they are six years of age, their understanding of number skills—that is, counting and number knowledge (the concept of numerosity)—is limited. In counting, a young preoperational child may become fixated on the very act of counting itself and may count a single object in a set more than once, or may count only some objects in a set.

When asked to count out ten items from a set of fifteen, the child may continue counting until all objects are counted. This child's actions are not dominated by the concept of number or the operation of counting; rather, the actions are dominated by the perceptual scheme that contains "things to be counted."

A child is given a set of 15 colored blocks and is asked to count all of them. He starts counting, but soon counts one of the blocks twice. His final count exceeds 15. The child is again asked to count the blocks and counts all but the blue ones. Again his counting is dictated by the perceptual characteristics of the situation. Finally, he is asked to count out five of the blocks. He counts to five and continues on to 15. He is enraptured by the act of counting, but is not cognizant of its symbolic relationship to a number of blocks.

Adults define one set of objects as larger than another because the larger set has more elements, a judgment that is based on the relative size of the two sets of objects. In contrast, the child less than six years old concludes that one set of objects is larger than another because the larger set has had elements added to it more recently than the smaller set, a judgment based only on immediate changes in the size of one of the sets of objects.

A child of five agrees that we each have ten poker chips. I add five chips to his collection and he reports that he now has more chips than I do. I then add one chip to my collection, and am astonished when he says that my collection now has more chips than his. The set with more chips is the one that has just been increased in size. The concept of "more" does not depend upon the relative size of the increases made in the two sets of chips.

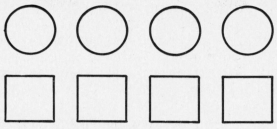

Phase 1
Younger children: Circles equal squares
Older children: Circles equal squares

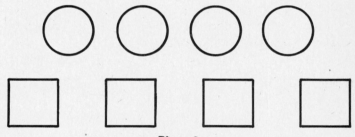

Phase 2
Younger children: Circles do not equal squares
Older children: Circles equal squares

Fig. 12.14

Two lines of chips are positioned in front of a five-year-old child. One line is made up of round chips, and one line is made up of square ones. The child correctly agrees that there are the same number of round and square chips. Without adding or subtracting any chips, one row is lengthened, as depicted in Phase 2 of Fig. 12.14. Now the child reports that there are more round chips. The concept of number is not understood; numerosity does not change unless elements are added to or subtracted from a set of objects.

The following example depicts the concept of number conservation as it is defined by Piaget. Conservation refers to the fact that conceptualized properties of an object do not change their value just because other properties possessed by the object change. Preoperational children do not exhibit an understanding of conservation, be it of number or of any other conceptual property.

A child is shown two identical balls of clay and reports that there is the same amount of clay in each ball. One ball of clay is rolled into a sausage; the child then reports that the sausage contains more clay. This child exemplifies the characteristics of the nonconserving, preoperational period of cognitive development. Attention was paid to a change in the characteristics of the object that was irrelevant to the concept of quantity, and the change was understood as a change in quantity.

Space

Preoperational children exhibit a number of problems in their concepts of space and spacial relationships. First, the children have difficulty conceptualizing the rearrangement of spatial relationships that can occur following the rotation of an object.

Three balls numbered 1, 2, and 3 are rolled in that order into the left end of a tunnel. If no reorientation of the tunnel occurs, the preoperational child can tell you that the balls will emerge from the right end of the tunnel in the order 1, 2, 3. That which goes in first must come out the other end first. However, if the tunnel is rotated or the child is asked the order in which the balls will emerge from the left-hand end of the tunnel, errors of various sorts can be observed. The child may actually report that ball 2 will roll out first.

A second problem encountered by the children in conceptualizing space is the measurement of distance. For an adult, the distance between two points, A and B, remains constant regardless of the objects that may lie between those points. For preoperational children, however, placing a barrier between points A and B may change the perceived distance between them.

Children four years old learn the physical location of objects under two conditions: some objects are separated by screens, while others are not. Children perceive those objects separated by screens to be farther apart than those not separated by screens.

The concentration of preoperational children on one characteristic of a situation results in still another problem of conceptualizing space and distance. If two cars stop at the same location, the child of two to six may report that the cars have traveled the same distance regardless of their original starting points or the routes by which they arrived at their destination.

Time

The preoperational child's conception of time is distorted relative to that of older children and adults. Time is associated with action, an association that is not always valid. The preoperational child focuses on the here and now. The past is a vague, disorganized memory, and the future is a speculative maze.

Ask a child to discuss what he or she thinks will happen far in the future. Often he or she will describe an event that is scheduled for tomorrow. Similarly, "a long time ago" may refer to yesterday or last year. Events that are perceived as occurring close to the present time are those that are most salient to the preoperational child, regardless of their actual time proximity to the present.

A child of four observes two persons walking for the same length of time (one minute). One man walks fast and covers 200 yards; the other man walks at a slower pace and covers only 50 yards. In spite of the men starting and stopping at the same time, the preoperational child will report that the man who walked farther had walked for a longer period of time.

CHAPTER 13

Individual Differences in Intellectual Development in the Young Child

The term intelligence is used not only by professional psychologists but also by ordinary nonprofessionals in their everyday conversation. In spite of its wide use, however, intelligence is a difficult word to define, even for psychologists and educators. Most often, individual intelligence is defined in terms of one or more abilities a person has: the ability to reason, to solve problems, to think abstractly rather than concretely, to adapt to new situations, and to generalize the solution of one problem to the solutions of other problems. The extent to which a person exhibits those characteristics, common sense suggests, defines that person's level of intelligence.

In this chapter we will see how intelligence is actually measured and computed, and take note of some factors that are thought to account for individual differences in intelligence.

Theories of Intelligence

The composition (or structure) of intelligence has been described in several different ways. One quite common approach has been statistical analysis, while other proposals have attempted to separate intelligence into habitual and novel forms and to organize it according to developmental stages. Each of these attempts has led to a theory of what constitutes intelligence.

Two-Factor Theory

In the early 1900s, English psychologist Charles Spearman (1863-1945) collected scores on various psychological test items and noted the correlations between them. He reasoned that because there were positive correlations between the scores in different areas—mechanical ability, musical ability, and mathematical ability, for example—there must be one common factor of general intelligence responsible for the relationship.

In addition, Spearman felt that each specific task, such as finding a solution for a mathematical problem, required specific abilities, such as memory and facility with numbers. His reasoning led him to describe intelligence as a general factor, which he called G, and a number of specific factors, which he called S.

Spearman's research resulted in the development of the statistical procedure known as factor analysis. Using factor analysis techniques, psychologists can identify and interrelate the many factors included under the heading of intelligence. Moreover, the study of many specific problem-solving tasks and their solutions allows psychologists using factor analysis to identify characteristics of intelligence that seem to be correlated.

Thurstone's Factors of Intelligence

L. L. Thurstone also used factor analysis to develop what he saw as the seven basic characteristics that appeared to make up intelligence. Thurstone identified these seven aspects of intelligence as follows:

1. *Verbal Comprehension:* Definition and understanding of words

2. *Word Fluency:* Being able to think of words rapidly

3. *Number:* Being able to do arithmetic problems

4. *Space:* Being able to understand spatial relationships

5. *Rote Memory:* Being able to memorize and recall

6. *Perceptual:* Being able to grasp rapidly the similarities, differences, and details of objects or stimuli

7. *Reasoning:* Being able to understand the principles or concepts necessary for problem solving

In addition to these factors, Thurstone, like Spearman, suggested that there is a general factor, or G factor, that represents some general intelligence linking these separate characteristics.

Guilford's View of Intelligence

J. P. Guilford rejected the idea of a general factor of intelligence. Instead, he developed a model for the structure of human intellect that is represented as a three-dimensional figure in which the dimensions are five kinds of mental operations, such as cognition and memory; four kinds of content involved in intellectual operations, such as semantic (verbal) or symbolic (nonverbal); and six different outcomes or products, such as units or classes that result from the various operations as they are applied to different kinds of content. Intelligence, Guilford argued, is the result of the interaction of these three dimensions.

To give a very simple example: in the task of studying a vocabulary list for a test, the content would be semantic (words), the mental operation would be memory, and the product would be the list of words or units the subject recalls when tested.

Guilford's model allowed for 120 separate factors of intelligence (five times four times six) and he devised tests to measure many of them. His model broadened the concept of intellect beyond that tapped in existing intelligence tests. He was also instrumental in linking divergent thinking (a type of creative thinking discussed in the preceding chapter) to intelligence. Research comparing results on traditional intelligence tests and those designed to measure creative thinking has shown that highly creative persons tend to be highly intelligent, but the reverse is not always true; that is, high intelligence is not a guarantee of creativity.

Piaget's Stages of Cognitive Growth

The developmental sequence of cognitive growth proposed by Jean Piaget (discussed in detail in Chapter 8) has been used as an approach to understanding intelligence. The cognitive growth stages suggested are as follows:

1. *Sensorimotor Stage* (birth to two years): Understanding of sensations and basic cause-and-effect relationships

2. *Preoperational Stage* (two to seven years): Conceptualization and representation by using language, drawings, or symbolic play

3. *Concrete Operational Stage* (seven to eleven years): Logic tied to concrete things; series of ideas

4. *Formal Operational Stage* (eleven years and above): Use of abstract concepts and formal rules of thought and logic

It has been proposed that an individual's intelligence can be estimated by comparing the particular characteristics of the person with the sequence proposed by Piaget.

Crystallized vs. Fluid Intelligence

In an attempt to describe intelligence, some psychologists, influenced by the work of Raymond Cattell, have distinguished between crystallized and fluid intelligence. Crystallized intelligence is observed in the application of what has been learned already; this use of intelligence tends to become habitual or unchanging. Fluid intelligence is seen in the ability of a subject to adapt or adjust to new and different situations. Fluid intelligence is thought to be flexible and is used when the person is confronted with new problems.

The ability to solve word usage problems, such as fill-in-the-blank definitions, requires reliance on previous learning and thus involves the use of crystallized intelligence. However, solving anagram problems requires both knowledge and flexibility, and thus involves fluid intelligence. Completing the sentence "Wearing apparel for a foot is called a . . . ." requires crystallized intelligence, while recognizing that the letters in the word "shoe" can be found in the word "honest" requires more mental flexibility, or fluid intelligence.

Measurement of Intelligence

To examine individual differences in intelligence, we must consider intelligence to be an attribute possessed in varying degrees by all people, and we must design methods to systematically measure the amount of intelligence attributable to a particular person. A variety of tests have been designed for that purpose. They all consist of problems whose solutions reflect the utilization of skills that are characteristic of intelligence.

A child is asked to rearrange the following four pictures so that they tell a story: (1) a masked man climbing in a window, (2) a masked man climbing out of a window and being greeted by a police officer, (3) a masked man rifling a desk, and (4) a masked man opening a window. This problem is one that is used in some tests of intelligence. Its solution requires that the child be able to take information available in the picture and organize it into a meaningful sequence of events. Such skill in organization is one characteristic of intelligence.

Tests of Intelligence

Some tests of intelligence are administered to people in groups, while others are administered individually. An individually administered test of intelligence has four advantages over a group-administered test:

First, it is more motivating to perform well when you are working directly with an examiner than when you are only one of many people taking a test. Second, the examiner is better able to insure that a person taking the test understands the procedures for the test. Next, a variety of problems that require special materials, such as blocks, can be employed in the individually administered test, but are difficult to use in group-administered tests. And finally, the examiner may be able to observe how the person arrives at a problem solution as well as recording whether the solution is correct or incorrect. For these reasons, group-administered tests of intelligence are satisfactory as screening devices for gross measurements of intelligence, but individually administered tests are preferred for clinical assessments of intelligence and for exacting measurements of that attribute.

The Stanford-Binet Intelligence Scale

One of the first standard tests of intelligence was designed in 1905 by Alfred Binet. The test was part of a set screening procedures used in Paris to determine which children might benefit from special educational opportunities. Since its original design, the test has been revised for American usage by Lewis Terman of Stanford University. The test items were most recently revised in 1960; the norms for computing intelligence quotients were revised in 1973. The test is still the one most frequently used to test the intelligence of individuals over two years of age.

The following are tasks representing two age levels from the Stanford-Binet Intelligence Scale

Age Two Years and Six Months

1. Identifying the use of objects

2. Identifying body parts

3. Naming models of common objects

4. Naming pictures of common objects

5. Repeating two digits

6. Obeying simple commands

Age Six Years

1. Describing the meaning of common words

2. Describing the differences between two objects

3. Identifying the missing elements in a mutilated picture

4. Number knowledge—picking up designated numbers of blocks

5. Opposite analogies, for example, a pound is heavy, an ounce is _____?

6. Solving paper and pencil mazes

A problem is included in the test if the percentage of people who solve it increases systematically with increases in age. If most children of a particular age can solve the problem, it is assigned to that particular age category. The term "most," however, is defined loosely. For some problems, 78 percent of the children in the age category arrive at the correct solution, while for other problems the correct solution is obtained by only 59 percent of the children in the age category.

To administer the Stanford-Binet test, the examiner begins by selecting a set of age-related items that are thought to be solvable by the person being tested (the testee). If the starting age level is properly selected, the testee should succeed at those tasks, and it is assumed that all tasks associated with younger ages would also be passed. Subsequently, the examiner administers test items representing older and older ages, and continues to do so until it is evident that no older age test items will be passed. Based on the number of problems correctly solved by the testee, an index of test performance can be calculated. In the case of the Stanford-Binet tests, that index is called the mental age. Mental age is calculated by awarding appropriate numbers of mental age months for each correctly solved problem and adding those months together.

The calculation of a mental age (MA) for a typical Stanford-Binet test would proceed as follows:

Test Item's Year Level	# of Items Passed	Months of MA Credited for Passing Each Item	Total Credit
4 yrs. (starting tasks)	6	*	48 mos.
4 yrs. 6 mos.	4	1	4 mos.
5 yrs.	3	1	3 mos.
6 yrs.	3	1	3 mos.
7 yrs.	2	2	4 mos.
8 yrs.	0	*	0

Mental Age = 62 mos. (5 yrs. 2 mos.)

It is assumed that having passed all tasks characteristic of the four-year level, the individual would have passed all tasks designed for younger children as well. Thus, credit is given for all months up through the age of four (forty-eight months). Similarly, having failed all the tasks designated as eight-year items, it is assumed that items designed for older children would be failed as well. Thus, those items are not administered.

While the calculated mental age is an index of absolute performance on the Stanford-Binet test, it is not a measure of the testee's performance on the test relative to the performance of others his or her age. A measure of age relative to performance, the intelligence quotient, will be discussed in a subsequent section.

Wechsler Intelligence Scale

A second set of widely used, individually administered tests of intelligence consists of three developed by David Wechsler. The three tests are constructed, administered, and interpreted on the basis of similar principles, but are designed for use with persons of different ages. The Wechsler Preschool and Primary Scale of Intelligence (WPPSI) is designed to be used with children from age four to six and one-half. The 1972 revision of the Wechsler Intelligence Scale for Children (WISC-R) is used with children from the age of six to the age of 16 years 11 months. The Wechsler Adult Intelligence Scale is used with persons over the age of 17.

Differences between the Wechsler and Stanford-Binet Tests

There are three major distinctions between the Wechsler tests and the Stanford-Binet test.

First Difference. In contrast to the Stanford-Binet test, in which tasks are arranged in chronological age groupings, tasks used in the Wechsler tests are grouped according to the skills needed to perform them. Within each skill grouping, test items of varying difficulty are administered, beginning with the simplest and progressing to the more complex. The examiner continues confronting the testee with progressively harder test

items until it is established that the testee would fail all subsequent items within that skill area.

The WISC-R utilizes ten skill areas in the assessment of
intelligence. (Two additional tasks can be administered, but are
not used in calculating a measure of intelligence.) The tasks
associated with those skills are:

Verbal Tasks

1. Information—the child is asked questions the answers to
which require commonly possessed information.

2. Similarities—the child is asked to describe how two objects or concepts are alike.

3. Arithmetic—the child mentally solves a series of arithmetic story problems.

4. Vocabulary—the child is asked the meaning of a series of
words.

5. Comprehension—the child is asked to describe appropriate behavior in various social situations, or the purpose
behind certain societal conventions.

Performance Tasks

1. Picture completion—the child tries to detect the missing
elements in pictures.

2. Picture arrangement—the child rearranges a series of
cartoonlike pictures to tell a logical story.

3. Block design—with a set of blocks having different
colored sides, the child reproduces a pictured design.

4. Object assembly—the child constructs pictures of common objects from pieces like in a jigsaw puzzle.

5. Coding—the child is shown a coding system in which each

of the numbers 0-9 have associated with them a meaningless symbol. With this coding system in view, the child places under each of a series of numbers its corresponding symbol. The task described is used for children over eight years of age. For children under eight, a similar task that employs geometric forms rather than numbers is used.

Optional Tasks

1. Digit span—the child is required to repeat a series of numbers presented orally.

2. Mazes—the child solves paper and pencil mazes.

The set of test items for the information task begins with a simple question, "How many days make a week?" and progresses to more difficult questions such as "Why does oil float on water?"

Second Difference. The Stanford-Binet test provides a single index of intelligence based on the individual's performance on all the tasks administered. In contrast, the Wechsler tests divide the skill areas into those that emphasize verbal abilities (verbal subtests) and those that emphasize perceptual and motor abilities (performance subtests). The division of the tasks into those groups allows for the determination of both a full-scale index of intelligence (one based on all tasks performed) and separate indices of intelligence based on either verbal or performance skill areas. This division of intellectual functioning allows a psychologist or educator to detect specific problems in intellectual functioning and to provide specific help to children in their individual areas of deficiency.

For example, the intelligence of three children was assessed using the Stanford-Binet test. All three were found to have average intelligence. The Stanford-Binet test did not discriminate among them. However, using the revised Wechsler Intelligence Scale for Children, three very different patterns of intelligence were observed. Although all three children exhibited average performance when the full-scale measure of intelligence was evaluated, the first child performed equally well on both the verbal and performance subtests; the second child exhibited strikingly good performance on the verbal subtests, but did poorly on the performance-based scale; while the third child performed well on the performance subtests of the WISC-R, but did poorly on those subtests emphasizing verbal skills.

Third Difference. Finally, while the index of absolute test performance used with the Stanford-Binet test is the mental age, the Wechsler test provides no such label for its test performance scores. It simply refers to them as raw scores.

Intelligence Quotient (IQ)

For each test of intelligence, an index of absolute test performance can be calculated. In the case of the Stanford-Binet test, the index is called a mental age, while in the case of other tests, it may simply be called a raw score. However, the same absolute performance index may be interpreted quite differently when achieved by persons of different ages. Thus, a numeric designation called the intelligence quotient (IQ) was developed to denote the relationship between a person's absolute test performance and the performance expected of persons the same age as the testee.

Let us assume that for a given test, the average test performance index for children seven years of age is 40. A seven-year-old who scores 40 on this test would have an average level of intelligence. A ten-year-old child who scores 40 on the same test would be performing well below the expectations for children that age and would have below-average intelligence, while a five-year-old with an identical score on the test would be described as performing well above the level of his or her age-mates.

IQ Ratio

The calculation of intelligence quotient has historically been based on an individual's mental age, which is an absolute index of performance on the Stanford-Binet test. IQ is calculated using the following formula:

$$IQ = \frac{\text{Mental age (MA)}}{\text{Chronological age (CA)}} \times 100$$

A person whose chronological age and mental age are identical would have an IQ of 100. If the chronological age were less than the mental age, the person's IQ would be above 100, and if the chronological age were more than the mental age, the person's IQ would be below 100.

Suppose two children of different ages receive identical absolute performance scores of five years five months on the Stanford-Binet test (according to the test, MA = 65 months for each child). One of the children, who was ten years and ten months old (CA=130) would have an IQ of 50; the other child, who was four years and four months old (CA=52), would have an IQ of 125:

$$IQ = \frac{65}{130} \times 100 = 50$$

$$IQ = \frac{65}{52} \times 100 = 125$$

While this method of calculating IQ was used for many years with the Stanford-Binet test, test imperfections posed two important problems. First, although the formula for the IQ suggests that the average IQ in an age group should have been 100, it was found in practice that this was not so. In fact, the average IQ for children differed from one age group to another. Second, the

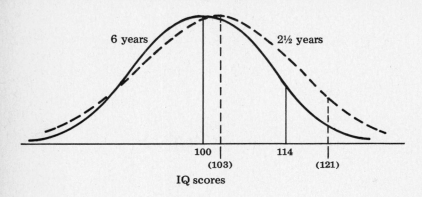

**Fig. 13.1 Distribution of IQ Scores for Children of Two Ages
(6-year-olds, M = 100, SD = 14; 2 1/2-year-olds, M = 103, DS = 18)**

variability of IQ scores (the standard deviation of their distribution) was not the same for all age groups. As a consequence of these problems, it was not possible to directly compare the IQs of children at different ages.

The graphs in Fig. 13.1 depict the distribution of IQ scores for children of two ages. Note that the IQ score of 100 does not reflect average performance for the two groups, as one would expect from the definition of IQ. Furthermore, 93 percent of the six-year-olds have IQs below 121, while only 84 percent of the two-and-one-half-year-olds score below that level. The same IQ score does not reflect the same performance relative to one's age-mates for the two groups.

Deviation IQ

The solution to the problem described above was to redefine the IQ score. The new IQ score is called a deviation IQ because it directly indicates how the testee's absolute test performance index differ from the mean absolute performance index for all persons the same age as the testee.

This method of conceptualizing the deviation IQ score was first used with the Wechsler test and is now used in the evaluation of the Stanford-Binet intelligence scale as well. It makes use of a standard deviation, which is a statistical device for describing the variability in a set of scores. By using the standard deviation, the tester can describe how a particular score that differs from the mean relates to other scores that deviate from the mean.

For a representative sample of each chronological age group, the mean and the standard deviation of the absolute performance index is calculated. These values are used in evaluating the performance of people who subsequently take the test. A testee who has an absolute performance score equal to the mean for his or her age group is said to have a deviation IQ of 100. Regardless of the age group, a deviation IQ of 100 is average.

On the Wechsler tests, if the testee's absolute performance score is one standard deviation above or below the mean of the age group, the corresponding deviation IQ scores will be 15 points above or below 100 (115 and 85, respectively). Regardless of the age group, the standard deviation of IQ scores for the Wechsler tests is 15. Consequently, deviation IQ scores obtained at different ages may be compared directly.

For tests other than the Wechsler tests, the standard deviation of the distribution of deviation IQ scores may be different from 15. For the Stanford-Binet test, for example, the standard deviation is 16. Consequently, one must consider the value of the standard deviation when comparing deviation IQ scores from different tests. A deviation IQ score of 70 on the WISC-R is comparable to a deviation IQ score of 68 on the Stanford-Binet test. Both scores are two standard deviations below the mean of the distribution of deviation IQ scores for their respective tests.

Reliability of Intelligence Test Scores

If a child is given an intelligence test at two different ages,

Table 13.1 Correlation between IQ Scores at Different Ages

Age at Test	.7	9	11	13	15	17
6	.86	.84	.78	.82	.72	.78
8		.91	.89	.88	.85	.84
10			.92	.88	.83	.86
12				.87	.85	.90
14					.87	.89
16						.89
18						.90

will the results be consistent? Findings show that (1) test results become more consistent as a person gets older, and (2) the closer together the two testing dates, the more consistent the scores. Table 13.1 provides correlations between the IQs of children tested at different ages.

A group of children are tested for intelligence at ages four, eight, and twelve. The correlation between IQ scores at ages four and eight will be smaller than that between ages eight and twelve. In spite of the fact that the same four-year differences exist between ages four and eight on one hand and eight and twelve on the other, the correlation between the latter pair will be greater because IQ consistency increases with age. However, the correlation between ages four and eight will be greater than the correlation between ages four and twelve.

Although correlations are reasonably high between tests administered at two different ages, there are instances in which individual test scores change dramatically. Goodenough and Maurer, in a study of mental growth from two years to fourteen years of age, report spontaneous changes in IQ of as much as 50 points over the course of nine years. Although reports of changes this large are valid, they are an exception. Typically, unless illness, emotional disturbances, or environmental changes take place, IQ scores obtained after the age of two remain within a fairly constant range over a lifetime.

A number of measures have been developed to assess infants' intelligence. These tests center around the evaluation of perceptual and motor skills, such as turning, pointing, or visually following a moving object. Tests at later ages focus more on language skills, which cannot be used when testing infants. As a result, with the exception of very extreme cases, correlations between scores obtained on infant intelligence tests and later tests of intelligence are generally quite low.

Exceptional Subjects

Those persons who obtain scores that differ from the mean by two or more standard deviations have been arbitrarily designated as exceptional. Those scoring two or more standard deviations below the mean often are referred to as mentally retarded, while those two or more standard deviations above the mean are called gifted.

Mentally Retarded

Designating a person as mentally retarded simply because he or she obtained an IQ value two or more standard deviations below the mean has proved to be an inadequate description of the individual's capabilities. As a result, subgroups within the category of mental retardation have been developed. These subgroups, along with their IQ cut-off points, are as follows:

70-50: Mildly retarded (educable)

50-35: Moderately retarded (trainable)

35-20: Severely retarded (minimal skills)

20-0:   Profoundly retarded (custodial care)

The Gifted

The exceptional subjects classified as gifted are not divided into further subgroupings. Some studies have shown that subjects with very high measured intelligence (IQs of 180 or more) may have adjustment difficulties because they are misunderstood by parents or peers. But most research indicates that the gifted, as a group, are better adjusted and healthier than are people of average intelligence.

Factors Influencing Intelligence

Genetics

Controversy exists concerning the role played by genetics in determining an individual's intellectual capabilities. Those who emphasize the role of genetics typically cite two sources of evidence to support their conclusions.

Twin Studies

Using the twin study method (described in great detail in Chapter 3), it has been found that the correlation between the intelligence of identical twins is significantly greater than among fraternal twins, siblings, or other persons of less similar genotypes. (See Fig. 13.2.) As you will recall, this pattern of differences is indicative of a trait with a hereditary origin.

Adopted vs. Biological Children

Adopted children are not genetically similar to their adopted parents; however, the environment in which the adopted children live is created by the adoptive parents. If genetics influence IQ, one would expect adopted children to have levels of intellectual

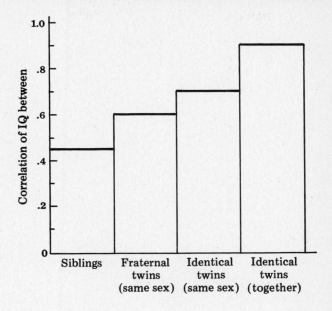

Fig. 13.2

functioning that correlate with their biological parents, while strong environmental determinants of intelligence would result in a high correlation between adopted children's IQs and their adopted parents' level of intellectual functioning.   Fig. 13.3 shows the correlation between adopted children's IQs and the educational level of their adopted and biological parents. These findings have been used to argue that genetics plays a significant role in determining individual differences in intelligence.

A brilliant writer once brought his adopted son into a clinic, complaining of difficulty in their ability to communicate with one another. The father could not understand why a boy reared in a stimulating environment would exhibit severe communication problems. Testing of the father and the son revealed that the father's IQ was 135, whereas the adopted son's IQ was only 90.

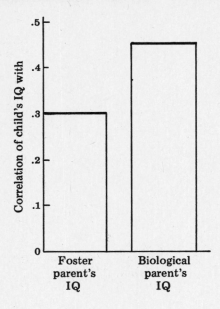

Fig. 13.3

The son's level of communication was compatible with his level of intellectual functioning but was clearly below the capabilities of his father. That discrepancy was creating the communication difficulty.

The Environment

While intellectual capabilities present at birth may account for some individual differences in intelligence test performance, the experiences of an individual are a significant influence on test scores. This influence is inferred when individuals who achieve similar scores on intelligence tests early in life show widely different performances on adult intelligence tests.

Social and Cultural Isolation

Various studies have shown that children reared in social and cultural isolation exhibit lower IQ scores than those children not so deprived. Furthermore, observed IQ differences increase with the age of the children. These studies have been conducted with children raised on canal boats in England as well as children from isolated mountain communities in the United States.

In the 1930s, villages located in the mountains of Virginia, west of Washington, D. C., were extremely isolated from the culture of the outside world. Because of transportation and communication difficulties, some of those communities were more isolated than others. When the IQ scores of children from the communities were compared, it was found that the children from those communities most isolated from the outside world produced, on the average, the lowest IQ scores.

The conclusion that the observed differences in average IQ scores reflect the effects of social and cultural deprivation is questionable. It is just as likely that persons with higher IQs left those isolated communities and, in so doing, lowered the mean IQ of the groups.

Subculture Experiences

Family environment and subculture norms play an important role in how well or poorly children do on standardized tests. These standardized tests are based on the assumption that all children have similar backgrounds, values, and language competencies. We know that is not at all the case, and that specific subcultures of our own larger culture demonstrate rich varieties of language expression, with idiosyncratic grammatical and semantic variations, different values, and different outlooks on social and cultural issues.

Socioeconomic Class

Persons from lower socioeconomic classes tend to perform

less well on tests of intelligence than those from middle socioeconomic classes. The difference is as great as 10 to 15 IQ points.

Socioeconomic classes are typically defined by the occupational level of an individual. The average IQ for four occupational groups are as follows: professional (115), skilled laborers and clerical workers (107), semiskilled workers (105), unskilled laborers (96).

This socioeconomic class difference in IQ test performance has been attributed to experiential deprivation. In homes where there are many children to care for and/or inadequate child care resources, children do not gain the benefits of one-to-one verbal interaction with a consistent parent. Nor do these children receive educational toys to play with or other forms of social and intellectual stimulation that middle-class children enjoy. Therefore, standardized tests such as IQ tests that include tasks involving material unfamiliar to some disadvantaged children have been criticized for not truly measuring their aptitudes, interests, and abilities. It has also been argued that the relationship between socioeconomic class and IQ test performance is the result of persons with lower IQs migrating toward the lower socioeconomic classes. Thus, genetic factors could account for their children exhibiting lower levels of IQ. Because of the correlational nature of these observations, one cannot, however, come to any clear conclusion about cause and effect. (See Chapter 2.)

Intervention Programs That Raise IQ

Experimental programs have been designed to assess the role that environmental factors play in the determination of intelligence. In these programs, a number of children are selected and randomly assigned to two groups. One group receives enriched environmental stimulation, and the other is maintained in a regular environment. If differences in IQ test performance are observed after this intervention, they can be ascribed to the intervention (environmental change).

When children from environments with minimal cognitive stimulation are placed in enriched environments, their IQs improve. The stability of that improvement, however, is dependent upon two factors. First, the children must be confronted with an enriched environment at an early age, that is, during the preschool years. Second, the enriched environment must be maintained by changing the home environment of the child. This change in home environment is accomplished most effectively by having the parents become part of the educational enrichment program for their children rather than simply teaching the parents to be better parents.

Children were randomly assigned to each of three experimental groups. One group was enrolled in a language-facilitating program designed specifically to teach children how to learn; a second group attended a traditional nursery school; and the third group received no preschool program. At the end of the kindergarten, the children in the first program had IQ scores that averaged 14 points higher than those in the second group, who in turn had IQ scores that averaged 7 points higher than those of the third group.

IQ and Creativity

The Creative Person

Very creative people tend to have high IQs, but the relationship does not hold the other way; that is, having a high IQ does not necessarily mean one is creative. Moreover, it has been suggested that any correlation that exists may result from variables such as the motivation of the subject, rather than from the trait of intelligence itself.

While measured intelligence does not seem to be an important aspect of creativity, there are several characteristics that seem to differentiate creative people from noncreative people. In general, the creative person is quite flexible in thinking patterns, interested in complex ideas, and shows a fairly complex personality pattern. Additionally, the creative person tends to be aesthetically sensitive, is interested in the unusual or novel, and shows a relatively open personality.

Measurement of Creativity

Several attempts have been made to develop measures of creativity. All have in common the aim of evaluating the unique or novel solutions to problems in a way that might reveal the characteristic of creativity. Among such tests are the following:

1. *Unusual Uses Tests:* Present an object and determine how many unusual uses the subject can generate for it.

2. *Remote Association Test:* Present several stimulus words and determine if the subject can "find" the associate that is common to all.

3. *Anagram Tests:* Present a stimulus word and determine how many and what smaller words can be created using the letters of the stimulus word.

4. *Drawing Completion Tests:* Present a partial stimulus and ask the subject to finish the drawing.

CHAPTER 14

Language Development in the Preschool Years

By the age of two, the preliminary steps to the acquisition of language have been taken. The child has babbled, learned to use words in expressing ideas, and, in many cases, has begun to combine words into simple two-word sentences. Still, there is more to be learned. Much of that language development takes place in the years from two to six.

This chapter traces the preschool child's mastery of phonetics, semantics, and syntax, and then discusses the major theories of language acquisition.

Phonetic Development

The two-and-one-half-year-old child has developed the ability to both discriminate and use all the vowel sounds in his or her language. However, the child has mastered only about two-thirds of the consonant sounds. This discrepancy in

Table 14.1

Three-year-olds:	Five-year-olds:
/m/ as in mama	/s/ as in sit
/n/ as in no	/sh/ as in ship
/p/ as in pin	/ch/ as in chip
/f/ as in feet	
/h/ as in house	Six-year-olds:
/w/ as in want	/th/ as in thin
/ng/ as in swing	/v/ as in very
	/t/ as in to
Four-year-olds:	
/y/ as in yell	Seven-year-olds:
/k/ as in cat	/z/ as in zip
/d/ as in dog	/th/ as in this
/g/ as in gone	/j/ as in jump
/r/ as in ran	/zh/ as in sure
/b/ as in boy	

development is due to the greater complexity of the motor responses used in producing the consonant sounds. Production and discrimination of the remaining consonant sounds is typically mastered between the ages of two and one-half and six. Table 14.1 depicts the various ages at which the use of different phonemes are mastered in all positions within words.

A child of three says "wun" instead of "run." This error would not be unusual because the phoneme /r/ is not well developed, while the phoneme /w/ is well developed in the three-year-old. A similar error in an eight-year-old would suggest a deficiency in phonological development.

Semantic Development

Semantics is the knowledge one has of the words in one's vocabulary. For many years, the study of semantic development consisted of determining the size and characteristics of children's vocabularies at various ages. More recently, developmental psychologists have become concerned with the meaning attributed to those words by children and how that meaning changes to more closely approximate the meaning adults attribute to those words.

Vocabulary

The vocabulary of a child may consist both of words the child understands and those the child spontaneously uses. The number of words in the first category typically exceeds the number in the second category. A child of two, for example, may not spontaneously use the word *underwear*, but when told, "Go get your underwear," the child will respond appropriately.

The size of the vocabulary understood by a child progresses slowly at first, but it begins to grow rapidly at about the age of two. By three years of age, there is an even more rapid spurt in vocabulary development. By the age of five or six, however, the speed of vocabulary growth levels off. (See Fig. 14.1.)

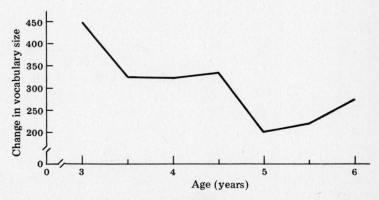

Fig. 14.1

Word Classes

The first words used by a child are those that denote concrete characteristics of his or her world: objects (nouns), actions (verbs), and the characteristics of those objects and actions (modifiers). As the child becomes older, new classes or words emerge in his or her speech. The development of these new word classes enables the child to express new relationships and a greater variety and complexity of sentences. It is difficult to associate the emergence of these new classes with particular ages because of the significant individual differences in the rate of language acquisition. However, the sequence of their emergence is rather uniform. New word classes normally develop between the ages of two and four.

Prepositions such as *in* and *on* constitute the first new class of words to emerge. When they are first used, those prepositions only designate locations and do not convey the more abstract meanings associated with them by adults.

A three-year-old child will say, "I am in a house" or "The salt is on the table," but is not likely to say, "I am in a hurry" or "I am on time." The latter two sentences denote states of the individual and not the physical location of a person or thing.

Other classes of words that quickly emerge in the vocabulary of the two-year-old child are possessives, such as *mine* or *yours*, pronouns, such as *he* or *you*, and articles, such as *an*, *a*, or *the*.

The plague of many parents is their child's development of a class of possessive words. Although the exact age may vary from child to child, sometime in the second year of life children will begin to express their possession of objects verbally with a screeching, "Mine!"

Some classes of words do not emerge in the vocabulary of a child until the age of three and one-half or four. These word classes include the auxiliary verbs such as *can*, *do*, *is*, *was*, and *were*.

Although a child of three may produce a sentence such as "I

can't fall down," a sentence such as "I can do that" is not typically produced at that age. In the latter sentence, the word *can* is used by itself. Psycholinguists interpret this observation as evidence that the child does not possess a class of auxiliary verbs such as *do* and *can*. The child considers *can't* and *don't* to be single words that are similar to *no* or *not* rather than contractions of an auxiliary verb and the negative word not.

Word Meaning

In language, most words other than proper nouns denote classes of objects or events rather than specific objects or events. Thus, the meaning of a word is dictated by the user's definition of the conceptual class symbolized by the word.

Children's thinking is concrete. They categorize objects and events on the basis of physical properties possessed by those objects and events rather than their abstract, unobservable properties. The consequence of this cognitive characteristic is that the words used by the child exhibit concreteness. The most commonly used words are those that symbolize objects, actions, and the physical properties of those objects and actions.

A child of three might be heard to say, "The black dog ran into the house," but would be unlikely to say, "The *scared* dog *felt* like *hiding* in the house." The word scared depicts an emotional state; the word felt denotes an unobservable fact; and the word hiding requires for its meaning an analysis of the dog's motive for running into the house.

Overextension

A child may symbolize a large class of objects or events with the same word that an adult uses to symbolize a much smaller conceptual class. It has been suggested that this overextension of word meaning results from the child using a small number of physical properties to define class membership, rather than the large number used by adults.

The child of three, for example, may call all objects in which one rides "car." This label is attached to trains, buses, and so on. The child is using two properties to define the concept: movement and passenger. The adult concept of car includes many other distinctive features.

While children may exhibit overextension in their spontaneous use of words, this overextension does not reflect an inability to distinguish between the various subclasses of objects or events, nor does it reflect an inability to comprehend the meaning of words used by adults to symbolize those subcategories.

A child may use the word *car* when referring to any mode of transportation in which people ride, but will act surprised if a bus is parked in the family garage. If the child could not discriminate the difference between the concepts of bus and automobile, no surprise would be expected. Similarly, a child who spontaneously exhibits overextension in speech may still respond correctly when shown a picture of a bus, an airplane, and an automobile and asked to point to the airplane. Apparently, overextension reflects the child's poorly developed formation of superordinant categories and the child's tendency to utilize these poorly defined classes in his or her spontaneous communication.

Underextension

Children overextend the meaning of words, but they also use words in too restrictive a fashion, symbolizing only a subset of the objects or events symbolized by the adult use of the same word. Unlike overextensions of word meanings, underextensions do not result in the clear misuse of words as symbolic labels. In the process of underextension, the objects or events that are labeled by the child are given appropriate names. Thus, underextension of a word meaning is a phenomenon much more difficult to detect in the spontaneous speech of children.

For example, a child calls the family cat "kitty" but does not use a word to label any other cat. This child's use of the word is appropriate when it is used; it is simply not used in all appropriate situations.

Underextension, like overextension, results from differences between the defining characteristics of the child's and the adult's conceptual categories.

A boy of four uses the word *fish* to refer to the fish in his family's aquarium, fish seen on a television program, and fish seen when he goes fishing with his father and mother. However, he does not call the fish on his dinner plate or the dead fish he sees in a store "fish." For this child, the property of movement is one of the defining characteristics of the class of objects symbolized by the word *fish*. For the adult, the property of movement is not a defining characteristic of fish; therefore, the adult labels both moving and stationary fish as "fish."

Syntactical Development

Although it would be ideal to associate the emergence of different sentence forms with children of particular ages, striking individual differences in the speed of language acquisition preclude that luxury. It has been noted by Roger Brown that one can characterize the development of language as a series of five stages through which a child progresses. Each stage is denoted by the initial onset of the use of a particular class of sentence structure.

The concept of stage as used by Brown reflects a sequential progression of sentence forms appearing in the child's language, beginning with those characteristic of Stage I and progressing to those forms characteristic of Stage V. However, the refinement of a sentence form characteristic of one stage may continue as the child enters subsequent stages. The perfection of past-tense expressions, first observed in Stage II, may not be complete until the child has reached Stage V.

Stage I (One- and Two-Word Utterances)

A detailed discussion of the characteristics of Stage I language has been presented in the discussion of infant syntax (see Chapter 9). For the most part, one can think of Stage I language as a characteristic of children close to their second birthday, although it does not always emerge as part of the child's behavior by that time.

Stage II (Inflections)

Stage II, which typically extends from about age two and one-half to about age three, is characterized by the emerging use of inflections. Although the emergence of Stage II language and the speed with which its development progresses varies for different children, the inflections characteristic of language in Stage II develop in a sequential order that is fairly consistent for most children. The emergence of these inflections marks the onset of the second stage of language development, but their development continues on through the other three stages as well. The typical order of emergence for some common inflections is shown in Table 14.2.

Although children use plural inflections early in Stage II development, the perfection of all plural forms is not complete until much later in their language development. Jean Berko showed children a picture of a single animal and called it by a nonsensical name: "Here is a wug." She then showed the children a picture of two of the animals and asked them to verbally complete the sentence: "Now there are two. . ."

By altering the nonsense words used to label the animals, she could determine which method of pluralization children were able to use. The words that required the addition of an /s/ or /z/ sound for their pluralization were responded to quite well by children four and five years old; however, children six and seven years old responded correctly to those words even more often.

Table 14.2 Typical Order of Acquisition of Morphemes

Morphemes	*Example*
Present progressive	I swim<u>ming</u>
<u>In</u> and <u>on</u>	Baby <u>on</u> chair; cookie <u>in</u> box
Plural(s)	Boat<u>s</u> in water
Past irregular	Bobby <u>swam</u>
Possessive	Fred'<u>s</u> train
Uncontractible copula	John <u>is</u> small
Articles	<u>The</u> chair, <u>a</u> car
Past regular	John look<u>ed</u> (overgeneralization—I swimmed)
Third-person regular	She run<u>s</u>
Third-person irregular	He <u>does</u> it; she <u>has</u> it
Uncontractible auxiliary	Sarah <u>is</u> <u>cooking</u>
Contractible copula	<u>He's</u> running fast
Contractible auxiliary	I<u>'m</u> cooking

In addition, when the words required the addition of an /ez/ sound (as in *fizzes*), preschool children were correct less than 30 percent of the time, while the performance of six- and seven-year-olds was correct only about 40 percent of the time.

Overgeneralization

When children first learn rules that govern their language, they often use them in every situation. The result of this overuse (called, overgeneralization, or, overregularization) is that children incorrectly use the rule in cases where there is an irregular exception to it in the language. In fact, children may often begin making mistakes in situations that previously have been responded to correctly. Later development of language involves learning exceptions to the established rules.

Irregular verbs are used in the past tense before regular verbs. A child will say, "I ate the apples" before using the regular past-tense inflection to create the sentence "I skated yesterday." However, when the child begins to use the regular past-tense inflections, he or she will very often attempt to apply them to previously correct cases and say, "I eated the apples."

Stage III (Reordered Sentences)

Stage III language, which emerges around the age of three and one-half, is characterized by the development of the ability to reorder the words of a sentence so as to express a new idea. Specific examples of this process are the evolution of questions and negative sentences. The precursors of negative sentences and questions may be observed as early as Stage I language, but in those earlier stages the child's implied meaning is conveyed through either intonation or the addition of a word to the front or end of the sentence rather than through the restructuring of a simple sentence.

The Question

For purposes of this discussion, questions may be broken into two forms, "yes/no" and "wh" questions. For "yes/no" questions, only a yes or no answer is required as a response. For adults, "yes/no" questions are formed by moving the first auxiliary verb of a sentence to the initial position or, when the sentence does not contain an auxiliary verb, first inserting one. This is called the question transformation.

With the question transformation, "John is swimming" becomes "Is John swimming?" "John swims" becomes "Does John swim?"

"Wh" questions are best described as sentences in which some important constituent of the sentence is unknown to the speaker and the speaker is asking another person to fill in the missing constituent. In the simple sentence "John is running" an important constituent element is the word *John*. If you are uninformed about the runner in the race, your sentence would read: "_____ is running," and you might ask someone else to help you fill in that blank. To do so, you would say, "Who is running?" which is a "wh" question.

"Wh" questions are formed by first using the question transformation and then adding an appropriate "wh" word—that is, *who, what, where, why, how,* and so on—to the sentence. The addition of that word is called a "wh" transformation.

"You *are* playing Mozart" is a simple sentence that contains the auxiliary verb are. If someone does not know the name of the composer but wishes to have that information, he or she would be forced to fill in the blank in the following incomplete sentence: "You are playing _____." To discover the correct answer, one must ask a question. The procedure for asking that "wh" question is to (1) use the question transformation to form "____ are you playing?" and (2) insert an appropriate "wh" word: "What are you playing?"

The development of questions in the child's language involves the development of the ability to use those two transformations appropriately.

Pre-Stage III Questions. Initially, a child conveys a question by the intonation in his or her voice or by tacking a "wh" word onto the beginning of a sentence. This is characteristic of the Stage I and II child.

"Mommy go?" may be a Stage I question denoted by intonation. "Mommy going?" is a Stage II question expressed by intonation. It is a Stage II question because its verb includes the progressive ending -*ing*, which is a Stage II characteristic. "Where mommy go?" is a Stage I "wh" question. Notice that there are no inflections. "Why mommy going home?" is a Stage II "wh" question. Notice that there is no insertion of an auxiliary verb. Such a restructuring of the sentence would be characteristic of Stage III language.

Initial Stage III Questions. The demarcation of Stage III language occurs when the child forms appropriate "yes/no" questions by using the question transformation and by inserting appropriate auxiliary verbs. However, initially those same transformations will not be used in "wh" questions. Instead, "wh" questions will use only the "wh" transformations but will not use a question transformation.

For example, "John is eating" will be transformed to "Is John eating?"; but "John is eating" will also be transformed to the inappropriate "wh" question "Why John is eating?" Apparently, the child in the initial phase of Stage III language knows the transformations needed to form all questions but cannot use more than one transformation at a time.

Later Stage III Questions. As the child's language progresses, he or she learns to coordinate more than one transformation at a time. In so doing, the child will produce questions of the form exemplified in Example 16. As is the case of other stage-related developments, this development overlaps with the emergence of more complex sentence forms characteristic of Stages IV and V.

Negation

The development of negation in children's language parallels the development of the question and represents another characteristic of Stage III language.

Pre-Stage III Negation. The child's initial method of negating a sentence involves the use of intonation or the addition of a negative word to the beginning or ending of a sentence. These methods of negation are characteristics of pre-Stage III language.

For pre-Stage III children, the affirmative statement "I play" could be negated by the statement "No I play." This negation in no way alters the form of the simple declarative sentence. Stage III negation emerges when the child transforms the elements in a sentence to convey the negation. In the case of negation, that transformation involves the movement of the negative word to a position in front of the verb. This transformation is called a negative transportation rule.

For example, "I play" becomes "I no play," and "She jumps" becomes "She can't jump." In contrast to the adult, who considers *can't* and *don't* to be contractions of the auxiliary verbs *can* and *do* with a negative not, the words *can't* and *don't* in ways that are conceptually similar to no and not.

Later Stage III Negation. Later the child acquires two additional tools to produce negative sentences that more closely approximate those of the adult. The first of those tools is the use of the auxiliary verbs *can* and *do*. Simple sentences now incorporate auxiliary verbs, and the negative transportation rule moves the negative word to a position between that auxiliary and the main verb.

	Affirmative	*Negative*
Stage I and II	I hide ball.	No I hide ball.
Early Stage III	I hide ball.	I no hide ball.
Later Stage III	I can hide the ball.	I can not (can't) hide the ball.

The second new tool is the ability to insert the auxiliary word *do* when an auxiliary word does not exist in the sentence. This is called the do-support rule.

	Affirmative	*Negative*
Early Stage III	I like it.	I no like it.
Later Stage III	I like it.	I do not (don't) like it.

Stage IV (Embedded Sentences)

The language of Stage IV is characterized by the child's ability to combine sentences to form more complex sentences. Specifically, sentences are used as constituent parts of other sentences. This is called embedding one sentence within another.

Consider the sentence "The boy who runs fast was hurt yesterday." This sentence actually contains two sentences: (1) "The boy runs fast" and (2) "The boy was hurt yesterday." In forming the more complex sentence, sentence 1 was changed slightly by substituting who for the boy, and it was then used to modify the subject of sentence 2.

In order of their emergence in child's language, three forms of embedding are observed in language. The use of a simple sentence as the object in a noun phrase occurs first. Then the child inserts a sentence containing a "wh" word as a substitute for a noun phrase. Later the child uses a relative clause to modify a noun phrase.

Simple Sentences

The first embedding to be observed in the language of children involves the use of a simple sentence as the object complement of a second sentence. Consider sentence (1) "You watch me" and (2) "I draw circles." When combined, sentences 1 and 2 become "Watch me draw circles."

Consider another pair of sentences: (1) "I believe" and (2) "We should go." When combined, sentences 1 and 2 become: "I believe we should go."

"Wh" Sentence Embedding

As noted in the discussion of the development of the question, "wh" words (*who, which, what, where*, and so on) may be substituted for constituent parts of a sentence. Those "wh" clauses that are developed in this way can be substituted for any noun phrase in a second sentence. This form of embedding emerges shortly after the embedding of simple sentences. Typically, the "wh" sentences are initially substituted for noun phrases that denote location and time. Subsequently, "wh" sentences are substituted for noun phrases that play other roles in the sentence.

The "wh" clause "when you come home," as used in the sentence "When you come home, I will go to bed," denotes time. The "wh" clause "where it is," as used in the sentence "I know where it is," denotes location. The "wh" clause "what I got," as used in the sentence "I will show you what I got," is a noun phrase in the role of the object of the verb.

Relative Clauses

A few months after the emergence of "wh" clause embedding, the child begins to embed relative clauses. A relative clause is a sentence that modifies a noun phrase. The initial embedding of relative clauses involves those relative clauses found in the predicate of the sentence.

Take two sentences: (1) "That is the car" and (2) "He rode in the car." When combined, sentences 1 and 2 become "That is the car he rode in." Sentence 2 modifies the noun phrase "the car."

Take another pair: (1) "The girl is in the car" and (2) "The girl went home." When combined, sentences 1 and 2 become "The girl in the car went home." Sentence 1 modifies the noun phrase "the girl."

Although some investigators maintain that Stage IV language can be observed in children as young as three years of age, other investigators maintain that Stage IV language is not manifested until after the age of six. This controversy has not yet been resolved it may reflect differences in the criteria used to define embedded sentences. It must be borne in mind that the initial emergence of embedded sentences, in the child's language marks the beginning of Stage IV language, but continued growth in the sophistication of that sentence structure will extend for many years after its first appearance.

Stage V (Compound Sentences)

The characteristic that denotes Stage V language is the

appearance of compound sentences. In contrast to embedded sentences in which one sentence is substituted as a constituent element of a second sentence, compound sentences contain two or more sentences, each of which express a separate idea.

There are different types of compound sentences. The simplest compound sentence, which emerges first in the child's language, consists of two simple sentences combined into a single sentence through the use of the connective *and*. For example, (1) "Mary ran" and "You chased her." When compounded, sentences 1 and 2 become "Mary ran, and you chased her."

In the example above, the subject and verb of the two sentences are different; thus, in the compound sentence both simple sentences are fully represented. When the same subject or verb is shared by two sentences, the compound sentence may be abbreviated. Abbreviated compound sentences appear in the language of children after unabbreviated compounds.

Later in the development of a child's language emerge compound sentences that imply relationships between events described in simple sentences. These compounds utilize the words *because*, *so*, *if*, and so on.

Consider these examples: (1)"Mary cried" and (2) "John hit Mary." When compounded, sentences 1 and 2 become "Mary cried because John hit her." Again consider (1) "I will go to the store" and "You give me some money." When compounded, sentences 1 and 2 become "I will go to the store if you give me some money."

The emergence of these sentence forms typically does not occur until after the age of six and is dependent upon the child's development of an understanding of a cause-effect relationship. Consequently, we will forego a discussion of this development until Chapter 18.

Explanations of Language Acquisition

There is much controversy in the field about exactly how children learn language. Several major positions have emerged: the behavioral position, exemplified by B.F. Skinner, and the biological propensity position, associated with Noam Chomsky. Two different theoretical approaches underly these positions— the empiricist perspective and the rationalist perspective.

Empiricist Perspective on Language Acquisition

The empiricist position is that a theory must concern itself with constructs that have the potential for possessing an objective reality. Furthermore, this viewpoint emphasizes that individual behavior is learned through one's experiences. Consequently, empiricists emphasize the role of environmental influences in the development of any behavior, including language.

For empiricists, biological determinants of development and the active participation of the child in the developmental process are de-emphasized. Language, to the empiricists, is a complex response system. Linguistic responses, be they overtly spoken speech or silent mediational speech, are elicited by the stimuli with which they are associated. Language is no different from any other behavior; its acquisition is governed by the learning principles that govern the acquisition of all stimulus-response (S-R) associations.

Within the context of the empiricist position, various specific theories of language acquisition have been developed, including reinforcement and social learning theories. One of the significant dimensions on which those theories differ concerns the role played by the environment in determining the acquisition of language behavior.

Skinner's Behavioral (Reinforcement) Position

Skinner argues that the principles of operant conditioning play a central part in the learning of language. As certain of the child's sounds and patterns of sound are reinforced, they become stronger, and the child begins to use them more readily.

Skinner explains these processes through the behavioral model, using the concepts of stimulus and response to describe language as behavior. That is, the baby associates "da-da" with a positive response from the environment (people make a fuss at the sound); as the baby begins to place words in their appropriate order, he or she is further rewarded. Skinner recognizes the complexity of language learning and the possibilities of innovation, but unequivocally suggests that the operant conditioning model takes all this into account.

Skinner's position has come under criticism, most notably by linguist Noam Chomsky and his followers. In an important review of Skinner's book on language learning, *Verbal Behavior,* Chomsky argues that the behavioral model cannot fully account for all the complexities of language learning. Moreover, he asks, if operant conditioning were the key, then why are the basic stages and processes of language learning the same everywhere in the world, throughout all cultures? The answer, Chomsky suggests, is that the human being has an innate mechanism for language learning, a kind of neurological pathway in the brain. The specific language we learn activates this pathway and provides the specific information, but the process itself is biologically determined by the capacities we have acquired over time through evolution.

This viewpoint is supported by the assumption that all languages have an underlying structure; that is, no matter how dissimilar languages appear to be on the surface, there are certain fixed principles, rules, and structures common to all of them. Analysis of language structure has confirmed this to some extent.

If this is true, it would be difficult to imagine identical conditioning processes from culture to culture.

Research on this debate has failed to resolve the basic issues. In recent years, physiological models have been used to account for both the innateness and universality of language acquisition. This approach is discussed in greater detail in a later section of this chapter, "Biological Propensity Theories," which amplifies Chomsky's position.

Social Learning Theory

Social learning theorists, like reinforcement theorists, stress that language is under environmental control; their explanation of its acquisition relies on the principle of generalization. Social learning theory, however, does not rely on the concept of external reinforcement to explain language development. Instead, according to this theory, the imitation of language produced by others is a significant contributor to language acquisition.

For example, John hears his father say, "Eat your dinner, John," and later, in a similar setting, repeats the utterance by saying, "Eat dinner." John has attempted to imitate his father, but his limited memory capacities result in the production of a fragment of the original utterance. As John grows older, he will imitate the entire utterance.

There are two major criticisms of social learning theories of language acquisition.

First, children may imitate their parents, but much of the language of a child is totally novel. Because the child has never heard it spoken before, he or she cannot have imitated this language. A child of 24 months may say, "All gone daddy." This is a common expression, but one that few infants would hear spoken by an adult.

The second criticism is that children who have never imitated language demonstrate by their comprehension that they have acquired a knowledge of the language. Eric Lenneberg reported the case history of a child who could not speak, yet comprehended language very well. The boy could not imitate the language he heard; thus, imitation could not explain his acquisition of language. He could not have been reinforced for speech because he never spoke.

A universal phenomenon is that children understand language before they speak it. A twelve-month-old child will not speak a word, but will go over and pick up a ball or bottle or book when requested to do so.

Rationalist Perspective on Language Acquisition

Unlike the empiricist, the rationalist accepts as elements in a theory certain constructs that may not have the potential for possessing objective reality. This characteristic of the rationalist philosophy of science allows for the inclusion in theories of language acquisition, and even in the definition of language, many abstract constructs that cannot be found in an empiricist theory. For the rationalist, language is defined as the process by which an abstract meaning is translated into a series of sounds that can communicate that meaning. When a person understands languages, he or she understands the principles governing that translation.

Competence vs. Performance

The rationalist maintains that language is knowledge, and like any knowledge, it may or may not lead to action. In the literature of language development, that knowledge is said to be the underlying competence of the individual to produce speech or to demonstrate through action an understanding of another's speech. Many factors may keep an individual from utilizing his or her capacities for language; thus, language performance, the actual speech we produce, may not totally reflect one's language competence.

The rationalist's emphasis is on language as a competence

that has no physical reality (it is not necessarily seen or heard). The empiricist, on the other hand, is interested in language performance—spoken or written—that does have a physical reality.

Sentence Structure and Sentence Meaning

The rationalist believes that the meaning of a sentence is not conveyed entirely by the words in the sentence. Instead, the sentence's meaning is conveyed in part by the relationship the words in the sentence have to one another.

"Mary hit John." "John hit Mary." These two sentences contain the same words but clearly have different meanings. To understand the meaning, one must recognize that Mary plays the role of the subject in the first sentence and the role of an object being hit in the second sentence.

Surface Structure. The series of sounds that we call speech have a structure. They are broken down into words, and the words are often clustered with one another by the pauses we make in a sentence and by the intonations in our voice. The clustering of the words in a spoken sentence is defined as the surface structure of that sentence. Sometimes we can tell that two sentences have different meanings by paying attention to the differences in their surface structure.

The sentence "They are eating apples" is ambiguous. It may have either of two meanings—that a particular type of apple is good for eating (as opposed to cooking), or that a group of people are eating apples. In this example, the intended meaning of the sentence is represented in the surface structure of the sentence. That structure is conveyed by the placement of pauses in speaking the sentence.

Meaning 1: (They) (are) (eating apples.)

Meaning 2: (They) (are eating) (apples.)

Deep Structure. Although sentences with different meanings may differ in their surface structure, surface structure is not sufficient for determining the meaning of a sentence. Two sentences may have very different surface structures but have the same meaning.

Sentence 1: Doris ate the cake.

Sentence 2: The cake was eaten by Doris.

Both sentences have the same meaning, but on the surface they do not have the same form.

It is also true that two sentences that on the surface appear to have the same form may have very different meanings. Examine the following two sentences. Both have identical surface structures.

1. (They) (are) (drinking glasses.)

2. (They) (are) (drinking companions.)

Each sentence begins with the pronoun *they*, which is followed by the verb *are*, which is followed by the progressive form of the word *drink* (the progressive form adds "-ing"); and they end with a plural noun. In spite of these identical surface structures, the two sentences represent different ideas, not just because the sentences contain two different words, but because those words play different roles in the meaning of the sentence. How can we tell?

If the words *glasses* and *companions* play the same role in the sentence, then we should be able to paraphrase the sentence in the same way and maintain their meanings. The following are paraphrases of the sentences. Notice that a paraphrasing that maintains the meaning of one sentence produces nonsense in the other sentence.

Paraphrase 1:

They are glasses that drink. (meaning lost)

They are companions that drink. (meaning maintained)

Paraphrase 2:

They are glasses used for drinking. (meaning retained)

They are companions used for drinking. (meaning lost)

Because the differences in meaning are not entirely represented in the surface structure of the two sentences in the above example, the individual who recognizes these sentences as having two different meaning must possess an understanding of a sentence structure other than that present in the sound pattern of the spoken sentence. That abstract structure reflects the true meaning of a sentence and is called its deep structure.

Transformational Rules. Because of the difference between the deep structure of a sentence, which reflects its abstract meaning, and the surface structure of the sentence, which characterizes it as a spoken communication, there must be some system of rules understood by a person who has knowledge of a language that allows him or her to translate the deep structure (meaning) into the surface structure (spoken sentence). Those rules are called transformational rules.

One transformational rule is a negative transformation rule, which allows us to negate the assertion contained in a simple declarative sentence. Take the sentence "Fred can run a mile," for example. This is a simple declarative sentence whose form in deep structure might be:

Fred   can run   a mile
(Noun) + (Aux + Verb) + (Noun Phrase)

To denote the negation of this sentence in the deep structure, we will simply mark the sentence with a symbol for negation. The sentence now reads: Negative, "Fred can run a mile."

Although the deep structure conveys the meaning we wish to express, it is not in a form acceptable in spoken English. Thus, the negative transformation rule is applied to transform the deep structure into an appropriate surface structure. That rule states:

"Put an appropriate negative word after the auxiliary verb *can*." When the rule is applied, the sentence reads, "Fred cannot run a mile."

Biological Propensity Theories—Chomsky's Position

Some rationalist theorists of language acquisition maintain that there are biological systems in the human organism specifically designed to direct language acquisition. Among the most notable of those theorists is Noam Chomsky. For Chomsky, language acquisition involves the child's discovery of the transformational rules appropriate for the language of his or her society. This discovery takes place through the child's attempts to comprehend that language and is further guided by an inherent knowledge of some of the parameters that define language. The model is often depicted by the diagram below.

Because of the assumed biological propensity for language processing and the active participation of the child in the language acquisition process, Chomsky and others with similar theories stress that environmental influences, such as reinforcement and imitation, play minor roles in language development. All that the child, the little scientist, requires to acquire a knowledge of language is a fairly good language laboratory— that is to say, an environment in which there are samples of language for the child to process and analyze.

Those who maintain that there is a biological propensity for language are not proposing that the specific language spoken by a child (for example, English or French) is biologically inherent, but that biological systems are available to ensure that some language is learned. Evidence for this position comes from five sources.

1. Special centers of the brain control language functioning. One hemisphere of the brain, typically the left, controls language processes. An anesthetic can be administered to temporarily paralyze one hemisphere of the brain at a time. In most people, when the left hemisphere is not functioning, both the expression and comprehension of language cease.

A structure called Broca's area, located in the front portion of the left cortical hemisphere, controls speech production. When it is destroyed, people have difficulty naming objects, confuse numbers when counting, and so on. Similarly, Wernicke's area (see Fig. 14.2) controls language comprehension. A person with damage to this area of the brain may speak, but will not understand what is heard.

2. All human beings who are neurologically intact and provided with minimal environmental stimulation possess a language.

3. Although wide variations exist in the environmental con-

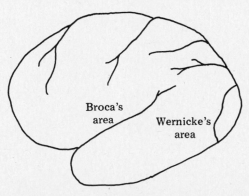

Fig. 14.2

ditions under which people are reared, little variation exists in the rate at which they acquire language or the ultimate level of complexity their language exhibits.

Josh is the son of a poor immigrant farmer who migrated from Mexico. He lives in poverty and comes from a family whose members have no education and who work long hours. Josh receives very little language stimulation. Edmund, in contrast, is the son of a highly educated professional parent who provides a stimulating linguistic environment. In spite of these vast environmental differences, the stages of language development through which the boys pass are identical. They speak their first words at approximately the same age, and the structure of the first sentences they form are identical.

4. The ages at which children achieve milestones in language development are highly correlated with the achievement of milestones in motor development. This does not imply that language development results from motor activity, but does imply that both dimensions of development are controlled by similar maturational processes. The motor milestones in development and their corresponding language milestones are listed in Table 9-1, Chapter 9.

5. There are common characteristics shared by all languages and common patterns of development shared by children learning all languages. These are called language universals. For English-speaking children, the earliest stage in the development of negative sentences is characterized by the placement of a negative word in front of a simple sentence, such as "No eat apple." In spite of the fact that negative sentences produced by adult speakers of Russian are very different in form than those of adult speakers of English, the same form of negation is used by both Russian-speaking and English-speaking children.

Cognitive Theories

In contrast to biological theorists of language acquisition, cognitive theorists such as Dan Slobin and Harry Beilin do not place great emphasis on the assumption of a specific biological propensity for language. Instead, these theorists maintain that the acquisition of language is a reflection of cognitive development. That development provides the child with the concepts and relationships he or she will express through language and with the capability to discover the transformations needed to translate abstract deep-structure meaning into verbally communicated sentences characterized by appropriate surface structures. The systematic nature of language acquisition and its universality are thought to result from the systematic and universal development of those cognitive capacities.

The young child does not clearly conceptualize the difference between events now, in the past, and in the future. When the child's concept of time is poorly developed, the use of verbs in past and future tense is also poorly developed. When the concept of time emerges in the conceptual world of the child, a language rule to express that concept soon follows. Early language acquisition as it is described by cognitive theorists is discussed in Chapter 8 under the heading "Semantic Theories."

CHAPTER 15

Personality and Social Development in the Young Child

Personality is the term used to describe the characteristic way in which an individual relates to his or her environment. It incorporates the combination of a person's thinking, feeling, and acting. The age span from two to six is a significant period in personality development because emerging conceptual abilities allow children to gain new perspectives on the world. They develop a greater awareness of the impact others have on them as well as their own impact on others. They can symbolize events in their life and create images of those events so that the events can influence their behavior at a later time. Their increased understanding of time and of cause-effect relationships allows children to conceptualize not only the here-and-now but also the future.

In this chapter we see how the preschool child becomes more independent, develops initiative, indentifies with his or her sex, and makes adjustments to social reality. We then see how pat-

terns of parenting affect the child's social and personality development.

Tasks in Personality Development

Although many people have attempted to describe the developmental tasks faced by the two- to six-year-old child, Erik Erikson's description is dominant in the literature of child psychology. He describes two related challenges of this period. First, there is the child's need to develop a feeling of autonomy, of independence as an individual, versus a tendency to feel dependent on others because of feelings of self-doubt. This leads to the child's need to develop initiative in undertaking actions versus feeling guilty about his or her behavior.

Autonomy vs. Doubt of Self

The conflict that children of two to four years of age must resolve is whether to be an autonomous individual or to doubt their own competence as individuals and maintain their dependency upon others. The resolution of that conflict is reflected in a variety of ways.

Negativism

The two- and three-year-old child is often seen as an individual who always wants to have his or her way. The child is negative about every idea that others suggest and every demand that is placed upon him or her. This attitude has been given the label negativism. Negativism is a natural phenomenon that reflects the child's attempt to demonstrate autonomy.

A mother calls her two-and-one-half-year-old child to lunch and is totally ignored. The child maintains that she didn't hear the call. Once at the table, the child refuses to eat her lunch; and when asked to carry her dishes to the kitchen, she runs outside blithely without responding.   This child is exhibiting the negativism typical of the two- to three-year-old child.

Dependency

Typical two-year-olds are very dependent. They cling to their parents and seek affection from them. Five-year-olds are quite different. They no longer cling and seek affection, but instead seek reassurance and attention for their autonomous actions, such as their newly discovered ability to dress themselves and perform most of their own personal hygiene activities in the bathroom. This change in behavior is a reflection of the older children's resolution of the conflict between developing autonomy and the development of doubt about self-worth.

The following situation can be used to show the reductions in dependency that occur with age: A child is brought into a room with his or her mother and allowed to freely explore the room. After this free exploration, a stranger is brought into the room, and the child's behavior is observed. Subsequently, the mother leaves the room, and the child is left alone with the stranger. How does the age of a child influence his or her responses to these three situations?

In free exploration, the distance that children move away from their mothers increases as the children become older: this is an example of decreased dependence with increasing age. The entry of the stranger will cause the two-year-old to cling to his or her mother and avoid the stranger. A three-year old may interact with the stranger, but will retreat to the mother on occasion if she is available. A child of four or more will not be affected by the presence of the stranger and may actually act in such a way as to attract the attention of the mother and the stranger.

When the mother leaves the room and the child is left alone with the stranger, a two-year-old may become upset. A three-year-old, in contrast, may interact with the stranger more than when the mother is present. This phenomenon is the result of the three-year-old's newly developed independence, which may not manifest itself fully when a crutch (mother) is available for retreat, but will emerge in full bloom when cues for dependent behavior are not available. Children of four, five, and six, of course, continue to exhibit their independence when left alone with the stranger.

Forms of Dependence

There are two types of dependence. *Instrumental dependence* is the tendency for a child to seek help from others. *Emotional dependence* is the tendency for the child to seek affection, approval, and close physical contact with others. In a child of three, instrumental and emotional dependence are correlated with each other. In a child of four, however, the amount of emotional dependence exhibited is not a good predictor of the amount of instrumental dependence exhibited.

For example, at the age of three, Duane, a highly dependent child, continually clung to his mother and cried frantically when she left his side. At the same time, he would seek his parent's assistance when confronted with the simplest task. At the age of four, Duane's behavior changed. Although he still sought assistance whenever he was confronted with a task, he no longer clung to his mother, nor did he get upset when she left him. By this age, the two types of dependence were emerging as independent personality traits.

Maintenance of Dependency

Although dependency will be exhibited more intensely under conditions that elicit anxiety, it is a characteristic exhibited by all young children. For some, however, dependence is maintained in later life as a personality trait. The stability of that trait over time is more pronounced in girls than in boys, possibly because girls are rewarded for their dependency and boys are encouraged to be independent.

In a longitudinal study of dependence, children were observed at the age of two and each year thereafter until the age of fifteen. At the ages of four and five, individual differences in the amount of dependence exhibited by the children were evidenced. For girls, the amount of dependence exhibited at the age of four was a good predictor of the dependency they exhibited later, at the age of 15. For boys, however, the predictive value of their dependence at the age of four or five was limited.

Children need to feel secure before they can take the risk of being independent. Any factor that disrupts security for young children can hinder their progress toward autonomy and result in a dependent personality.

Three factors stand out as contributing to insecurity and the maintenance of dependence:

1.   If children have not formed an adequate attachment to another person during their first two years of life, they may continue to seek that attachment and maintain their dependency in later life. (See Chapter 10 for discussion of attachment.)

2.   A lack of consistency in discipline imposed by parents produces an environment in which the children do not know the rules by which society plays. If one doesn't know the rules of the game, making errors out of ignorance can be anticipated. Thus, insecurity can stem from inconsistent discipline, and the result of that insecurity is the maintenance of dependent behavior.

3.   Parents who threaten children with the loss of love create an insecure atmosphere and, in so doing, enhance the maintenance of dependent behavior.

A father, for example, continually threatens his four-year-old adopted daughter by saying that if she does not obey his demands, he will send her away to live with another family. Although one might speculate that the young child would respond to this love withdrawal threat with anger or rejection of her own, in reality she clings to her parents and becomes disturbed when they leave her with a baby sitter, leave home for vacations, or tell her she will attend a nursery school.

Characteristics Associated with Dependency

Children who exhibit dependent characteristics also exhibit more nurture toward others than children who are not so dependent. It is as if children who need to have others express love and affection toward them say to themselves, "If I give love and kindness to others, maybe they will return the favor."

Initiative vs. Guilt

Children of four and five begin to initiate more and more actions on their own. Five-year-olds can dress themselves, can be responsible for their own personal hygiene, and so on. However, with this ability to initiate actions and accept responsibilities comes a potential for failure, frustration, and guilt for having done something wrong. The challenge to four- and five-year-olds is to develop the ability to cope with the feelings of frustration and failure that occur, so that they can continue to take the risks involved in the initiation of activities.

The number of emotional outbursts observed in children fluctuates with age. One of the peak periods for such outbursts is at the age of four. These outbursts reflect the conflict generated between children's desire to initiate activities and the feeling of guilt that can be associated with failure.

Parents play an important role in determining the extent to which the child experiences the conflicts characteristic of the four- and five-year-old. If the parent encourages the independent initiation of actions and praises the fact that they have been undertaken rather than just the fact that they are successful, then little guilt will be felt by the child. In contrast, parents who expect performance on tasks to exceed the abilities of the child will foster feelings of guilt for failure.

Identification

Identification is the process by which an individual takes on the personality characteristics of another person (typically a parent). The process of identification is important in the evolution of personality between the ages of two and six.

Theories of Identification

Three theories attempt to explain the identification process.

Psychoanalytic Theory

According to Freud's psychoanalytic theory, two forms of identification exist, anaclitic identification and identification with the aggressor.

Anaclitic Identification. This form of identification takes place in both boys and girls and results from a fear of losing the love of a significant person. Because the mother nurtures the young child and is the child's primary source of love prior to the age of three or four, both boys and girls experience anaclitic identification with her.

Identification with the Aggressor. At about the age of four, the child enters the phallic stage of psychosexual development. In that stage, the male child begins to experience sexual fantasies about his mother and fears that his chief rival for his mother's affection, his father, will punish him for those fantasies. The conflicts generated by these fears and fantasies are called the Oedipus complex.

The resolution of the Oedipus complex is the motivation for the male child to identify with his father. This form of identification is called identification with the aggressor. It is as if the boy of four or five says, "My father is likely to punish me severely for my fantasies about Mom. However, he wouldn't punish anyone who is a lot like him, so I'll try to be as much like him as I can. Furthermore, if I am like Dad, then I can vicariously enjoy the power that he has and also his relationship with Mom."

Girls, in contrast to boys, do not exhibit a fear of their father and consequently do not engage in identification with an aggressor. Their identification continues to be of the anaclitic form, and the object of the identification continues to be the mother.

Social Learning Theory

For social learning theorists, such as Albert Bandura, identification is little more than a special form of observational learning. In contrast to the psychoanalytic theory of identification, which stresses the importance of the early years in the process of identification, social learning theory proposes that the process of identification begins early but continues throughout the child's life.

It is well known that children imitate the behavior of significant people in their lives. The significance of an individual stems from two characteristics: the amount of nurturance and love that the person has provided the child, and the extent to which the child's receipt of rewards and punishments is governed by the person. Because mothers and fathers are both nurturing to children and powerful forces in their lives, it is the mother and father who are likely candidates to be imitated.

Boys tend to identify with their fathers because imitation of that behavior is socially acceptable and thus results in reinforcement. It is not socially acceptable for boys to imitate their mothers; rather, it results in punishment or at best being ignored. Girls identify with their mothers for the same reason: it is socially acceptable behavior that is reinforced.

Cognitive Theories

In contrast to both psychoanalytic and social learning theories, the cognitive theory espoused by Lawrence Kohlberg emphasizes the role of cognitive development in the identification process. Children of three are capable of categorizing people on the basis of various characteristics. The first step in the identification process is that the children categorize people on the basis of their sex and place themselves in one of those categories. Having identified themselves as members of a particular sexual class, children make an effort to be as much like the others in that class as they can. Because the same-sex parent is one of the child's best available examples of the characteristics possessed by persons in that sexual class, the child imitates that parent.

In a study conducted in the early 1970s by Spencer Thompson and Peter Bentler, children were shown dolls that had female genitals but short hair, other dolls with male genitals and long hair, and still other dolls with mixtures of various sex-identifying characteristics. The children were asked if each doll was a girl or a boy. Four-, five-, and six-year-old children based their categorization of the dolls on their body proportions, body form, and the length of the doll's hair. They did not base their judgment on the sexual organs possessed by the doll.

Consequences of Identification

Identification results in two important developments in the child: sex typing and the acquisition of moral standards.

Sex Typing

In all societies, there are some behaviors that are typically thought to be masculine and others that are thought to be feminine. The establishment of these sex-role behaviors in the child is called sex typing and is one of the outcomes of the identification process. Sex typing is demonstrated in a variety of ways.

1. At three, the child correctly labels his or her own sex, and by the age of four or five, can identify the sex of others. Sex identification is not thought by the young child to be constant property possessed by a person, and the young child may consider the possibility that the sex of a person will change later in life. However, the six-year-old child conceptualizes sex as being a constant property of an individual.

A child of five is heard to say, "My brother is a boy." When asked, "Will he be a boy when he is as old as your father?" the child responds, "I don't know." By the age of six, the same child would consider the question trivial or stupid because there would be no doubt about the constancy of sex.

2. By the age of three, boys typically demonstrate a preference for toys that are defined by their society as being associated with the male sex role. After the age of six, that sex-appropriate toy preference increases dramatically. For girls, the development of toy preference is less systematic, than it is for boys. Although the preference for sex-appropriate toys increases in girls between the ages of three and four, it does not increase dramatically from the ages of six to nine, as it does for boys. (See Fig. 15.1.) After the age of ten, girls do begin to increase their preference for sex-appropriate games and toys. (However, adult females are more likely than adult males to express a willingness to take on the role of the opposite sex.)

3. By the age of four, children prefer to play with others of their own sex. This sex preference is initially exhibited for sex-specific activities, such as playing house or playing cowboys. By the age of five, playmate sex preference is well developed and extends to general as well as sex-specific play.

While talking to a five-year-old girl, a researcher mentioned that he had met a boy who was very talented at gymnastics. The girl, who herself was involved with gymnastics, said, "Foo on boys, I don't want them in our gym."

Sex typing on the part of any child is most likely to occur when the parent of the child's own sex is nurturant and possesses the characteristics that make him or her an individual who is likely to be imitated. At the same time, sex typing is more likely to occur when both parents reward any evidence of the sex-role behavior that is determined by their society. Given these circumstances, stable sex typing is established by the age of five or six.

As one might expect, sex typing can be influenced by the absence of the parent of the same sex. To exemplify that point, the sex-type behavior of boys who were living with their fathers was compared to that of boys who had been separated from their

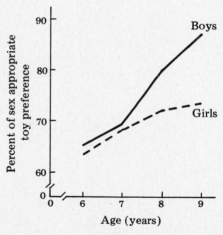

Fig. 15.1

fathers. The latter group of boys exhibited less firmly established sex-type behavior.

Moral Development

Morality is thought to be an internalized set of principles that govern the behavior of an individual and incorporate characteristics based, at least in part, on societal norms. The establishment of those moral principles requires the interaction of two factors.

First, persons who possess characteristics that encourage the child's imitation of the behavior must exhibit for the child a system of moral standards. The importance of this factor in the development of morality is emphasized by social learning theories of moral development.

Second, the child must have lost the extreme egocentrism of youth and developed the cognitive capacities to conceptualize the abstract principles of morality exemplified in the model's behavior. The role of cognitive factors in the development of morality is emphasized by the theories of moral development espoused by Jean Piaget and Lawrence Kohlberg.

The majority of research concerning moral development has involved the observation of children over the age of six. Thus, a detailed discussion of that research will be postponed until Chapter 19. Those studies that have examined the moral behavior of children under six years of age have been concerned with the effects of parental practices on that behavior. The results obtained have been ambiguous, reflecting limitations in the children's development of the cognitive capacities necessary to understand the abstract concept of morality. Rather, children less than six years old can be considered premoral. Because of their limited cognitive capacities, the behavior of two- to six-year-olds is governed almost entirely by the immediate consequences of that behavior upon themselves.

One principle of Western morality is that a person can resist temptation. Resisting temptation, by definition, means that one

denies oneself a positive but forbidden pleasure. Prior to the age
of six, the child's ability to resist temptation is very poor.
Whether or not a young child resists temptation seems dependent
upon the (positive) value of the temptation and the anticipated
(negative) consequences of not resisting the temp- tation; factors
such as the "rightness" or "wrongness" of giving in to the
temptation do not seem to play an important role.

Socialization

Prior to the age of two, the typical child associates with few
other children in the course of the day. That number increases
significantly from the age of four onward. (See Fig. 15.2.) Of
course, this increased companionship simply may reflect an
increased opportunity for associating with other children and not
a change in the child's need for companionship. That need,
however, is exemplified by the tendency of children from ages

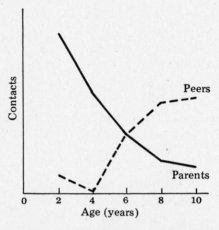

Fig. 15.2

two through five to invent imaginary friends who serve as companions when real associations are not available. Similarly, the need for companionship is reflected in the importance attached to pets by the child between the ages of three and six years.

Social Play

Play is part of the child's development as a social being. While to the child, and perhaps to the parents, play is a diverting, pleasurable, almost haphazard activity, psychologists have long recognized its importance in socialization and cognitive development.

Ethologist Konrad Lorenz, who studied the behaviors of animals through the evolutionary process, has suggested that play is an integral part of the human being's development as a species. Lorenz believes that the functions of play include the refinement and sharpening of cognitive capacities. He points out how play is based on curiosity behavior, which is tied to the ability of a species to survive and prosper.

Erik Erikson, who studied children's play in order to better understand the child's developing sense of reality, argues that play is one of the major functions of the ego and its development. He noted that children's play is not the equivalent of adult's play—it is not simply recreation. Rather, Erikson believes that through play the child is able to advance to new developmental stages and to deal with life experiences, which the child attempts to repeat, to master, or to negate. Play, he argues, involves self-teaching and self-healing, for in the play situation, the child can make up for frustrations and defeats in the real world. The child who fails at a task in the outer world can retreat into what Erikson calls the "safe island" that play provides and can overcome the feelings of failure within his or her own set of boundaries. Erikson describes the different stages of children's play, from the original focus on the self to the point at which the child can reach out and play with others, demonstrating the crucial role of play as a socializing factor.

The developmental sequence of play has been studied in much detail because it reveals, step by step, how the child socializes and, more important, how the child's social development is related to other areas of growth, such as cognitive growth, language learning, moral reasoning, and psychomotor development. While infants' play is limited to activity with their own bodies and with the nipple or the breast that supplies milk, by the time children reach elementary school age, play brings together all their subjective feelings and thoughts, along with all the people in the environment, transforming simple subjective expression into complex social interactions.

Three forms of social play have been identified in the pre-six-year-old child: parallel play, associative play, and cooperative play.

Parallel Play

The child of two loves to play in the company of other children. Interestingly, however, when children two and three years of age play alongside one another, they often engage in two different activities. This form of playing alongside one another is called parallel play.

Two children are sitting on the floor, playing. One is drawing with a pencil on paper, the other is building a tower with blocks. Although they are playing in close proximity, there is no shared experience between them. This lack of shared experience characterizes parallel play.

Associative Play

By the age of three, children play in groups. Still, while they appear to be playing at the same activity, children at this age are often playing with the same materials but using them in different ways. This associative play sometimes results in behavioral contagion. One or two children will become engaged with some game, and quickly all the children in an area will want to play with the same toys.

Ask a number of children who are apparently playing the same game to explain what they are doing. In spite of the fact that they are playing together, individual children may report that they are playing very different games. This phenomenon exemplifies the principle of associative play, in which children play together at the same activity but do not coordinate their activities.

Cooperative Play

Around the age of four, it is not uncommon to see children playing on a teeter-totter or one pushing the other on a swing. These activities, which require coordinated actions on the part of two or more children, exemplify the principle of cooperative play. Cooperative play can be observed in children older than four but is rarely observed in younger children.

Aggression

Prior to the age of four, most children are aggressive, and the form of that early aggression is often physical. They shout, cry, hit, kick, and throw things. The aggression exhibited by older children most often manifests itself in more socially acceptable ways. In contrast to the three-year-old, who may physically attack another child over the use of a toy, the five-year-old is more likely to call the second child names, tease him or her, or otherwise use verbal skills in the attack.

"Sticks and stones may break my bones, but names will never hurt me." Among the five- and six-year-old set, this old phrase is a popular verbalized defense against teasing. Its popularity probably stems from the increased frequency with which the five- and six-year-old is confronted with verbal aggression from within the peer group. Prior to that age, little thought would be given to the development of defenses against verbal attacks.

Individual Differences in Aggression

Popular children appear to play more aggressively than unpopular children, although their aggression is more controlled. Rather than blowing up and exhibiting general aggression toward everyone in their vicinity, popular children pick a target for their aggression and direct it in a controlled fashion. Unpopular children are more submissive than popular children, but when aggression does manifest itself in the unpopular child, it is uncontrolled and undirected.

When a group of three-year-olds are playing with one another, one boy stands out as a leader, while another child stands out as the group outcast. Not only can these roles be detected by interviews with the children, but they can be seen clearly in the aggressive activities of the children. The popular leader roughhouses with the rest of the group in a playful way and leads the attack on the group outcast when it is undertaken. At all times, this boy seems to be in control. In contrast, the outcast hangs around the edge of the group and avoids contact. When he is finally prodded into action by the group, he cries, hits wildly at whoever is near him, and runs away.

At three years of age, there are few sex differences in the aggression exhibited by children. At four, however, boys begin to exhibit a greater amount of physical aggression than do girls, while girls become more inclined toward verbal aggression.

A typical scene shows a five-year-old boy playing with his four-year-old cousin when a problem arises over who will play with a particular toy. The boy is much more likely to hit his cousin or simply pull the toy away. The girl, in contrast, is more likely to threaten her cousin verbally or tell a parent about the problem.

Consistency of Aggression

Aggressive behavior is a consistent pattern of responding for children from three to five years of age. Children who are highly aggressive when they enter nursery school tend to maintain that high level of aggression relative to their peers in later years.

Behavior Disorders of Childhood

Along with the so-called normal development of personality during childhood, we should consider some of the maladaptive conditions. These are enumerated in the DSM-III-R, the *Diagnostic and Statistical Manual of Mental Disorders*, published by the American Psychiatric Association. The following represent some of the disorders relatively common among children.

Eating Disorders

These disorders, which may occur in childhood or adolescence, are characterized by a major disturbance in normal eating patterns. They can be serious, requiring medical attention for concomitant problems, such as malnourishment, vitamin deficiency, and ulcers. The main disorders are anorexia nervosa, bulimia nervosa, pica, and rumination disorders of infancy.

Anorexia Nervosa

Anorexia nervosa is characterized by a refusal to ingest the minimal amount of food necessary to maintain a normal body weight. The child suffering from this condition loses appetite and finds food repulsive. While he or she loses weight drastically over a relatively short period of time, there still persists a feeling of being fat or distended, which is totally out of touch with reality. While this is more commonly found in adolescence, it may appear during prepuberty as well.

Bulimia

Bulimia is similar, except that it also includes binge eating and self-induced vomiting. The binge is characterized by immoderate eating, lack of control, failure to differentiate among different foods, and gobbling rather than chewing. In many cases, vomiting is induced, and there may also be a preference for laxative use or enemas.

Pica

Pica is an eating disorder associated with early childhood. It is characterized by the persistent eating of nonfood substances, such as paint, plaster, hair, etc. It can lead to illnesses caused by ingesting toxic substances such as paint.

Rumination Disorder of Infancy

The rumination disorder of infancy is characterized by the repeated regurgitation of food, with accompanying weight loss. This causes the infant to be irritable and often results in weight loss and physical illnesses. While the disorder is rare, it can only be determined when all physical causes (such as esophageal obstruction) are ruled out.

Sleep Disorders

This category includes insomnia, sleep-walking, and sleep terrors.

Insomnia

The main symptom of insomnia is the inability to fall asleep. The insomniac usually thinks about sleep during the day but experiences anxiety at bed time. In children, the disorder is often compounded by the parents' failure to see it as a psychological problem and to treat it instead as a behavioral problem.

Sleepwalking

Sleepwalking disorder is characterized by a sleeping person leaving the bed and walking about, without that person being consciously aware of it. This disorder usually begins between the ages of six and twelve and will typically disappear during adolescence.

Sleep Terrors

Sleep terrors, like nightmares, arouse the sleeper into a frenzied wakened state. The child who experiences this will often awake with a panicky scream, and will generally be unresponsive to others who try to comfort him. Morning amnesia often follows, with the person having no memory of the episode.

Elimination Disorders

These include the common childhood disorders of functional enuresis and functional encopresis. *Enuresis* is the involuntary voiding of urine, either while awake or asleep. *Encopresis* is the involuntary movement of the bowels, usually with feces being deposited inappropriately. With both these disorders, there are usually accompanying mental disorders, such as schizophrenia, organic brain disorders, or retardation.

Anxiety Disorders

Children who suffer from anxiety disorders exhibit many of the same signs as do adults. But these symptoms are grouped together in the DSM-III-R under a separate heading of "Anxiety Disorders of Childhood and Adolescence." These may include *separation anxiety* (an inappropriate panic at being separated from the parents or caretaker), *avoidant disorders* (fear of relating to unfamiliar people, shirking social situations) and *over-anxious disorder* (excessive anxiety that interferes with functioning for six months or longer). *Phobias* are also common, especially school phobia, where the child is prevented from attending schools by inordinate levels of fear.

Patterns of Parenting

Among those controversial and popular issues in the field of child psychology is the question of how to raise children. Every parent would like to know the "correct" way to raise a child, but realistically there is no "correct" way. The effectiveness of any technique depends a great deal on the characteristics of the parent, the characteristics of the child, and the kind of child the parent wishes to raise. Recent research has identified three general patterns of child rearing, each of which is associated with the development of children bearing unique characteristics.

Authoritative Parents

Authoritative parents display confidence in themselves as parents and as people. They are nurturant and loving toward their children, but not overly so. They establish and communicate behavioral standards for their children to follow that take into consideration the needs of children as well as the needs of the parents and society. They discipline their children when those standards are broken, explain the rationale for their discipline, and tend not to use physical force as a means of punishment. They encourage their children's independence and expect them to act maturely and respond appropriately to other people around them and to the societal demands placed upon them. When the children do so, they are praised by the authoritative parent. In short, these parents present a model of mature, well-socialized, loving adults.

The children of authoritative parents tend to be the most mature, independent, self-reliant, explorative, self-controlled, and assertive. Perhaps most important, they are content with themselves.

Mary and David Brown are authoritative parents. They consider their own needs as well as their child's needs in establishing standards for conduct. For example, these parents believe that it is important that a child not disrupt the eating of others at the dinner table. At the same time, they understand that their child is not always ready to eat certain foods. While their son is not expected to eat his food just because it is set in front of him, he is expected to refrain from playing with uneaten food or crying for special foods. If he chooses not to eat, he can politely excuse himself from the table. This behavior is praised by Mary and David when it occurs.

However, when the child does act up at the table, a simple form of punishment is administered. Either Mary or David says, "That is not acceptable behavior at the table. Go and sit in your chair for five minutes." The child's chair is isolated from the rest of the family and from television sets and other forms of entertainment. A timer with a bell on it records the five-minute period; when it rings, the child is free to play. If a protest is made, an additional five minutes is added to the punishment time. This punishment is effective, yet it involves no physical abuse.

Authoritarian Parents

Like authoritative parents, authoritarian parents control their children, but do so in a very different way. They tend to establish rigid standards of conduct that do not take into consideration the needs of the children, nor is the rationale for those standards communicated to the children. When the standards of conduct are broken, the result is physical punishment administered in a no-nonsense fashion, with little or no explanation. While expecting conformity to their parental standards of conduct, these parents tend to minimize the amount of love, nurture, and praise given to their children.

Although the children of authoritarian parents exhibit self-control and some self-reliance, they seem withdrawn, discontented, and apprehensive about their own actions. Apparently, when all control is administered by machine-like, nonnurturing parents, there is a limited amount of internalization of their standards.

Jane, a girl of five, knows that there are strict rules that must be followed at home and knows that to disobey those rules will result in punishment. She doesn't argue about the rules even when they seem unfair to her, because she believes that to express her feelings would be a waste of time. Jane's parents are authoritarian. When the child is away from home, she continues to obey rules that are set for her Unfortunately, rules are not always prescribed, and when she is in an unfamiliar situation, a voice inside her says, "I don't know what I'm expected to do; yet if I do something wrong, I know I'll be punished." Because of her apprehension, Jane tends to avoid unstructured situations and to act unsure of herself when confronted with new experiences.

Permissive Parents

Permissive parents are characterized by insecurity in their role as parents. They tend to assert little control over their children and demand little in the way of mature behavior from them. They seem to be afraid to exert themselves because they do not know an effective way to back up their demands.

These parents, however, are nurturing, at least more so than authoritarian parents. When permissive parents believe it is time for their children to go to bed, they may request the children to do so. If the children resist, however, voicing a plea to watch one more favorite television program, the parents typically back down and grant the children their wish.

Permissive parents exhibit the characteristics of insecure people, and their children reflect that pattern of behavior. Of the three types of preschool children studied, the children of permissive parents are the most insecure, immature, dependent, and the least self-reliant and self-controlled.

PART V: Middle Childhood

Middle childhood extends from the age of six years through the age of twelve. It has been characterized as a period of crystallization, inasmuch as the developments that take place during middle childhood are slow, uniform, and provide reasonably stable predictors of the child's characteristics as a young adult.

Although the family continues to play an important role in the developmental processes of middle childhood, school becomes a significant contributor to the child's growth at this time. Not only does school provide an environment for the development of cognitive and academic skills, but it also represents a setting in which peer groups can influence the socialization of the child.

CHAPTER 16

Physical Development in Middle Childhood

Between the ages of six and twelve, the child grows steadily in height and weight. Muscles become larger, the neurological system matures, and strength and coordination increase.

Physical Growth

As shown in Fig. 16.1, physical growth in middle childhood is uniform.

Height

Height increases from an average of 45 inches at age six to about 60 inches at age thirteen.

Weight

In middle childhood one observes a continuous and stable

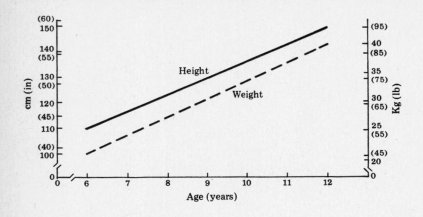

Fig. 16.1

gain in weight. The average six-year-old weighs approximately 45 pounds, while the average child on his or her thirteenth birthday weighs approximately 95 pounds.

Body Proportions

As the child ages from six to twelve, he or she develops a body that is like that of a small adult. The body proportions of a twelve-year-old are nearly the ratios one observes in the adult.

Gender Differences in Growth

The growth of boys and girls is parallel until the average age of nine and one-half. Between eight and one-half and eleven and one-half years of age, girls experience a prepubescent growth spurt. On the average, girls are taller and heavier than boys of the same age. This difference is maintained until about the age of thirteen. By that age, boys, who experience the same growth spurt between the ages of ten and one-half and fourteen and one-half, catch up and surpass the girls in both height and weight.

Because of the growth spurt experienced by girls shortly after their ninth birthday, it is not uncommon to see girls of ten and eleven years old who are superior in athletic competition to their male peers. This fact has both positive and negative consequences. On the one hand, it provides girls the opportunity to participate effectively in activities such as Little League baseball and soccer. On the other hand, some boys may react adversely to girls who are their physical superiors. For a young girl who may be developing a romantic interest in boys, there may be a conflict between the expression of her natural physical superiority and her emerging desire for heterosexual relationships.

Effect of Growth Spurts on Personality

Whether a child is an early or a late physical maturer may have significant effects on his or her later personality. The effects of early or late maturing differs in boys and girls.

Early Maturers

Girls who mature early often develop aggressive behavior patterns that carry over into their adult personalities. Those aggressive patterns may be viewed by others as undesirable personality characteristics. In contrast, boys who mature early exhibit characteristics that allow them to be leaders in their group. Those leadership experiences stay with the early-maturing boy and are viewed as positive personality characteristics in the adult life of the individual.

Late Maturers

Late-maturing boys and girls exhibit patterns of personality in their adult life different from those of early maturers. The late-maturing girl tends to adjust well to her development and continue with her pattern of normal social and sexual adjustment as she moves into adulthood. The late-maturing boy, however, may maintain his little-boy personality long after he has achieved physical maturity. Of course, the maintenance of that personality is viewed as a sign of poor adjustment in the adult male.

Neurological Development

The neurological system of the child is near full maturity by the time he or she reaches middle childhood. Although some myelinization of nerves continues through adolescence, that process for the most part is complete by the age of six or eight.

When injuries occur to the brain of the young child, recovery is rapid and the prognosis for complete recovery is good. This ability of the child to overcome brain damage stems from the fact that in infancy and early childhood, the brain is growing rapidly; thus, it can compensate in its growth to account for the injuries it sustains. In contrast, chances of recovery from brain injuries suffered toward the end of middle childhood are poor. The brain has accomplished its task of growth and cannot compensate for the injuries.

Motor Development

Throughout middle childhood, children's bones become longer, their muscles become larger, and children become consistently quicker, stronger, and more agile. Studies of children's reaction time according to age demonstrates this growth.

The reaction time of a five-year-old child is about twice that of the adult. If a five-year-old child wants to catch a ball thrown from ten feet away at the speed of 15 feet per second, he or she will need to begin reacting to the ball as soon as it leaves the thrower's hand. In contrast, an adult could very well ignore the ball until it was halfway between the thrower and himself or herself. This improvement in reaction time observed during middle childhood accounts for many of the simultaneous improvements observed in the athletic ability of children as they age from six to twelve.

Studies of strength provide data consistent with these findings. The average grip of a six-year-old boy is 9.66 pounds; of a nine-year-old, 14.94 pounds; and of a twelve-year-old, 20.38 pounds. Notice that this increase in strength is a nearly linear function of the age of the child.

Of particular interest to many persons concerned with educational problems in children is the relationship of motor skills and educational accomplishments. Often these educators will become concerned when children are unable to perform such tasks as rhythmically hopping from one foot to another. However, research suggests that only 50 percent of six-year-old girls and 15 percent of six-year-old boys can perform that task. By the age of nine, those percentages have increased to 90 percent and 67 percent, respectively. Thus, while significant increases in performance do occur in middle childhood, it is not unusual to find normally maturing boys exhibiting a certain amount of poor coordination.

In throwing a ball, seven-year-old boys will usually outperform their female peers by a little over 8 feet on the average. By the age of eleven, boys can throw a ball 94 feet on the average, while girls can throw a ball only about 58 feet.

Asked to balance on one foot with their eyes shut or to walk along a 2 × 4 board, girls will tend to outperform boys at all age levels. However, the performance of all children on these balance and coordination tasks improves with age.

CHAPTER 17

Cognitive and Perceptual Development in Middle Childhood

A significant change occurs in the thinking of children between the ages of five and seven—the use of a system of logic that Piaget called concrete operations. As the child discovers more and more of these principles of logical thinking, he or she can solve problems of increasing complexity and wider variety.

Concrete operations are enhanced by other advances associated with middle childhood. These are improved memory, higher levels of attention and concentration, greater facility in generating hypotheses, and the ability to ignore irrelevant information.

Characteristics of Middle Childhood Cognition

The changes that occur in the thinking of children from about age five to age seven overcome the limitations that inhibit the effective cognitive functioning of the younger preoperational child.

Concrete Operations

Initially, the world of middle childhood, like that of the preoperational child, is still concrete. The problems that can be solved are still those that can be experienced in concrete ways. However, as the six-year-old matures toward the age of twelve, he or she is better able to use concrete thinking to deal with abstract concepts.

Diminished Egocentrism

Unlike younger, preoperational children, children in middle childhood no longer view the world from their own unique vantage point. They are able to realize that others perceive the world differently. As the children become older, they may even seek out an understanding of other perspectives in order to appreciate more fully the problem at hand.

Teachers of children as young as six or seven years of age are beginning to recognize that their students are not as egocentric as was once believed. When one child in the class is being picked on by others, for example, teachers find that they are able to ask their students and obtain a realistic response to the question "How do you believe it makes another person feel to be picked on?" Directing the aggressors' attention toward the feelings of the person they are attacking often helps to reconcile conflicts among children who have reached the age of six or seven.

Decentration

Children of seven are able to decentrate. They can consider

more than one aspect of a problem at the same time, and their attention is not dominated by the perceptual characteristics of a stimulus array. In essence, they can look from one tree to another rather than focusing on the biggest tree. In so doing, they can see the forest as well as the individual trees.

A child, for example, is given an odd-shaped bottle of juice and a second bottle that is a standard shape. The standard bottle actually contains more juice than the odd one. When asked which bottle contains more juice, the child of four or five might well pick the odd-shaped bottle. The oddness of its shape would attract the child's attention and dominate the decision-making process. Children of seven or eight would be more likely to say that they were unsure of the answer or to give a correct answer. They would not be dominated in their decision- making by the perceptual salience of the odd-shaped bottle, but instead would shift their attention to characteristics of the situation more relevant to the problem's solution.

Causality

Children at this age begin to understand cause-and-effect relationships with increasing sophistication. They understand this in terms of physical action (hitting a ball makes it go faster), in terms of time (the concepts of "not now," "soon," and "later") and in terms of space (two blocks cannot be in the same place at the same time). This ability helps them piece together the logical world with a sense of interconnectedness that is lacking at earlier cognitive levels of functioning.

Attention to Transition As Well As States

An important acquisition in the cognition of middle childhood is the ability to conceptualize both the states through which one moves in getting from one situation to another and the processes that allow for those changes to take place.

In disciplining a child, it is the parent's intent to teach the child the consequences of his or her act so that the anticipation of those consequences will inhibit the action on subsequent occasions. A young child is hard pressed to acquire the complex understanding of why discipline follows certain actions; however, by the age of seven or eight, the child can both explain and understand specific reasons for punishment.

Reversibility

One critical consequence of the child's ability to conceptualize the transitions that exist between states as well as the states themselves is the understanding of the concept of reversibility. In addition to symbolizing the transition from state one to state two, the child can symbolically represent the reverse transition, which returns things to their original state.

A six-year-old child is confronted with a conservation-of-liquid problem in which two identical glasses, A and B, are filled equally with liquid. The contents of glass A are poured into a third glass, C, which is taller and thinner than the original glasses. After observing this transfer, the child is asked, "Is there the same amount of liquid in glass C as in glass B, or is there more, or is there less?" The child not only responds correctly that the two glasses have the same quantity of liquid, but justifies the response using the logic of reversed operations: "They're equal. If I poured the liquid back into glass A, they would be the same again."

Logical (Concrete) Operations

According to Piaget's theory, thinking in middle childhood is characterized by the use of an organized system of logic to structure and manipulate objects and events in the world. Piaget described the thinking processes used in this period as concrete cognitive operations, and the period of middle childhood is often referred to as the period of concrete operations.

Logical Operations Defined

A cognitive operation is similar, but not limited to, mathematical operations of addition, subtraction, multiplication, and division. A cognitive operation, like a mathematical operation, possesses the property that once a simple principle is understood, it can be applied to the solution of an infinite number of problems.

A child learns to add together any two single-digit numbers (3 + 4 =), and also learns the principle of carrying. With the discovery of these simple principles, it is possible for the child to add together any set of whole numbers.

The transition from preoperational to concrete operational thought may involve the discovery of only a few operations, but the acquisition of those operations affects the way the child goes about solving a vast array of problems.

Expanding Operations

Changes that occur within the period of concrete operations reflect the continued discovery of concrete operations; but equally important, they reflect the use of those operations already acquired under an ever-widening variety of conditions.

In a conservation-of-quantity task, a child is shown two equal balls of clay. One ball is then rolled into a long sausage shape, and the child is asked if the two balls contain equal quantities of clay. The preoperational child incorrectly responds that following the clay ball's change of shape the two pieces of clay have different quantities. The child of five or six, who has just acquired an understanding of a concrete operation, will provide a correct response.

However, if the question asked of that child is whether or not the two balls of clay are of equivalent weight, he or she will continue to make errors. The ability to conserve weight does not emerge until the age of eight. Conservation of volume, in which the question asked of the child concerns which of the clay balls will displace more water, does not emerge until the age of eleven or twelve.

Groupings of Concrete Operations

The concrete operations discovered by a child can be divided into eight groups. Each group contains a set of interrelated operations that can be applied in the solution of particular types of problems. Four of the eight groups apply to problems that concern classes of objects, while the other four groups apply to problems that concern the ordinal relationship among objects or events. Although it is beyond the scope of this book to provide a detailed description of all eight groups, a representative sample will be discussed to provide the reader with examples of concrete operations and their uses.

Primary Class Addition

Let us say that there is a class of living things that we will call fish. We will label those living things we call fish (F). Because living things must be either fish or not fish, there is a second class of living things we will label (F'), signifying living things that are not fish. Notice that if I join all the fish (F) together with all the nonfish (F'), I have all the living things (L). That is, $(F) + (F') = (L)$.

This joining of elements from two classes to form a larger class is called the operation of primary class addition. Having joined the elements of two classes together, we can reverse that class addition operation by using a class subtraction operation that separates the superordinate class (L) into its component parts: $(L) - (F') = (F)$. For each operation, there is always a second operation that allows the first to be reversed. This property is called *reversibility*. The ability of the child to reverse operations is one of the milestones of concrete operational thought. Knowledge of the operations in the group of primary class addition allows children to solve problems for which they previously produced errors.

For example, a child is shown a set of wooden beads, some of which are brown and some of which are red. She indicates that the red beads are wooden and the brown beads are wooden. However, when asked if there would be any wooden beads left if all the red ones were removed, the child answers, "No." This child has not appropriately applied the reverse operation of primary class addition and is preoperational in her thinking. Thus, red beads + brown beads = wooden beads; wooden beads − red beads = no beads.

The child who is in the period of concrete operations, however, correctly says, "Yes, the brown wooden beads would be left." This child has used the reverse operation of primary class addition. Thus, brown beads + red beads = wooden beads; therefore, wooden beads − red beads = brown beads.

Class Multiplication

We sometimes group objects or events together because they share two or more common characteristics. For example, I have a set of pictures, some of which are flowers (F), some of which are butterflies (B). Some of the pictures are red (R) and some are yellow (Y). I formed four piles of pictures: red butterflies (RB), red flowers (RF), yellow butterflies (YB), and yellow flowers (YF). The pictures in each pile or class share in common two characteristics, color and content. This type of organizational scheme is often depicted by a matrix. (See Fig. 17.1.)

The creation of a matrixlike scheme of categorization is useful in the solution of many problems. It can be constructed by the use of operations referred to as class multiplication. As in the case of primary class addition, class multiplication can be reversed.

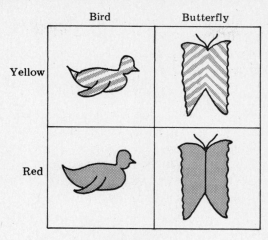

Fig. 17.1

A child is shown the incomplete matrix depicted in Fig. 17.2 and asked which of the two objects below the matrix fits into the empty space. A child not utilizing the class multiplication opera-

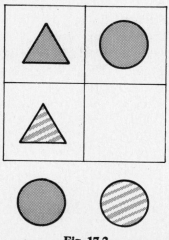

Fig. 17.2

tion will often respond incorrectly by attending to one or the other of the defining characteristics of each class, but not both. A child who uses the class multiplication operation, however, will respond correctly.

Addition of Relationships (Transitivity)

Consider the following problem: Bill is older than John. John is older than Fred. Who is older, Bill or Fred?

The solution to this problem requires combining the relational information contained in the first and second statements. The combination of that relational information involves the operation of relational addition, or transitivity.

Using symbolic representations to depict those relationships, the problem could be solved as follows:

$$(a > b) + (b > c) = (a > c).$$

A variety of problems call for solutions based on the utilization of this logical operation. The preoperational child does not use the operation and thus arrives at inappropriate solutions to those problems. The child in the period of concrete operations can, and does, solve these same problems.

A child is shown two sticks: a short yellow one and a longer red one (Fig.17.3, Phase l). Then the child is shown the red stick

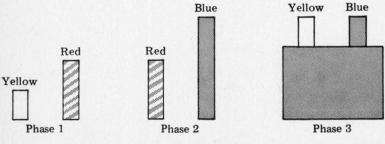

Fig. 17.3

and a longer blue one (Phase 2). Finally, (Phase 3), the child is shown the yellow and blue sticks in a special holder that hides their length and is asked to point to the longer of the two. The preoperational child will guess at this answer, sometimes correctly and sometimes incorrectly. The child in the period of concrete operational thought, however, will use the available system of logic, apply appropriate operations, and consistently arrive at the correct answer.

Children are given three objects of equal size but with different weights. Object A is the lightest and Object C the heaviest. They are told to place the objects in a row, with the heaviest at one end and the lightest at the other. The only trick to solving this problem is that the children can lift only two objects at a time. Preoperational children may lift Object A and find A lighter than Object B. They may then lift Object A and C and find A lighter than C. Following those observations the children will immediately place the objects in the order A, B, C.

While this answer is correct, on another occasion the same children will place the same objects in the order A, C, B. Preoperational children have not arrived at the answer using operational logic; thus, they are inconsistent in their responses. Children in the period of concrete operations lift A and B to discover that A is lighter, and lift A and C to discover that A is lighter. They know, however, that this information is irrelevant in determining how to place the objects in order. To solve that problem, they must know the relative weight of B and C. They lift B and C, discover that B is lighter than C, and correctly order the objects A, B, C.

Extralogical Development

While Piaget emphasized the acquisition of concrete operations as a basic change that demarcates the thinking of middle childhood, others emphasize that problem solving depends on many processes in addition to logical operations. These researchers believed the increased efficiency of these extralogical processes produces the changes in thinking observed in middle childhood. For example, Jerome Kagan describes the child of seven as having acquired better "executive capabilities" to organize and direct those extralogical processes.

The extralogical processes discussed below are attentional processes, memory, classification, hypothesis generation, and evaluation.

Attentional Processes

The attention of children in middle childhood changes in four ways:

Tune-Out Information

The child is better able than younger children to ignore irrelevant information. Children in kindergarten, second grade, and fourth grade listen to two voices, a man's and a woman's, simultaneously speaking different words. Before hearing this presentation, the children are told that they will be asked to report only the word spoken by the woman's voice. The accuracy of reporting that word improves with age. Furthermore, the number of errors resulting from the report of words spoken by the male voice decreases with age. Apparently, older children are better able than younger children to filter out the irrelevant information.

Selective Attention

Even when the child does not tune out incoming information, the older child is better able to respond only to those aspects of the stimulation that are important to the solution of a problem. This skill increases with age. While a six-year-old is better than a four-year-old at selective responding, a twelve-year-old is better than either of these younger children.

Flexibility

Another attentional characteristic whose development enhances problem-solving capabilities is attention flexibility—the extent to which an individual can shift attention from one characteristic of a problem to another in order to arrive at a correct solution.

A problem is presented to a child. The solution requires that the child pay attention to the size of objects in the problem. Having solved that problem, the child is given another problem in which attention to object size is irrelevant to the solution but attention to the number of objects in the problem is important. Older children are better able than younger children to make this attentional shift; thus, they solve the second problem more easily.

Reduced Perceptual Dominance

A fourth change in attention is the child's movement away from attentional processes dominated by salient physical properties of the stimulus. The stimulus characteristics of color, shape, size, brightness, and so on are quick to attract the attention of young children. However, many problems are not solved by attending to those stimulus characteristics. With increased age and experience, the child seeking a problem's solution discovers, and subsequently attends to, more subtle stimulus properties, such as the angles between lines, the orientation of objects in space, or the relative size of two objects.

Memory

Coding Strategies

The capacity for memory is a second extralogical process that improves significantly around the age of six or seven. This improved memory results from improvements in coding strategies. The production deficiencies noted in young children are overcome by children of six or seven, and they spontaneously use effective coding strategies rather than requiring that those strategies be imposed upon them. There are three important strategies:

1. *Chunking.* When young children hear the string of numbers 5, 4, 0, 4, 2, 7, 2, 0, 0, they may be unable to remember them, for they are heard as nine separate numbers. Older children, however, may group the numbers as follows: 540- 427-200. When this is done the nine separate numbers become three units, which can be remembered much more easily.

2. *Associating things to be remembered with well-learned information already in storage.* In this strategy, recall of the new information is generated by recall of the old. To remember the license plate number JK 1963, for example, one might remember that (J)ohn (K)ennedy was assassinated in 1963.

3. *Clustering information for coding purposes.* A young child is shown twenty pictures; five are animals, five are plants, five are buildings, five are fruits. The child will recall a few of these pictures, and those recalled may come from all four classes. An older child, however, will recall more pictures and, regardless of their order of presentation, will tend to recall the pictures in clusters based on their content: first animals, then fruit, and so on.

Role of Memory in Cognition

The importance of memory in those capacities Piaget called concrete operations is exemplified by the following observation:

Children are given a problem whose solution requires the use of the logical operation of relational addition. Specifically, the children are shown two sticks, a shorter yellow stick and a longer blue stick. Subsequently, they are shown the blue sticks and a still longer red stick. Finally, they are asked, "Which stick is longer, the blue or the red?"

As Piaget would predict, four- to six-year-old children do not solve the problem correctly. However, those children who do not demonstrate the use of the logical operation of relational addition tend not to remember the two relationships originally shown to them, that is, (yellow/blue) and (blue/red). When children the same age are given extensive training in remembering those initial pieces of information, they solve the transitivity problem in the same way older children would.

Classification

As children become older, they tend to group objects and events together on the basis of characteristics that formerly were not used for grouping. These new classification patterns are more conducive to solving problems in an adultlike manner.

Subordinate Classification

An intelligence test might ask, "How are an elephant and a giraffe alike?" Young children are likely to respond that the elephant and giraffe are alike because they have four legs, because they can reach high into a tree, or because they are both found in the jungle. Older children are apt to say that the two objects are alike because they are both animals. This is called a superordinate classification because the relationship is based on an abstract attribute shared by the two objects or events.

Analytic and Functional Classifications

When objects are classified together because they share a similar physical property, that classification is referred to as an analytic similarity. When objects are classified as belonging together because they are found in similar locations, the classification is referred to as a functional-locational relationship. The use of analytic and superordinate classifications increases with age, while the use of functional classification decreases with age.

Jerome Kagan constructed many triads of pictures similar to those in Fig. 17.4. In the first triad, pictures (a) and (b) are related in that the squirrel lives in the tree (a functional relationship); (a) and (c) are related in that both are animals (a superordinate class relationship). In triad two, pictures (d) and (e) are related because both are writing instruments (a superordinate class relationship), while (d) and (f) are similar because both depict feathers (an analytic relationship).

Kagan showed each picture triad to a child and asked which two pictures went together. Older children used more analytic and superordinate classifications to answer the questions than did younger children, while the number of functionally based classifications decreased with age. When words symbolic of the pictures were used rather than the pictures themselves, older children used more superordinate than analytic classifications.

Hypothesis Generation

Effective hypothesis generation facilitates problem solving. The young child tends to establish hypotheses in a trial-and-error fashion, while older children and adults are able to ask questions whose answers provide a great deal of information about how one should proceed to arrive at solutions to problems.

In the game of Twenty Questions, one person thinks of an object, and the other person attempts to discover the target object by asking a series of questions that can be answered "Yes" or "No." When young children play this game, from their first questions onward they will guess specific objects to be the target: "Is it the lamp?" "No." "Is it the cup?" "No." This hypothesis-generation strategy is very ineffective. One might go through the entire list of potential objects to arrive at a solution.

In contrast, older children ask questions to which the answers significantly narrow down the range of possible solutions to the

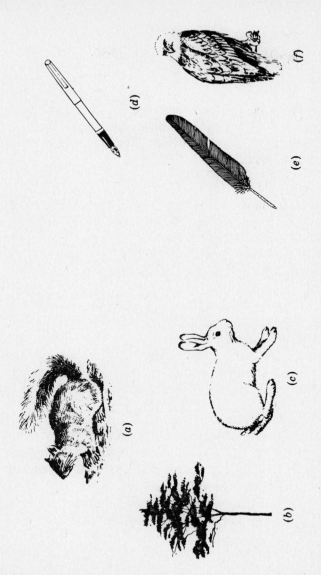

Fig. 17.4

problem: "Is it or was it alive?" "No." "Is it in the front half of the room?" "Yes."

Evaluation

Age differences exist in the styles used to evaluate solutions to problems. In addition, people within the same age group differ systematically in their cognitive style. Two evaluative styles have been studied extensively.

Impulsivity

As children become older, they become less impulsive in judging the solution to a problem as being correct or incorrect. Although impulsivity decreases with age for all people, individuals who are the most impulsive at one age continue to be the most impulsive individuals within their age group as they become older.

A child is shown a standard picture and is asked to select from among a series of other similar pictures one that is identical to the standard. Because all the pictures are very similar, the correct response requires concentration. The young child responds more quickly than the older child to the problem, but also makes more errors.

Field Dependence

Some individuals are more influenced than others by perceptual information extraneous to a problem's solution but present in the environment. Those people are said to be field dependent. Persons who can ignore irrelevant perceptual information in the environment when making a judgment are said to be field independent. With increased age, children become more field independent.

As is true for impulsivity, however, there is evidence that in spite of increased absolute field independence, persons who are the most field dependent in relation to their peers at one age tend to remain the most field dependent within their age group as they become older.

CHAPTER 18

Language Acquisition in Middle Childhood

It has often been suggested that except for increases in vocabulary, the acquisition of language knowledge is complete by the age of six. However, this premise has been disproved in recent years. There is now general agreement that additional language development occurs after the age of six and may continue through adolescence. This chapter considers the phonologic, semantic, and syntactic components of advanced language development.

Phonology

Although six-year-olds can comprehend and produce nearly all the sounds of a language, a few sounds and sound combinations still give them trouble. Often these troublesome sounds will be produced adequately when they occur at the beginning of words, but will be difficult to produce when they occur in the middle of a word, and impossible to produce when they occur at the end of a word.

The following are some sounds that children of different ages do not produce adequately in all word positions:

Six-year-olds:	*Seven-year-olds*:	*Eight-year-olds*:
/t/ as in tin	/th/ as in thin	/hw/ as in white
/th/ as in this	/z/ as in zip	
/v/ as in above	/zh/ as in vision	
/l/ as in little	/j/ as in jump	

One of the most difficult sounds for children even as old as nine or ten is that corresponding to /elfth/, as in *twelfth*.

When sounds are mispronounced, the substituted sound closely resembles the mispronounced one but is easier to produce. It is as if the child has a good idea about the gross distinctions among sounds but has not fully mastered some of the subtle differences.

The most common substitutions in phoneme production are: /f/ for /th/ and /v/ (paf for path, or glof for glove); /th/ for /s/ (kith for kiss); /k/ for /t/ (rak for rat) and /n/ for /m/ (sane for same).

Semantics

Of course, the vocabulary of the child improves dramatically from age six through age twelve. It is estimated that each year the child adds nearly 1,000 words to his or her personal dictionary. However, semantic development during middle childhood involves more than simply adding words to a vocabulary. It also involves changes in the meaning attributed to the words. The same word often has a different meaning to an eight- and to a twelve-year-old. This is illustrated clearly in how we learn to use parts of speech called intensifiers.

Consider this sentence: "That box is slightly larger than this box, which is large itself." Modifiers like *rather*, *slightly*, *some-*

what, *unusually*, *very*, and *extremely* denote the extensiveness of the word they modify. If one were to construct a scale to depict the extensiveness represented by each word, that scale would be different for adults and children. First-grade children (age six) perceive the word *rather* to mean "less than slightly," which means the same as *somewhat*. For those same children, the words *very* and *extremely* have the same meaning, and both reflect greater extensiveness than the word *unusually*. Fourth-graders (age ten) perceive the words *rather* and *somewhat* to be equal, and both to mean greater extensiveness than the intensifier *slightly*. *Very* and *unusually* mean the same thing to the fourth-grader, and both depict less extensiveness than the word *extremely*. College students differentiate between the words *rather* and *somewhat*, and consider *unusually* to mean the same as *extremely*.

Some words, such as *hard*, have both a physical meaning and a meaning that denotes a psychological state, as in "It was a hard floor" and "He was hard to understand." Five- and six-year-old children do not use these words to denote their psychological meaning, nor do they understand the psychological meaning attributable to the words. By seven or eight, children begin using the words to denote both physical and psychological meanings, but they cannot describe the relationship that exists between the two meanings. It is not until the age of ten or eleven that most children consistently use these words appropriately and convey an adult understanding of their meanings.

We also see signs of development in how children learn to use connective words. Cause-effect relationships are denoted by adults through the use of connective words such as *because*, *if*, *so*, and so on: "John ran away because I yelled at him;" "I obtained a job, so I will not be able to sleep late tomorrow." Words such as *then* denote the temporal sequence of events: "I fell down, then I started to cry." Although many sentences produced by children appropriately use words such as *because*, *if*, *so*, *therefore*, and so on, careful examination reveals that these words do not denote cause-effect relationships in the language of middle childhood. Instead, these words merely indicate a temporal relationship of one event following another (such as that denoted by the word *then*) or the occurrence of two events within a similar time frame (as denoted by the word *and*).

Syntax

For many years, it was believed that knowledge concerning syntax was fully acquired prior to the age of six. However, it is now generally agreed that syntactical development continues gradually beyond the age of six, with two major growth spurts occurring at about six and again at eleven or twelve years of age. These growth spurts are interesting in light of the simultaneous occurrence of cognitive growth spurts. This common growth pattern reflects the close relationship between linguistic and cognitive development.

The syntactic development that occurs in middle childhood consists primarily of (1) increasing the complexity of sentence units used in speech, by using embedded sentences and modification in noun phrases; (2) learning exceptions to general syntactic rules; and (3) increasing the use of syntactic structures seldom used even in adult speech.

The Minimum Distance Principle

The sentence "Peter told Fred to wash" contains two nouns. One noun (Peter) is the subject of the verb *told*. The second noun (Fred) is the subject of the infinitive *to wash*. To understand this sentence, one must have a rule to specify the noun that is associated with each verb. In most sentences, the appropriate rule is called the minimal distance principle: The noun associated with the verb is that which is closest to it.

When the minimal distance principle applies, children as young as five or six comprehend sentences with more than one verb. However, some verbs disobey the minimal distance principle, as in the sentence "Peter promised Fred to wash." In this sentence the principle is violated, because Peter does both the promising and the washing. Six-year-old children will confuse the meaning of this sentence by applying the minimal distance principle in an inappropriate situation. They will interpret the sentence to mean that Peter is promising that Fred will wash. Not until the age of seven or eight will sentences that are exceptions to that principle be consistently understood.

The verb *ask* exemplifies an even more difficult problem in the application of the minimal distance principle described above. When *ask* is used in sentences such as "John asked Peter to run," the minimal distance principle applies. However, when *ask* is used in a sentence such as "John asked Peter what to do," the minimal distance principle is violated. John, not Peter, is the person who will engage in the doing. The sentence could be paraphrased, "John asked Peter what he [John] could do." Children acquire the ability to consistently understand sentences that use the word *ask* after they have learned to understand sentences that employ the word *promise*, as that described above.

The Passive Voice

Children at an early age can understand sentences in the active voice, such as "Fritz hit Frieda." But children have age-related difficulty understanding sentences in the passive voice, such as "Frieda was hit by Fritz." Although the rules needed to understand passive sentences are acquired at about the age of six, children do not apply them perfectly.

However, semantic restrictions allow children of five or six to understand some passive sentences. "The steak was eaten by Jason" is understood, as is "Jason ate the steak," because it would not make semantic sense to have a steak doing the eating. But not until the age of eight or nine do children consistently comprehend passive sentences whose meanings are not dictated by semantic considerations. The sentence "Frieda was hit by Fritz" is an example of a passive sentence whose meaning is not dictated by semantic considerations. No characteristic of the nouns *Fritz* and *Frieda* dictate the actor in the sentence.

CHAPTER 19

Personality and Social Development in Middle Childhood

By the time children enter school, they have become relatively independent. They are better able to handle the failure that sometimes follows risk-taking, and they have made adjustments to social reality. As we saw in Chapter 15, the kind of parenting children receive at this time has an important effect on these aspects of development.

In the middle years, patterns of parenting continue to have an impact on social and personal growth. Other strong influences are birth order, peer relationships, and mass media. This chapter discusses these factors in social and personal attainments and looks at some of the adjustment problems of this period.

Characteristics of Middle Childhood

Sigmund Freud called the middle years of childhood the

latency period; to Erik Erikson, they are a time in which a child resolves the conflict of industry versus inferiority. These years have also been described as a period of consolidation, or crystallization, of personality.

Latency Period

According to psychoanalytic theory, the latency period is a time when the libidinal energy of the individual is not directed toward any particular body part, but instead lies dormant, waiting for the onset of adolescence. Just how dormant sexual interest is at this stage has been debated by psychologists over the years. Certainly, children of ages six through twelve are curious about sex and may engage in sex play.

The Conflict of Industry vs. Inferiority

Erikson characterized the period of middle childhood as a stage in which children discover that they are capable of producing something and that through production they can achieve social acceptance and a feeling of self-worth. This effort to produce is called industry; its failure results in feelings of inferiority.

The production can be material, such as producing a piece of artwork at school or weeding a garden. It may be an intellectual effort, such as getting good grades at school. Or, it may be behavioral, such as demonstrating (to please the parents, no doubt) quiet and tranquillity at home. If a child does not discover his or her potential for industry, the result will be a feeling of inferiority.

Consolidation

Because the personality of the child is not in a dramatic state of flux during the elementary years, personality tends to stabilize

Table 19.1

Child Behavior	Adult Behavior
Boys	
Behavior disorganization and aggression	Anger arousal
Heterosexuality	Sexual behavior
Achievement	Intellectual concern
Sex-typed activity	Sex-typed activity
Spontaneity	Spontaneity
Girls	
Achievement	Intellectual concern
Sex-typed activity	Sex-typed activity
Spontaneity	Spontaneity
Passivity	Withdrawal

into that pattern which characterizes the child throughout the later period of his or her youth.

A longitudinal study measured various personality traits of children in middle childhood and again when the individuals were adults. Table 19.1 provides a list of childhood traits that correlate 0.4 or better with corresponding traits in the adult.

The Changing World of Middle Childhood

In this section, we will explore the impact on children's development of parents, the family, and the social and cultural worlds of the child.

Patterns of Parenting

Patterns of parenting and their impact on younger children were discussed in Chapter 15. The two dimensions that can be used to describe parenting patterns that influence development in middle childhood are acceptance-rejection (warmth-hostility)

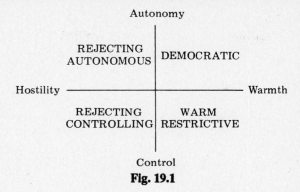

Fig. 19.1

and control-autonomy. By constructing a graph (see Fig. 19.1) with these two dimensions represented by the x and y axes, it is possible to characterize any parenting pattern as a point on the graph. The fact that there are an infinite number of points on this graph indicates that there are an infinite number of parenting styles. However, it is possible to discuss parenting styles representative of each of the four quadrants of the graph.

Democratic Parents

Democratic parents are similar to the authoritative parents described by Baumrind and discussed in Chapter 15. They are accepting of their children, but at the same time, they set limits for the children and maintain a structured environment within which the children have some freedom of choice. The children of democratic parents tend to be active, outgoing, socially assertive, independent, and creative. While they may be somewhat aggressive, they are not generally hostile.

However, all democratic parents do not produce the same type of children. If the control they exert is firm, children of democratic parents tend to be responsible, self-confident, and purposeful. However, if that control is lax and inconsistent, the children tend to be more assertive individuals who are not as well organized as they might be, are lacking in goal-directed behavior, and are a bit of a behavior problem. In contrast to many other behavior problems, however, the children's difficulties stem from a lack of control rather than an overabundance of hostility.

Warm but Restrictive Parents

Warm but restrictive parents are loving persons who want so much to be good parents that they overcontrol their children. It seems that such parents are not willing to allow their children to take risks and make mistakes because such mistakes would reflect negatively on their worth as parents. The children of warm but restrictive parents tend to be highly dependent, less friendly or creative than other children, and either highly persistent in completing tasks or else entirely lacking in persistence.

Although these children do not manifest overt signs of aggression during middle childhood, they do demonstrate hostility in their fantasies. One wonders whether this hostility is exhibited later in life through passive-aggressive acts.

Rejecting and Controlling Parents

Parents who exhibit little love while insisting on rigid control of the children tend to generate anger and hostility in their offspring. However, that anger cannot be exhibited overtly because of the fear the children have of the parents. Instead, the children often turn the anger on themselves. These children often become neurotic, self-punishing individuals who have little confidence in themselves and withdraw from social interactions.

Rejecting and Autonomous Parents

These parents exhibit little love for their children nor do they care enough about their parental role to exert the energy required to try to control the children or provide them with any behavioral guidelines. When control is attempted, it is usually inconsistent and based on irrational expressions of the parents' frustrations, rather than exemplifying guidelines for behavior that can be learned by the children. Rejecting parents who provide little or no structure for their children produce the classic delinquent whose lack of love has resulted in an overabundance of anger, who has little control over his or her behavior, and who consequently exhibits external aggression.

Family Structure

While the parenting patterns of the family play an important role in the child's personality development, the structure of the family is also important.

Parental Absence

The effect on child development resulting from one parent's absence from a family has been a subject of interest for some time. Because the absence of fathers is a the prevalent phenomenon, research in this field has concentrated on it. The impact of a father's absence is different for boys than for girls. For boys, its effects depend on the age at which the father leaves, and for girls, they depend more on the cause of the absence.

Boys. Sons who have absent fathers tend to exhibit more hostility, delinquency, and social ineptness than boys whose fathers are present. Furthermore, boys of absent fathers tend to have greater difficulty with sex-typed behavior than do peers who grew up with their fathers. In contrast to the typical pattern of cognitive skill development, in which boys are better at perceptual motor skills than at verbal skills, boys with absent fathers tend to exhibit a pattern of cognitive skill development similar to girls' patterns; that is, they perform better on verbal than on perceptual motor tasks. These sex-typed patterns are more prevalent among those boys whose fathers are absent prior to their fourth birthday than among those whose father's absence begins after the child has reached his fifth birthday.

Girls. Girls from father-absent homes exhibit more emotional and school problems than those who are raised in homes where the father is present. They maintain a female sex role but act out more of their aggressive feelings, and as adults, they are more dependent than other females. Their relationships with men are also affected by their absent father. In general, these girls will exhibit more anxiety concerning their relationship with men; however, the way in which that anxiety is manifested will depend in part on the reason for the father's absence.

Very often, girls whose fathers are absent because of death respond to that loss by withdrawing from relationships with men. In comparison with other girls, they date at a later age, are less likely as adolescents to engage in sexual activity, and so on. In contrast, although girls of divorced parents are also anxious about their relationships with men, they have a tendency to respond to that anxiety by seeking out male companionship, becoming sexually aggressive, and dating earlier.

Ordinal Position (Birth Order)

Does ordinal position, the order of one's birth in the family, play a role in shaping one's personality and influencing behavior? This question has long been a source of speculation and research. Over one hundred years ago, Francis Galton, investigating great minds for his study of hereditary genius, noted that elder sons were twice as likely as younger ones to achieve academic success. Alfred Adler, whose contributions to theories of personality development and to psychotherapy were substantial, argued that ordinal position is an important factor in personality development.

Adler noted that eldest children are likely to develop leadership qualities in adult life, but because they were "dethroned" in early childhood by the arrival of the second-born, they are also likely to feel insecure and to develop problems later on. Second or middle children, according to Adler, may resent the older child's authority and develop a rebellious nature. Because youngest children never experience being replaced by another sibling, they tend to be spoiled.

Although there have been hundreds of studies on this subject, there is still no general agreement about the specific influences of ordinal position on development. For every finding, it seems, there is often another study that produces conflicting results, for it is difficult to control all the relevant variables, such as the size of the family and differences in age between the siblings being studied.

The Eldest Child. Historically, birth order has played a crucial role in inheritance rights (hence the term "birthright"), marriage, and social position. The first- born male has traditionally held the position of heir to the parent's estate. It is not surprising, then, that the first-born child was the subject of several early studies, most of which found that first-born children tend to be competitive, achievement-oriented, and motivated toward competency.

Stanley Schachter, in a study of affiliation behavior, found that when under stress, first-born and only children are more likely to seek the company of others and to conform to group values than are later-born children. Many studies have shown that first-born children, having had for some period of their early lives only adult models in their immediate families, are more adult- oriented—that is, more at ease socially with adults than with their peers—than are later-born children.

Birth order is only one of several factors, however, that affect personality, and for that reason it is difficult to single out its effects. Some of these other factors are sex of the child, social class, maternal attitude and expectation, and size of family. Still, most of the evidence indicates that first-born girls, though not necessarily first-born boys, do tend to be adult-oriented.

The Middle Child. It is often said that the middle child bears the heaviest burden in the family. The older child, first on the scene, probably enjoyed the undivided attention of the mother.

Because the older child is able to outperform the second child and can usually walk by the time the second child arrives, he or she is probably capable of eliciting more attention from others.

Moreover, the mother of two children is unable to lavish as much attention on the second-born as she did on the eldest. If a third child comes on the scene, the second-born then becomes the middle child, not only competing with the older sibling but also finding that much attention is given to the new arrival. The middle child has been found to suffer a number of problems not typical of others in the family, including a greater dependency need than the youngest or the eldest child.

The Youngest Child. Probably the circumstances surrounding the birth of the youngest child play a more crucial role in development than the simple fact of being the last-born. How many years separate the birth of the previous child from the birth of this child? Are there other siblings around the same age? How old was the mother at the time of the child's birth? All these factors are significant.

A number of researchers have emphasized the advantages of being a last-born child, particularly socialization. Having the opportunity to observe his or her siblings, he or she can learn appropriate social responses through modeling. The youngest also enjoys the benefits of having more experienced parents, who are more comfortable in the role of parenting.

Social Interactions

Middle childhood is characterized by the formation of social groups. Belonging to "the gang" is an important part of the child's life. Identification with this small group is a stabilizing element during middle childhood, when the family unit is no longer continually available to provide stable interpersonal relationships.

Group Structure

Between the ages of six and ten, groups are rather informal, and membership is based more on availability and fortuitous factors (such as being neighbors or being the children of parents who are friends) than on common interests. In its early stages, a "gang" may contain both boys and girls, but by the age of seven or eight, the groups with which children identify will typically be restricted to children of the same age and the same sex. This division of the sexes in their social interactions at approximately age seven or eight is referred to as sex cleavage.

A school in a certain neighborhood draws students from a geographic radius of two miles. The groups that form in the primary grades are often based on the route children take in walking to school. Children who walk together, talk together. These groups are informal in the sense that no official rules exist for membership, nor is there a code of conduct unique to a given group.

At about age ten, groups become more formal. We see the emergence of the structured social groups such as Boy Scouts, Campfire Girls, and so on. In contrast to the younger cliques, these groups are more cohesive. However, like the younger gangs, ten- to twelve-year-olds maintain sex cleavage in their group. Boys in particular strongly reject "feminine" activities; and although girls continue to enjoy activities identified as masculine, they tend to engage in them within the context of all-girl groups.

Popularity

Throughout middle childhood, a social hierarchy among children can be observed. The characteristics of the children at the top of that hierarchy differ for boys and girls, and for girls, those characteristics change with age. For boys of all ages, the characteristics are leadership, enthusiasm, outspokenness, cheerfulness, friendliness, athletic ability, boldness, and daring.

For girls up to the age of nine, the characteristics are friendliness, quietness, lack of bossiness, and lack of quarrelsomeness. For girls over the age of nine, the characteristics are physical attractiveness, physical activity, friendliness, quietness, lack of bossiness, and lack of quarrelsomeness.   We see that the major difference here is the addition of physical attractiveness as a key characteristic of social acceptance.

Social Conformity

Prior to the age of eight, children are fairly autonomous individuals. They are so egocentric that their judgments are influenced little by the judgments of those around them. However, between the ages of eight and twelve there is a marked increase in the extent to which the children's judgments will be influenced by the expressed judgments of others.

In one experiment, children of ages four, eight, and twelve were shown a standard line 6 1/4 inches long and asked to pick from a set of three other lines the one that was the same length as the standard. The alternative choices presented were 6 1/4 inches, 6 1/2 inches, and 8 inches long. Before a child made a choice, four other children responded to the question by picking

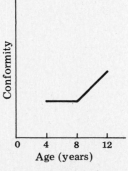

Fig. 19.2

the line 8 inches long as the one that was the same as the standard line. Fig. 19.2 depicts the extent to which children at different ages went along with the group and made incorrect responses.

Influences of Culture

The social development of the child is influenced not only by the family and the peer group but also by the culture, particularly the mass media, as expressed through films, radio, music, and television. The mass media provide important information about expected behaviors and values to the child. This information may agree with or contradict other information and values. When it agrees, it reinforces what the child is learning at home or at school. When it contradicts, it may cause the child to question some values or to feel a sense of conflict between what he or she has learned and the way he or she wants to act.

The average school-age child spends more time watching TV than in the performance of any other single activity. Television and films provide role models for social behavior. Children of this age not only imitate what they see but begin to sense it as a portrayal of the real world, of life, and as a guide of what is expected in terms of their reactions to other people. Studies have demonstrated that aggression and gender role development are influenced by what children see on TV.

Moral Development

In discussing moral development, one must distinguish between judgments and behavior. *Moral judgment* refers to the judgment an individual makes about the morality of a behavior or about the worthiness of a punishment. *Moral behavior* refers to the specific behaviors in which one actually engages. For example, Martin Heidegger, a brilliant philosopher, was a great moral theorist who was able to justify at a high intellectual level his blatantly immoral behavior of burning books written by Jews during the Nazi regime.

Moral Judgment

Moral judgment is a cognitive act, and as such, it has been studied most intently by researchers who emphasize the importance of cognition in development.

Piagetian Morality

Jean Piaget described three stages of moral development through which children pass: premoral judgment, moral realism, and moral subjectivism. For Piaget, passage from one stage to another was dependent upon the changing cognitive capacities of the child.

Premoral Judgment. Piaget suggested that the young child does not possess the cognitive capacities or inclinations to make moral judgments; thus, the young child seemingly has no morality. Because this period is characteristic of the preoperational child, it has been discussed in Chapters 10 and 15.

Moral Realism. As the child enters the period of concrete operations during the early years of middle childhood, he or she becomes a moral realist. Moral realism is characterized by three qualities.

1. A belief that rules are omnipotent and cannot be changed. A boy of seven is asked to describe the rules that apply to going to bed. He says that seven-year-olds go to bed at 8 p.m. When questioned about the possibility of that rule being changed because of a special event, he denies that it can be changed or at least denies that such a change would be legitimate.

2. A tendency to evaluate actions as good or bad on the basis of their outcomes rather than the intentions of the actor. In a classic experiment reported by Jean Piaget, children were told

two stories about boys who got into trouble. In one story, a boy had the good intention of helping his father, but in trying to help, he made a big mess. Another boy, engaged in behavior with bad intentions, accidentally made a small mess. The experimental subject was asked which boy was the naughtier. Young children tend to base their judgments on the amount of mess that was created and tend to ignore the intention of the child.

3. A belief that punishment is controlled by nature and an inevitable result of negative behavior. A child of seven is told, "A boy steals a candy bar from a store and runs away. As he runs across the street, he is hit by a car." The child is then asked why the car hit the boy, and she responds, "Because he stole the candy bar."

To these moral realists, punishment is retributive. Its purpose is to make the offender suffer in accordance with the committed offense, rather than to serve as a tool for changing future behavior. The punishment suggested by these children is typically harsh, physical, and has no relationship to the offense itself, nor do the children suggest that the person being punished be informed about the relationship between the offense and the punishment. For example, a child is told that another child lied to the teacher about why he had not completed an assignment. The child is then asked to describe a punishment for the liar. The seven- to eight-year-old child would be likely to suggest a whipping.

Moral Subjectivism. The middle years of middle childhood are a period of transition from the stage of moral realism to the stage of moral subjectivism. This more mature stage is characterized by the following qualities:

1. Rules are viewed as being creations of people, for the benefit of people. As such, they can be altered by mutual

consent or by recognized legal processes to meet the changing needs of those they serve. While the younger child sees rules as immutable, the older child recognizes their utility and potential for flexibility and revision.

Some ten- to twelve-year-old boys are asked to describe the rules of a game. After carefully describing the rules in detail, they are asked if the game will be legitimate if certain rules are changed to accommodate some unique circumstances. While a child in an earlier stage of moral development would deny the legitimacy of those changes, the moral subjectivist would accept the new game as different but legitimate.

2. Value judgments about behavior are based on the intention behind that behavior as well as the outcome of the action. A twelve-year-old, unlike a younger child, would judge the child whose positive intention resulted in a terrible outcome to be less guilty than the child whose bad intentions resulted in only a minimal problem.

3. Punishment prescribed by moral subjectivists will more likely fit the crime and will serve as a lesson for the offender. A child is asked to prescribe a punishment for a girl who goes to a movie rather than fulfilling her family responsibility to mow the lawn. A moral subjectivist, taking circumstances into account, would likely suggest that the girl be denied the right to go to a movie for two weeks and that she be required to wash the car as well as to mow the lawn.

Kohlberg Morality

Lawrence Kohlberg agreed with Piaget that individuals advance through stages in their moral development, but he described the stages somewhat differently.

Preconventional Morality. Preconventional morality is characterized by a morality based on egocentric hedonism. Good acts are those that result in good outcomes, and bad acts are those that result in negative consequences to the actor. Kohlberg further divided the preconventional stage of morality into two substages:

1. *Punishments and Obedience:* A period when the physical consequences of an action determines its goodness.

2. *Naive Hedonism:* A period when good acts are those for which an individual receives a positive consequence in return.

In one experiment, children were asked to describe unfair behavior. Sixty-four percent of the children six to eight years of age responded by saying that it was behavior forbidden by parents. Only 27 percent of those children indicated that inequality in the punishment administered to people committing the same offense was unfair behavior. In contrast, for older children the corresponding percentages were 7 percent and 73 percent, respectively.

In another experiment, children were asked why people should follow rules. Children in the primary grades, ages six to eight, tended to respond that behavioral standards should be met in order to avoid punishment and receive pleasant outcomes such as special treats. Children in middle school, ages ten to twelve, responded to this question by noting that rule conformity is a benefit to society.

Conventional Morality (Morality of Rules and Conformity). In contrast to the child of six or eight, the ten- to twelve- year-old is more concerned with the maintenance of social order than receipt of personal pleasure. This characteristic is a defining property of conventional morality, a period also divided by Kohlberg into two substages. In the period of conventional morality, the value of behavior is judged on the basis of the extent to which it follows the rules that maintain social order. The two subdivisions are:

1. *Good Boy/Girl Morality:* Good behaviors are defined as

those behaviors that follow the rules established by others and thus please others. When asked why she had chosen to participate in an organized athletic program, a girl of nine responded, "I don't like it much, but my mom really wants me to play."

2. *Morality of Authority:* Good behavior is behavior that maintains social order, even if it may not be appreciated by others. A child observes a group of his peers stealing from a store. In spite of the fact that his friends will be angry with him for doing so, the child reports their stealing to the store owner, because to do otherwise would cause the store owner to lose profits and the friends to continue stealing because they believed they could break the rules of society and get away with it.

Postconventional Morality. Postconventional morality is characterized by moral judgments that reflect the subjective nature of value judgments as well as the importance of those judgments for the maintenance of interpersonal relationships. Postconventional morality is also subdivided into two substages:

1. *Social Order:* Social order is maintained by rational and potentially changeable contracts among individuals. Because social order is important, changes in those contracts are established by the use of methods developed by the society.

2. *Universal Morality:* Ultimately, an individual may reach a point where ethical principles that transcend social systems are used as a basis for moral judgments. This final stage of development is rarely observed.

Stories similar to the following were read to children ages seven, ten, and thirteen:

A boy's dog was very sick and would die unless it received a special medicine. The medicine cost a great deal of money and

**Table 19.2 Percent of Responses Reflecting
Moral Judgment**

Age	Stages 1 and 2	Stages 3 and 4	Stages 5 and 6	Stage 6
13	24	55	21	46
10	60	38	2	0
7	95	5	0	0

could only be purchased from one animal doctor. The boy came from a very poor family and had no money with which to buy the medicine. He tried to get a job to earn the money, but because he was only eight years old, he could not find work that paid enough to buy the medicine. He went to the animal doctor and asked if he could work in the animal hospital to pay for the medication. The doctor told the boy that no help was needed at the hospital, and that he would need to have money before he could receive the medicine. The boy was very upset and broke into the doctor's office and stole the special medicine for the dog. Should the boy have done that? Why?

After hearing the story, the children were asked to judge the morality of behavior exhibited by the main character. Table 19.2 depicts the percentage of children at each age whose response was characteristic of the three periods of moral development described by Kohlberg.

Factors Influencing Development of Moral Judgment

Two factors are thought to be most important in the development of moral judgment: cognitive development and social interactions.

Cognitive Development.   Cognitive theories of moral development emphasize the role that cognition plays in moral judgment. Particularly important for the development of higher levels of moral judgment is the child's shift away from the egocentrism and realism of preoperational thought to the more sophisticated thinking of later childhood.

Social Interactions. According to cognitive theorists such as Piaget and Kohlberg, changes in moral judgment are stimulated by changes in the child's social interactions. For a child of six or seven, the world is dominated by authoritarian adults who administer what appears to the child as arbitrary punishment. From the child's perspective, these adults have little concern for the feelings or needs of those who are being punished. This subservient role is reflected in the moral realism that the child manifests.

With increased peer interactions, however, children begin to find themselves in a cooperative society, where they play a role in establishing rules and punishments. This new social system, coupled with the ascendance of concrete operations, stimulates the emergence of a higher level of moral judgments.

Children were asked to make moral judgments about various behaviors that others had engaged in: stealing candy, breaking a trust, and so on. Each child's judgment was coded, either as (external if it suggested that the act was wrong because a person would be punished for it) or as internal (if the judgment suggested the act was wrong because it had a negative consequence for the victim, destroyed a relationship of trust, and so on). Children whose parents used physical punishment and denial of material objects as forms of discipline proved to be far more external in their judgments than children whose parents gave explanations for requiring a change in their child's behavior and emphasized the impact of the child's behavior on others.

Moral Behavior

Although one may engage in sophisticated value judgments

about behavior, it does not follow that one's own behavior will adhere to those judgments.

It was noted above that children aged ten to twelve tend to report that rules should be followed because they help to maintain social order. However, when these same children are asked why they actually follow rules, their responses suggest a preconventional level of morality. Even at age ten or twelve, children report that they follow rules in order to avoid punishment and receive rewards.

Factors Influencing Moral Behavior

Most behavior results in mixed consequences, some positive and some negative. To the extent that the risks of negative consequences are greater than the pleasures afforded from the potential positive outcomes, a person will tend to avoid engaging in a behavior. However, when the potential positive outcome is greater than the negative risks, one will tend to engage in the behavior.

Of course, many factors determine the amount of risk or payoff one anticipates from an act. Thus, a variety of factors influence the extent to which a child will engage in a moral behavior commensurate with the level of moral reasoning of which he or she is capable.

External Factors. External factors may influence the risk or payoff potential of an act. A child will be less likely to engage in a forbidden activity if there is an adult nearby or if there is a good chance of being caught.

Internal Factors. Internal factors may also influence the risk or payoff potential of an act. If a child has been deprived of candy by his or her parents and wants candy very badly, he or she will be more likely to steal candy than a child who has free access to it.

Experiential Factors. Some factors influencing payoffs and risks for behavior are experiential. A child who has been punished consistently when caught engaging in an unacceptable behavior is less likely to engage in that behavior than a child who is sometimes punished and sometimes not.

Observational learning (modeling) also plays a role. Children exposed to models who engage in unacceptable behavior and get away with it are more likely to imitate that behavior than children who have observed others caught and punished for unacceptable behavior. All the variables that affect imitation influence the extent to which exposure to models will determine moral behavior; some of these variables are the status of the model, the similarity between the model and child, and the extent to which the model controls rewards and punishments.

Cognition. Children's ability to attend to more than one aspect of a situation at a time, to put themselves in the role of others, and to consider both the here-and-now as well as the future influences the payoffs and risks they will be able to anticipate for their behavior.

John and Pete are both confronted with a jar of candy they have been told not to open. John is seven years old and still possesses the characteristics of a preoperational child. Specifically, he has trouble attending to more than one aspect of a situation at a time, is very egocentric, and centers his attention on the here-and-now. When confronted with a temptation, John centers his attention on his own immediate needs. In so doing, he does not consider the other factors that will determine the real consequences of his behavior should he give in to temptation. This cognitive characteristic results in John opening the jar and eating the candy when he feels the need.

Pete, on the other hand, is twelve years old and is capable of viewing his potential behavior from a number of varying perspectives. For example, while he is aware of his immediate need—that is, to eat the candy—he attends as well to the impact of his actions on others (they won't have any candy). His behavior is also informed by other, indirect factors that affect the ultimate consequences of his actions (punishment, should he be caught). Weighing all those factors, he decides that although satisfaction of his immediate need would be pleasant, it would be offset in the long run by negative consequences. Thus, he resists the temptation.

Adjustment and Learning Problems of Middle Childhood

Problems of adjustment and learning tend to occur when dramatic changes take place in a person's life. Middle childhood is initiated by both a cognitive and a social change. The child progresses from the period of preoperational thinking to the period of concrete operations, and typically he or she enters the world of formal education. Middle childhood ends with other dramatic changes: the onset of puberty and movement into the teen-age years. Because of these two periods of dramatic change, it is not surprising that there is a high incidence of adjustment and learning problems for children in the middle years.

The peak periods of childhood referrals to psychological clinics occur between the ages of four and seven, and again between the ages of ten and fourteen. These referrals are often made because of behavioral problems that cause disruptions in the child's home and school. However, as we shall see, children also manifest serious problems such as depression, obsessive-compulsive behavior, psychosomatic illnesses, and phobias.

If mild disturbances are included as adjustment problems, 33 percent of children in the age range of six to twelve experience some emotional problem. Ten percent of these children require clinical assistance to overcome their problems.

Interestingly, four times as many boys as girls experience problems. This fact may be attributable to actual differences in the problems experienced by the sexes, or it may be that boys exhibit their problems in a more socially unacceptable way than do girls and thus are referred for help more often.

Sources of Adjustment Difficulties

Three factors contribute most to adjustment problems in middle childhood: parents, social relationships, and school.

Parents

The relationship between parents and children changes in middle childhood. It is a time when parents must begin to recognize the independence of their child and encourage the development of that autonomy, while at the same time providing support for and acceptance of the child. For the child, it is a period of life in which he or she begins to identify with people and groups outside the family. These changing relationships often result in a conflict between the needs of the parents and those of the child, a conflict that can be resolved. However, in some cases the conflict produces in the child negative emotions against which he or she must defend. In the case of many emotional defenses, the behavior produced is often dysfunctional.

A ten-year-old boy observes that many of his friends are allowed to stay home by themselves at night while their parents are gone. He feels like a child when he is left with a baby sitter. His parents view the situation differently. They feel strongly that a ten-year-old should not be left alone and observe that the friends to whom their son is referring are twelve years old. The needs of the child and those of his parents are clearly in conflict. The response of the boy in this example is to become angry with his parents, blame them for all the problems he is experiencing, and finally to rebel and act uncooperatively with the baby sitter.

Social Relationships

The middle years of childhood are important for the development of social relationships. Being accepted by others is one of the most important goals of children from age six to twelve. In an effort to be accepted or to defend against the negative emotions that accompany rejection, children often develop unusual behaviors.

A ten-year-old client reveals to a psychologist that he has no friends. His classmates tease him and call him names. The boy's response has been to establish a territory on the playground that he declares to everyone is his kingdom. At recess he runs to his kingdom and prances around defending it. Of course, the other children accept his defensive position as a challenge and attempt to take over the territory.

The result has been daily fights in which the client is hurt physically, teased, and called names. Although it would appear that his behavior would cease because of the pain it produces, the boy says, "If I asked them to play with me, they would all run away. If I fight with them, I have someone to play with." This client engages in behavior that appears maladjusted to many, but it serves the purpose of giving him boys with whom to play.

Likewise, a twelve-year-old girl engages in sexual activities with the boys at her junior high school. In discussing her behavior, she points out that she does not have many friends and her sexual behavior at least makes her feel like part of a group.

School

It is estimated that 25 percent of all children experience school failures that significantly affect their behavior. During middle childhood, school places demands on children that have not been placed on them before. For example, they are expected to learn arithmetic and reading skills, which were unimportant in their earlier life. Many children confront this challenge and succeed. For others, school is an experience in failure. When one anticipates or experiences failure, it is natural to develop defenses against the negative emotions that are generated. Those defenses, however, often result in behavior problems.

A seven-year-old boy is referred to a clinic after crawling under a table to hide at school. As it turns out, the boy had failed to learn basic reading skills and was afraid to demonstrate his ignorance to the rest of the class. As long as he hid under the classroom table, he was labeled emotionally disturbed and was not expected to perform normally in class. Although his behavior was viewed as bizarre and dysfunctional by his teacher, it served a useful purpose for the child. He was able to avoid exhibiting his academic failure.

Types of Adjustment Problems

The conflicts of middle childhood may result in various forms of behavioral problems.

Aggression

Physical and verbal aggressiveness is a common behavior problem in middle childhood. Eighty percent of children will exhibit a tantrum at least once a month. However, for about 10 percent of children, such tantrums occur daily. Often the aggressive act is a response to anger, anger that is generated by the frustration of not having needs satisfied that the child thinks are important. The aggressive act, however, is often directed against people or property unrelated to the source of the anger, or is directed in subtle, indirect ways.

Joan is a ten-year-old who has always achieved well in school. She has come into conflict with her parents about wearing makeup and nylons. Joan wants to wear them, but her parents do not approve. Joan is afraid to confront her parents directly with her anger and begins instead to be a listless student. In addition to allowing her academic work to fall behind, she begins to talk back to her teacher.

In family counseling, it soon becomes evident to the

psychologist that Joan's behavioral change is a subtle and indirect attack on her parents, who in the past have always felt proud of themselves because of their ability to raise a smart, well-behaved daughter.

An eight-year-old boy is brought to a psychologist's office by a parent who is concerned because the boy has chased the baby sitter with a knife and threatened her life. After a few minutes' discussion, the boy breaks down crying. He says that his parents are always away and that no one pays any attention to him. He threatened the baby sitter with the knife because she spent all her time on the phone, and he continued to feel rejected.

Withdrawal

It is natural to attempt to avoid negative emotions. One way to accomplish that objective is to avoid situations that might potentially elicit those emotions. For some children, this defense results in withdrawal from many social contacts or intellectual challenges.

In its simplest form, withdrawal may appear to be of shyness. More severe withdrawal may result in the creation of a make-believe world whose reality cannot be tested because of the child's total lack of communication with other people. This severe withdrawal is characteristic of psychotic disorders such as schizophrenia.

A twelve-year-old boy spends most of his nonschool hours in his room, singing and listening to the radio. His withdrawn behavior does not concern his parents until he begins to report that he is talking to a dead relative who comes to visit him on a regular basis. The dead relative gives the boy advice and comforts him when he feels lonely. In therapy, the boy reveals that he is afraid of people because they might not like him. Rather than risk the empty feeling of rejection, he avoids people entirely by withdrawing to his room.

Regression

On occasion, a person confronted with stress will begin to act as he or she might have acted at an earlier age. Such regression is not uncommon in middle childhood.

A girl of six years old has been toilet trained for three and one-half years. One day there is a birthday party for one of her classmates, and she is not invited. That same week, she fails a test in school and is put in the lowest reading group of her class. At this time, she begins to urinate in her pants and wet the bed. The emotional stress of the week resulted in her behavior regressing to that of an earlier period in her life.

Fears

The fears of children six to twelve differ from those of younger children. While younger children tend to fear physical injury and make-believe creatures, those in middle childhood fear social rejection and the unknown. At the age of eight, death is a major source of fear in many children. Some fears become overpowering for children, and they will do almost anything to avoid the feared objects. Those strong fears are called phobias.

School phobia to some degree affects about ten children in every thousand. These children are fearful of school buildings, teachers, or any other objects associated with school. Needless to say, these children develop a variety of behaviors that help them to avoid contact with school-related situations. They may become ill or make up stories about beatings they anticipate if they go to school or about wild animals that lurk on the school grounds.

The cause of school phobias is not always known. In some cases, they stem from a fear of failure; in other cases, from a fear of being deserted by parents when the child leaves home to go to school. In all cases, however, the underlying fear has been transformed into a fear of being anywhere near a school-related object.

Physical Symptoms

One of the most common reactions to emotional stress is a physical symptom—usually a rash, a stomachache, or a headache. However, more severe problems have been observed. A boy eight years old is to be given a test in school on Tuesday morning. Tuesday morning he has diarrhea, an upset stomach, and all the symptoms of the flu. His parents allow him to stay home from school, and of course he misses the test. By 11 a.m. the flu symptoms are gone, and the boy goes back to school in the afternoon.

This pattern of illness, brought on by the anticipation of threatening events such as tests, is a major cause of absenteeism in schools.

PART VI:
Adolescent Development

Adolescence is the transition from childhood to adulthood. It is distinguished by significant physical changes that culminate in sexual maturity. These physical changes, especially puberty, are often viewed as a mark of entry into adolescence. But adolescence is more than a period of physical change; it is a period of cognitive development as well. The adolescent moves from thinking about the concrete here and now to abstract thinking and possibilities for the future. Adolescence is also an important time of social development, the length and quality of which varies from culture to culture. In some cultures, social adolescence is brief or nonexistent, while in other cultures (particularly the United States), social adolescence is drawn out well beyond the limits of pubescent change. Some studies indicate that a true psychological transition into adulthood may take place as late as age 28.

CHAPTER 20

Physical Changes in Adolescence

Adolescence is traditionally divided into three parts: puberty (early adolescence); middle adolescence; and late adolescence, the transitional period to adulthood. This chapter is concerned with the physical changes that accompany puberty—body growth and the development of primary and secondary sexual characteristics—and the hormonal activity that brings these changes about.

Puberty

Puberty is the period of life that links childhood and adolescence. Though it occurs simultaneously with the early period of adolescence and the two terms are used interchangeably with some degree of freedom, puberty describes more the physical period of development, while adolescence is used more to describe a psychological period.

While there is no specific age that clearly marks the beginning of puberty, some general norms have been established. Boys are believed to enter puberty between the ages of 12 and 14.5, while girls are generally believed to enter this period slightly earlier, between about 10 and 13 years old. If we consider the hallmark of puberty to be sexual maturity, then these figures are basically accurate.

A number of factors have been identified as important forces during puberty. Social constraints, which check and stifle the burgeoning forces of sexuality, may become objects of rebellion. In the school, where the pubescent spends a large portion of time, teachers and other personnel may be viewed as oppressors, who by their mere presence encourage, rebellion and rage. This is also a period of sexual awakening and often sexual confusion, met with ambivalent reactions by both sexes.

Psychologists have identified three key challenges as central to the pubescent's growth: (1) the challenges posed by the biological changes of puberty; (2) the challenges posed by entry into a new social system, the junior high school; and (3) the challenges derived from sudden entry into a new role status (as a member of the adolescent subculture).

Physiological characteristics of puberty include menarche— the first menstruation—for the girl, and reproductive potency— the presence of sperm in the semen—for the boy. Just as significant is the appearance of the secondary sex characteristics, which for boys are pubic hair, facial hair, deepening of the voice, heavy muscular development, and angular body build, and for the girl, breasts, triangular pubic hair patterns, and an increase in subcutaneous fat, which gives the body its rounded body contour. While these physical changes are the clearest signs of puberty, there are also marked psychological changes—changes in attitudes, interests, emotions, and cognitive ability—that become the crux of the adolescent experience.

Body Growth

From the age of two, children grow at a steady rate. However, early in adolescence they experience a spurt in the rate of growth.

During puberty, the adolescent's rate of growth nearly doubles to an average of 4 inches per year (10 cm/year) for boys and 3.6 inches per year (9 cm/year) for girls. Of course, there is variability in the amount of growth that occurs from one adolescent to another, ranging from 2.8 to 4.8 inches (7 to 12 cm) for boys and 2.4 to 4.4 inches (6 to 11 cm) for girls. The average age at which the peak of the growth spurt occurs is approximately 12.5 for girls and 14.5 for boys. In both sexes, however, some adolescents may have completed their growth spurt before others have even begun theirs. (See Fig. 20.1.)

These individual differences in adolescent development apparently have far-reaching effects on personality and social adjustment. However, the age at which girls experience their growth spurt does not appear to have the significant long-range effects on their behavior patterns that is evidenced for boys.

Late-maturing boys are rated by their peers as less attractive, not as socially adjusted, more tense and attention-seeking, and less popular than other adolescent boys. Furthermore, their own

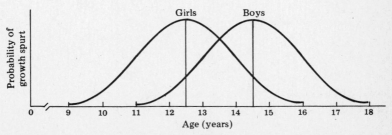

Fig. 20.1

ratings of themselves indicate greater feelings of inadequacy and more negative self-concepts. These personality characteristics are often maintained throughout the individual's adolescence and into adult life.

The amount of growth occurring during the adolescent growth spurt is not entirely related to the preadolescent height of the child. The correlation between pregrowth-spurt height and adult height is approximately 0.8, meaning that approximately 35 percent of the variability in adult heights is attributable to changes in height that occur during adolescence.

While it is unusual for extremely short children to become extremely tall adults, it is not uncommon for boys or girls who are below average in height before adolescence to grow to above-average height as adults.

Body Proportions

Growth during adolescence is not uniform. An adolescent's legs grow first and are followed by growth in the trunk. This pattern of growth results in the long-legged, clumsy appearance that popularly exemplifies the adolescent. By the time the adolescent's growth is completed, the trunk comprises approximately 37.5 percent of the total body height, the head 12.5 percent, and the legs 50 percent. This compares with corresponding percentages for preadolescence of 40 percent, 14 percent, and 46 percent, respectively.

Strength

Until adolescence, there are small but systematic differences in the strength of boys and girls. Boys exhibit slightly greater strength than girls. With the growth spurt of adolescence, however, there is an accelerated development of muscle tissue in boys, which is accompanied by a significant acceleration in their strength. Corresponding acceleration in the development of muscle tissue and strength is not apparent in girls. This results in a marked difference in the strength typically exhibited by males and females after the onset of adolescence. Of course, there are individual differences in strength, so some girls are stronger than some boys of the same age.

By the age of 12, the average arm-pull strength of boys is approximately 44 pounds (20 kg), while that of girls is approximately 37 1/2 pounds (17 kg). By the age of 12, boys' strength has increased to approximately 61 1/2 pounds (28 kg), while that of girls has increased to about 44 pounds (20 kg). By age 17, the average boy's arm-pull strength has increased to 108 pounds (49 kg), while his female counterpart's strength has increased to 57 pounds (26 kg).

Primary Sexual Characteristics

Those physical structures that are involved in the reproductive process and are present at birth are referred to as primary sexual characteristics. For the male, they include the testicles, penis, prostate gland, and seminal vesicles. For the female, they include the ovaries, uterus, vagina, and clitoris. Although adolescents vary in the age at which primary sexual characteristics mature, the maturing process tends to proceed in a sequential manner for all adolescents.

Male Development

The development of primary sexual characteristics in males occurs in five stages:

Stage One: The small testes and penis of childhood characterize Stage One development. This is a prepubescent stage.

Stage Two: The first sign of change in primary sexual characteristics is the enlargement of the testes and the wrinkling of the pouchlike structure, the scrotum, in which they hang. The emergence of Stage Two occurs between the ages of 10 and 14.5, with an average age of 12 years.

Stage Three: The lengthening of the penis marks the beginning of Stage Three. This growth is accompanied by the growth of the prostate gland, which produces the semen in which sperm cells are transported, and the seminal vesicles. The onset of Stage Three usually occurs about one year after the onset of Stage Two.

Stage Four: The beginning of Stage Four is characterized by the first potential ejaculation of semen and sperm. This stage is typically achieved one year after the onset of Stage Three, or at an average age of 14 years. The first experienced ejaculation may not correspond to the onset of Stage Four because that event depends, in part, upon cultural factors. For most boys, initial ejaculation results from masturbation or a spontaneous nocturnal emission (wet dream). During the fourth stage of development, there is continued growth of the testes and an increase in the diameter of the penis.

Stage Five: Complete development of the testes and penis characterize Stage Five, which is achieved nearly one year after the onset of Stage Four. The range of ages at which full development of the primary sexual characteristics is achieved may vary from 13 years to 18 years. Thus, some boys reach Stage Five development before others have entered Stage Two.

Female Development

Because direct observation of their growth patterns is easily accomplished, stages in breast development are used to denote the stages of primary sexual development in the female. While the development of breasts is accompanied by the growth of the internal sex organs—the uterus and ovaries—as well as the external genitalia—the clitoris, labia, and vagina—breasts themselves are considered secondary rather than primary sexual characteristics.

Stage One: Prepubescent, childlike breasts characterize Stage One. The nipple of the breast is not raised and the areola (the dark portion of the breast surrounding the nipple) is small and light in color. The uterus and ovaries are small and inactive.

Stage Two: The development of "breast buds which is" a darkening, swelling, and enlargement of the areola, signifies the emergence of Stage Two. During Stage Two, no protrusion of the nipple is observed. Accompanying this obvious change in the physiology of the adolescent girl is the initial growth of other primary sexual organs. Stage Two may occur between the ages of 8 and 13, but the average age of onset is 11.

Stage Three: Because of increased fat deposits, girls at the average age of 12 begin to develop larger, conical-shaped breasts. This marks the third stage of primary sexual development. Throughout this period there is an increased growth and maturation of other primary sex organs.

Stage Four: In contrast to Stage Three, in which breast development results from increased fat deposits, breast development, results from the emergence of the mammary glands themselves. The product of that development is a rounder, more mature breast, with the areola becoming a part of the surrounding breast and the nipple protruding.

Stage Four occurs on the average at about age 14. *Menarche,* the most significant event in primary sexual development, often occurs during Stage Four (although menarche has increasingly been occurring earlier—at about 12.8 years—according to statistics gathered during the 1980s). Menarche, or the first menstrual flow, signifies that the unobserved growth of the ovaries and uterus has been progressing. They are now beginning to function in a mature way. The average age of menarche is a little over 13.5 years in today's Western society, but may vary from 10 to 16.5 years. For most adolescent girls, menstruation is at first an irregular event and may be anovulatory, that is, not actually accompanied by the release of an ovum. Thus, for some time following menarche, adolescent girls may be sterile. There are, of course, exceptions to the rule of post-menarche sterility.

Secondary Sexual Characteristics

The same biochemical changes that stimulate the primary sexual characteristics to mature also stimulate other physical changes. Those changes are called secondary sexual characteristics. Secondary sexual characteristics include the appearance of body hair, changes in the texture of the skin, changes in the functioning of subcutaneous glands, and changes in the voice. For girls, breasts are also considered secondary sexual characteristics.

Hair

Pubic Hair

The emergence of pubic hair has been the most widely studied secondary sexual development. That development begins shortly after the first signs of primary sexual development (shortly after the age of 11 in girls and the age of 12 in boys), and typically its emergence follows a series of systematic stages:

Stage One: This is an infantile stage in which no pubic hair is present, or at most there is a downlike hair with little or no coloration.

Stage Two: The emergence of true pubic hair characterizes Stage Two. The hair is coarse and straight and covers only small portions of the pubic region. In girls the average age of Stage Two onset is 11.25 years, while for boys it is 12.17 years.

Stage Three: Pubic hair in Stage Three exhibits a slight curl and begins to spread over a larger surface of the pubic region. In girls the average age of Stage Three onset is 12.5 years, while for boys it is 13.25.

Stage Four: Stage Four is characterized by the spread of twisted, dark pubic hair over the pubic region. However, the spread does not yet correspond to the mature mass of pubic hair characteristic of the adult. For girls Stage Four development occurs at an average age of 12.66 years, while for boys the average age of Stage Four development is 13.75 years.

Stage Five: Mature pubic hair, which is fully pigmented, twisted, and covers an inverted V-shaped region of the pubis, characterizes Stage Five development. Mature pubic hair development occurs on the average at 14 years of age for girls, while for boys the average age is 16 years.

Axillary and Facial Hair

Other body hair develops later than pubic hair. Axillary hair (the hair under the arms) as well as facial hair emerges two years after the first signs of pubic hair. Facial hair begins to make its appearance on the upper lip; only later does it appear on the lower lip and finally on the cheeks. Soft, downy facial hair initially appears on both boys and girls. The development of coarse, dark facial hair is a male secondary sexual characteristic.

Body Hair

Hair on the lower legs and forearms appears along with axillary hair and facial hair, and in some cases, there may also be a tuft of hair on the chest of a boy. However, male development of chest hair and heavy hair masses on the arms, legs, and back typically occurs only in late adolescence, as a last stage in body hair development.

Glandular Activity, Skin and Voice Changes

Puberty is marked by the development of sebaceous and apocrine sweat glands in the axillae (underarms), genital, and anal regions. The development of those glands gives rise to the body odor associated with maturity. Inasmuch as it is stimulated by the male sex hormones, this development is more pronounced in males than in females.

Adolescence is characterized by a roughening of the skin and pore enlargement. Changes in skin structure, coupled with preglandular activity, cause the acne so common among adolescents.

The voices of both the male and the female change during adolescence. That change is a gradual process resulting from a rapid growth of the larynx and a lengthening of the vocal cords.

Biochemical Stimulators of Adolescent Changes

The accelerated growth observed in adolescence is the result of dramatic hormonal changes. These changes occur at three levels: the hypothalamus, the pituitary gland, and the peripheral glands and organs. The structures at each level provide stimulation for the activity at the next lower level. The resulting activity of the peripheral glands serves as a feedback loop to inhibit further stimulation by the hypothalamus. In this way the hormonal balance of the organism is maintained.

Level One (The Hypothalamus)

The hypothalamus is a small structure located near the base of the brain. It is sensitive to the level of sex hormones in the body, and among its various functions, it releases neurohormones that control the pituitary gland. When the level of sex hormones in the body falls below a critical value, the hypothalamus releases neurohormones that signal the pituitary gland to stimulate the production of additional sex hormones.

Prior to puberty, even extremely low levels of sex hormones in the body inhibit the hypothalamus from executing that signal. However, when the hypothalamus matures, its sensitivity to sex hormones diminishes and the prepubescent level of sex hormones in the body no longer inhibits the release of the neurohormones that activate the pituitary gland. Thus, those pituitary-activating neurohormones are released by the hypo-thalamus, and in turn, the pituitary gland initiates the production of additional sex hormones. The production of those sex hormones continues until their level in the body reaches that level required to inhibit the activity of the now-mature hypothalamus—a level great enough to stimulate the development of primary and secondary sexual characteristics.

Level Two (The Pituitary Gland)

The pituitary gland is a major control mechanism for the human endocrine system. It secretes hormones that act as stimulators for the growth and activity of many other organs. When the level of sex hormones in the body falls below the critical level established by the hypothalamus, that structure executes a neurohormonal signal to the pituitary gland, causing that gland to release three types of hormones: *growth hormones,* which directly stimulate the physical growth observed in adolescence; *adrenocorticotrophic hormones,* which stimulate the activity of the adrenal cortex; and *gonadotropic hormones,* which stimulate the growth activity of the gonads.

The two gonadotropic hormones secreted by the pituitary gland are follicle-stimulating hormone (FSH) and luteinizing hormone (LH). *FSH* stimulates the growth and development of the follicles of the female ovaries and, in so doing, stimulates the production of estrogen, a female sex hormone. In the male, FSH stimulates the growth of the testes and, in so doing, initiates the active production of sperm cells. *LH* plays two roles: it regulates the production of the female sex hormone, estrogen, and it stimulates the growth and activity of the Leydig cells of the male testes, which produce the male sex hormone, testosterone.

Level Three (The Peripheral Organs and Glands)

Adrenal Cortex

In both males and females, the adrenal cortex produces small amounts of the female sex hormone, *estrogen,* and the male sex hormone, *testosterone.* In addition, it produces small amounts of other adrenal androgens (male sex hormones). It is the adrenal cortex that maintains the small amounts of estrogen and androgens found in the bloodstream of both males and females before puberty.

At puberty, the surge of activity by the adrenal cortex, stimulated by the release of adrenocorticotrophic hormone from the anterior pituitary gland, results in the rapid increase of androgens for both sexes. These androgens are important for the normal development of secondary sexual characteristics, particularly body hair.

Body hair develops more profusely on males than on females because male androgen levels are supplemented markedly by the production of testosterone (a primary androgen) in the testes, while the androgens in the female system are limited to those secreted by the adrenal cortex.

Gonads

The gonads of the female are called the *ovaries*. The ovaries serve two functions. First, they are the source of developing ova, or female germ cells. The development of the ovaries and the initiation of this first function is stimulated by the follicle-stimulating hormone (FSH) secreted by the anterior pituitary gland. The second function of the ovaries is the production of the female sex hormone, estrogen. Estrogen controls the development of most female secondary sexual characteristics and is also important in the maintenance of the primary reproductive functions of the female body. Estrogen administered to a male in high enough doses will result in the development of female secondary sexual characteristics, such as breasts.

The male gonads are called *testes.* Like the ovaries, testes serve two functions. First, they are the source of the male germ cell, the sperm. The growth of the testes and the development of sperm cells is stimulated by the follicle-stimulating hormone (FSH) secreted by the anterior pituitary gland. A second function of the testes, and specifically of the Leydig cells located in them, is the production and secretion of testosterone, the primary male sex hormone. The growth and activity of those cells is stimulated by the secretion of luteinizing hormone (LH) from the anterior pituitary. Testosterone, along with smaller amounts of other androgen hormones secreted by the adrenal cortex, is responsible for the development of male secondary sexual characteristics as well as the male sex drive.

CHAPTER 21

Cognitive Development in Adolescence

The primary transition in thinking between middle childhood and adolescence is the increased capacity to consider concrete events in relation to possibilities. The child of this age understands not only the actual realities with which he or she comes into contact but also the potential realities (future realities) that may or may not physically exist at this time. This capacity is referred to as formal thinking and depends on the mental processes that Piaget called formal operations. Formal thinking allows the thinker to conceptualize abstractions as well as concrete events.

The capacity for formal thinking not only increases adolescents' ability to solve problems that previously went unsolved, but also leads to the idealism that is typical of their age group. The ability to conceptualize the world as it might be often leads adolescents to question why the real world does not conform to that ideal.

Characteristics of Formal Cognition

Six properties characterize the formal cognitive capabilities of adolescents:

Focus on Logical Conclusions Rather Than Factual Information

Consider the following series of statements indicating a certain type of reasoning:

1. All green birds have two heads. (Statement of Premise)

2. I have a green bird at home named Charlie. (Statement of Premise)

3. How many heads does Charlie have? (Question)

4. Based on premises 1 and 2, Charlie must have two heads. (Conclusion)

The first statement in this problem may be viewed as a proposed description of reality and evaluated on the basis of its correspondence to reality. The statement may also be viewed as an assumption made solely for the purpose of this problem—an assumption whose validity is irrelevant in determining the answer to question 3. Preadolescents tend to approach problems by evaluating their correspondence to reality, while adolescents are able to appreciate the potential of drawing, from available information, logical conclusions that are independent of their correspondence to experienced reality.

For example, an eight-year-old boy confronted with the problem described above might respond by saying, "There aren't any two-headed birds. Charlie can have only one head." This child, who does not yet possess formal operational thinking, focuses on the factual content of the problem and relates it to his own experience with reality. A 12-year-old child, on the other hand, might focus on the conclusions one can draw from the premise found in the initial two statements rather than from the content of the statements themselves, and say, "If Charlie is green and you have assumed that all green birds have two heads, then Charlie would have two heads."

Hypothetical-Deductive Reasoning

The adolescent's focus on the possible conclusions one can generate from a set of assumptions allows for hypothetical deductive reasoning. In hypothetical-deductive reasoning, an individual first establishes a theoretical hypothesis about the possible ways in which the elements of a theory relate to one another. Next, from those hypotheses, deductions are made about the observations one would expect to make of actual reality if the hypotheses were true. To determine the adequacy of the initial hypotheses, comparisons are made between the predicted observations and actual observations of reality. Finally, a reformulation of the theoretical perspective about reality is made to account for discrepancies between the predicted observation and the actual observations.

The first two phases of hypothetical-deductive reasoning involve thinking about the way reality might be; thus, they require formal thinking. It is only in the last phase of hypothetical- deductive reasoning that the reasoner must confront actual reality.

An adolescent girl notes that the rigidity with which her parents enforce their curfew rule fluctuates over time. She is curious about the factors influencing that fluctuation. "It could be that when my parents are relaxed and enjoying themselves, they are more lenient," she hypothesizes. "If it is their emotional state that influences the enforcement of their rules, then I could anticipate that the curfew rule might be less rigid when the whole family is on vacation, but that it would be affected very little by my being on vacation if my parents are still working. I can find out if this hypothesis is true by looking at the facts. This summer when school let out, the curfew remained in effect and was enforced. As soon as Mom and Dad took their vacation, however, I was free to stay up late. That provides some support for my theory."

Notice that the adolescent developed a theory of how the external world (specifically, her parents) might operate and then examined the validity of the predictions generated by the theory. Rather than generating a general theory, a younger child would have developed a list of encounters he or she had experienced with the parents and would have drawn a specific conclusion from that list. The younger child might even have focused on the first experience that came to mind and arrived at a conclusion based only on that experience.

Generation of All Potential Combinations and Permutations of Events

To facilitate hypothetical-deductive reasoning, the adolescent is capable of systematically generating all the possible ways in which the elements of a problem can be combined to form potential problem solutions. In contrast, the preadolescent generates those combinations in a nonsystematic, trial-and-error fashion that is frequently directed by past experience and, more often than not, results in his or her ignoring many potential perspectives on the problem.

Consider an experimental situation in which children are told to make as many words as they can from the letters A, E, S, T, and M. Preadolescents may quickly see some obvious words such as "steam" and "mates." They may manipulate the letters haphazardly to discover one or two additional words. The adolescent, in contrast, may quickly switch to the systematic strategy of creating all 120 possible letter combinations and then discover that six of them are actual words.

Generate Higher-Order Operations from Single Operations

In order to discover which number, when added to 8, becomes five times its original size, preadolescents will select one number after another and insert each number in the formula $x + 8 = ?$ and in the equation $5x = ?$ to determine if the answers are the same. Adolescents, however, are capable of reorganizing the original problem into the formula $x + 8 = 5x$. Subsequently, adolescents may systematically solve that equation to arrive at an answer. They do not require the use of trial-and-error approximations to discover the problem solution.

In a classic experiment, Jean Piaget gave children four flasks of perceptually identical liquids and a fifth flask containing a liquid that was perceptually distinct from the other four. (See Fig. 21.1.) He then demonstrated that a yellow liquid could be created by combining the liquid from the fifth flask with certain other liquids. He asked the children to discover how the yellow liquid could be created by combining liquids. (The solution to the problem required the child to combine the liquid from three different flasks.)

Preadolescent children will attempt to solve this problem by combining the liquid from the fifth flask (E) with each of the other four liquids (A, B, C, and D). Sometimes preadolescents forget one of the four flasks. When they do not achieve the yellow-colored chemical by combining only two liquids, they give up or simply repeat their experiment. Prompting by the experimenter may result in preadolescents discovering the components of the yellow liquid, but the discovery is accidental and typically cannot be repeated.

Adolescents will begin seeking a solution to this problem in

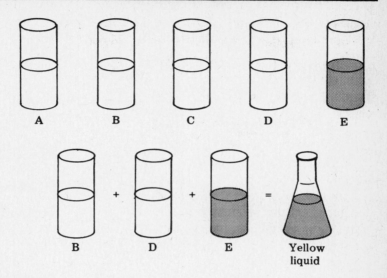

Preadolescent attempted solution:

A + E ≠ yellow
B + E ≠ yellow
C + E ≠ yellow
D + E ≠ yellow

Adolescent attempted solutions:

A + E ≠ yellow
B + E ≠ yellow
C + E ≠ yellow
D + E ≠ yellow
(A + B) + E ≠ yellow
(B + C) + E ≠ yellow
(B + D) + E = yellow

Fig. 21.1

the same way as the younger child. However, in contrast to the
younger child, adolescents will not give up when combinations
of only two chemicals do not produce the desired result. Instead,
systematic combinations of the first four chemicals will be
created, and then the fifth chemical will be added to each mixture
until the correct mixture is discovered. The major distinction
between these two performances is the adolescents' ability and
willingness to systematically generate all combinations of the
five chemicals in an attempt to discover the correct problem
solution.

Simultaneous Contemplation of More Than One Aspect of a Situation and the Relationships Among These Aspects

The preadolescent examines events sequentially; he or she does not explore the relationship or potential relationship among events. The adolescent, however, is able to consider the logical relationship among a variety of events.

A child observes the following events: (1) Father says he wants his family to be healthy and enjoy each other for many years; (2) the television announcer says that smoking may be hazardous to your health and cause you to die earlier than normal; (3) Father is observed smoking.

Preadolescents respond to each of these events as a separate entity. They do not contemplate the lack of logical consistency that is exhibited. With the acquisition of the capacity for formal thinking, adolescents become aware of the logical inconsistency in these events. The adolescents' attempts to reconcile the logical consistency of an ideal with the illogic of experienced reality often results in confusion. For preadolescents, such confusion seldom exists.

Future Orientation

The adolescent considers future consequences in making plans and considering the implications of certain behaviors. This is made possible by his or her ability to think about possibilities, not just actualities. During the formal operational period, the teenager becomes capable of logical thought about what *might* occur rather than being restricted to consideration of actual events. "What if the Japanese had won World War II?" the adolescent might consider, extrapolating the possible situation today.

A further extension of this capacity is the ability to derive implications about future events from present data so that during formal operations the adolescent can give logically correct and "sensible" answers to questions such as "What will happen in the future if I do this now?" or "What will happen to me later in life if I choose not to go to college but go to work instead?" This type of question requires cognitive processing that has not yet developed in the child at the concrete operational stage.

This ability allows the adolescent to plan and assess in terms of ideals—higher, abstract principles—rather than being limited to the concrete situations and materials of the world of today. Many of the commitments of the adolescent are reflections of this new idealized thinking, including political beliefs, religious values, and the guiding forces behind dating, bonding, and sexual relationships.

Prevalence of Formal Thought

Although textbooks often depict the thinking of adolescents and adults as formal operational cognition, it is more correct to say that formal operational cognition becomes more prevalent as individuals become older. Individuals reared in some environments do not require the development of formal operational cognition for their normal functioning, and these individuals may not develop their capacity for that form of cognition.

Even individuals who have developed the capacity for formal cognition may not consistently use it. There are many situations in which formal cognitive processes are less efficient than concrete operational thinking. Furthermore, as in the case of the younger child, personal motives and emotions may interfere with an individual's full utilization of his or her formal cognitive capacity.

In an experimental situation, the individual may have little emotional involvement with the task in which he or she is involved. In contrast, a personal involvement with the problem places the individual in an emotional condition that may reduce his or her use of formal logic by focusing attention on only a limited number of situational factors while making a judgment. For example, Peter, a 17-year-old, might exhibit the capacity to use formal operational thought in an experimental situation involving moral judgments, but exhibit less mature levels of thinking when asked to judge the morality of an individual who, while speeding to the hospital with a sick friend, crashed into Peter's car.

CHAPTER 22

Personality and Social Development in Adolescence

As they approach adolescence, most children have made important social adjustments—to parents, to peers, and to school. Now they must define themselves against a new set of conditions. They must take a giant step toward independence, come to terms with their sexual selves, develop a personal code of moral conduct, think seriously about a career, and explore new social roles toward an adult lifestyle.

The psychologist G. Stanley Hall, writing in 1916, viewed adolescence as a period of Sturm und Drang (storm and stress). Whether this need be so (anthropologist Margaret Mead held that adolescent turbulence is culturally linked) is still being debated. A certain amount of psychological tension and anxiety is normal for this period. However, for some young people, the conflicts and confusion of adolescence result in deviant behavior such as drug abuse, delinquency, and psychophysiological dis-

trubances. This chapter traces the adolescent's passage toward maturity, noting some of the pitfalls along the way.

Identity vs. Role Confusion

Erik Erikson has identified the years of adolescence as a period during which the developing person must establish a sense of social and personal identity. If difficulty is experienced in the achievement of that objective, the end product is role conflict. Personal identity, in Erikson's model, is defined as a sense of contentment about one's own physical, intellectual, and emotional attributes, a sense of purpose and objective, and the anticipation of recognition from other people who are considered significant to the individual.

The search for identity is stimulated by three factors. First, dramatic changes in one's physical appearance at puberty result in the question "Who am I, and how am I viewed by others?" Second, the capacity for formal cognitive processing allows the adolescent to conceptualize the many possible identities that one might have, thus prompting the question "Which of these possibilities is really me?" And third, societal expectations for the individual change, causing a rejection of the established child identity and forcing an exploration of various possible adult identities.

Tasks in the Search for Identity

In searching for an identity, the adolescent confronts four specific tasks, each of which will be discussed in turn. They are (1) the establishment of independence, (2) sex-role adjustments, (3) the establishment and maintenance of peer relationships, and (4) the determination of a vocational role.

Independence

The establishment of independence is a universal phenomenon. The difficulty one experiences in establishing independence is determined in part by cultural factors. Some cultures provide a gradual shift from dependent childhood roles to independent adult roles. This gradual establishment of independence reduces the confusion and conflict that could be associated with that task.

In one New Guinea tribal society, a girl is selected as a wife at a very early age. Likewise, a young boy is engaged to his future wife long before adolescence. During their childhood, the two children interact regularly and informally with each other's families, and the girl takes on an increasing number of responsibilities in the home of her future husband. Because of the limited roles available to an individual in that society, the boy, too, makes a gradual and unconfusing transition to maturity. Following a puberty rite in which his adult status is recognized, he formally accepts his share of the responsibility for the care of his family—a role he has observed others play throughout his life and one he has practiced informally since he was a child.

Other cultures demand sudden shifts from dependent to independent roles. These sudden shifts in roles can be accompanied by anxiety and conflict. The confusion and corresponding anxiety that a sudden shift in dependency expectations creates can be reduced in part if two things occur: (1) the role of an independent adult is clearly defined by the society, and (2) the process of role change is initiated by some formal event denoting entry into the adult world.

Anthropologist Ruth Benedict has described the traditional rites of puberty in a North African tribe for which honor in warfare is the significant goal in the life of a man. In a dramatic puberty rite, boys torture themselves by cutting strips of skin from their body, cutting off fingers, and so on. After this torture, the tribe believes the man is prepared for his warrior life and will exhibit prowess in that role.

Independence of the Adolescent in the United States

The search for independence in the United States is more difficult than in many primitive cultures. The reasons for this difficulty center on the following factors:

Diversity of Training for Independence. Parents do not always have clear guidelines for training their children for mature independence. Some parents provide their children with little or no experience at being independent and then abruptly thrust them into an independent role during adolescence. The children of such authoritarian parents suffer the greatest anxiety during their search for independence.

The adolescents who experience the least confusion and anxiety in their adolescent search for independence are those reared by democratic, or authoritative, parents. Democratic parents are characterized as gradually providing increasing experiences at independence for their children based on the children's demonstrated capacity to be independent. Furthermore, democratic parents openly discuss the rationale for the restrictions they place on their children, and they encourage their children to play a role in the establishment of the structure within which the children function. Children with democratic parents are more likely to report that their parents are fair in their demands and restrictions. Those children are also more likely to disagree with their parents, be more independent of pressure from their peers, and feel comfortable in their independent role.

Conflicting Expectations for Independence. Our society does not provide universally accepted puberty rites, unless one can consider the rights to obtain a driver's license, to purchase liquor, or to vote as comparable. The consequence of this societal void is that a diversity of expectations is placed on adolescents by different segments of the society, by the same people at different points in time, and even by the adolescents themselves.

Some forms of dependence are acceptable during adolescence, while others are less acceptable. Instrumental dependence—that is, dependence on parents to provide food, housing, money, and other commodities—is an acceptable form of dependence for adolescents in American society. However, emotional dependence—that is, dependence on parents for affection and emotional support—diminishes in adolescence and is particularly unacceptable for boys.

Diversity of Available Roles. If there are few role choices available to a person, there is little opportunity for confusion and conflict. American society, in contrast to many other societies, provides a diversity of roles toward which one can aspire. This wealth of potential roles requires choices on the part of the American adolescent and consequently increases the potential for confusion and conflict.

It is often reported that in earlier days, the crisis of adolescence appeared to be less dramatic. A more moderate degree of adolescent conflict would be expected because American society formerly did not allow for as much flexibility in adult roles as is allowed in today's society. It has also been noted that until recently, boys suffered greater conflicts in their search for independence than girls, and society emphasized a much narrower set of acceptable female roles than male roles. Up through the 1950s, most girls were expected to become wives and mothers; prior to attaining those roles, they might serve as teachers, secretaries, nurses, or social workers. Following the sexual revolution of the mid- to late 1960s, when studies in feminine psychology and sociology shed light on gender-related development, many more career opportunities became available to women.

Sexual Adjustment

The relatively rapid pace of sexual maturity during adolescence makes adjustment to one's sexual self a compelling and crucial task, one that has profound influence on social standing and social behavior. The size of a girl's breasts may help or hinder her popularity with boys; they may make her an object of jokes, an outcast, or an object of admiration, respect, and lust, pursued by the socially prestigious older boys. Likewise, a boy's lack of facial and body hair may place him at a disadvantage in comparison with his more hirsute peers, who equate facial and body hair with virility.

Not only do adolescents have to come to terms with changes in physical appearance, they have to deal with the emergence of a strong sexual drive. Accommodation to this drive represents one of the milestones in the search for identity. The importance of the sex drive forms the basis of psychoanalytic theories of adolescent development.

Psychoanalytic View of Adolescent Sexuality

In psychoanalytic theory, adolescence marks the reemergence of directed libidinal energy. In this stage, libidinal energy is directed toward the genitals, thus the term "genital period" of psychosexual development. For the early adolescent in the United States, the sexual drive often cannot be directly released; thus, it is sublimated into socially accepted releasing activities, such as sexually oriented jokes, intense interest in hobbies and athletics, and so on.

For the 12-year-old, the sexual drive creates enough threat that boys overreact and belittle girls or belittle any interest in heterosexual relationships, while girls have their last fling at being tomboys. Subsequently, idealized friendships evolve with same-sex individuals who possess qualities the adolescent wishes to possess. Often these individuals are older idols, such as an athlete, an older adolescent, or a teacher. In this way, the sexual drive is vicariously released.

In mid-adolescence, libidinal energy can no longer be suppressed, and heterosexual relationships emerge. They emerge, however, in an atmosphere of considerable confusion, because the experience is new to the adolescent, and there is often a lack of parental support or clear social guidelines. In fact, most early sexual behavior is "experimental," in the sense of trial-and-error learning about something new, different, and exciting—but also scary. To facilitate this adjustment, initial heterosexual contacts are often group-oriented.

With experience, the adolescent establishes a unique and independent identity, or ego synthesis, that allows for comfortable interpersonal relationships. However, not all people achieve this stage of ego synthesis; for those that do not, adolescent patterns of sexual adjustment may continue throughout life.

Dating

Dating, or courtship behavior, serves to define, clarify, and strengthen sexual or gender identity. It becomes the basis for later, permanent attachments, and is an important factor in an individual's socialization.

As heterosexual relationships emerge, so does the potential for direct physical release of the sexual drive. It is a classic belief that boys possess a greater sex drive than girls and that this results in the greater ease of sexual arousal for males and their more direct expression of sexuality. However, cultural mores rather than biology may account for these sex differences.

At the very point in life where sexuality becomes a compelling force, parental disapproval and the risk of pregnancy encourage the limitation or postponement of sexual activity. Adolescents have to learn to express their sexuality in rewarding yet responsible ways.

Peer-Group Relationships

During the adolescent years, as the young person begins to establish his or her own identity outside the nuclear family, important new social roles are explored and tested. These roles are increasingly, though not exclusively, defined by the peer group. They comprise, to a large degree, the beginnings of what will ultimately emerge as a coherent adult lifestyle. Most people have their first sexual exploration (not necessarily intercourse or even genital sex), as well as their first serious intimate relationship, during their adolescent years. These experiences constitute an influential part of adolescent socialization, which is integral to sound psychological adjustment.

The peer group is more important during adolescence than at any other stage of development. This fact can be accounted for by four characteristics of the adolescent years.

1. The adolescent is seeking independence and must break ties with parents and family to do so.

2. Peer relationships are prototypes of mature adult relationships; thus, they serve as a proving ground for the development of adult social skills.

3. The adolescent needs a trustworthy confidant with whom to talk about shared experiences.

4. Although in a state of fluid change, the adolescent still seeks some stability. The peer group can fulfill that need.

The importance of being accepted by one's peers is particularly evident in the compulsive concern often shown by adolescents about their body proportions, complexion, body odor, clothes, hair style, and, generally, the acceptability of their physical appearance to other people. Evidence suggests that this concern is particularly prevalent in girls and reaches a peak intensity at about the age of 16.

Conformity Among Peers

Early adolescence is the age of greatest peer-group conformity. Those individuals who are self-confident, autonomous, and who have established a sense of identity will conform to their peers less than individuals who have not achieved these characteristics. This fact can account for the greater conformity of younger adolescents. It is also reflected in the tendency of adolescents from democratic families to be comfortable in conforming less to the standards of their peers or parents than children from authoritarian families.

In studies of adolescent judgment conformity, a subject is shown a standard line and asked to judge which of three other lines is the same length as the standard. Before the subject makes a judgment, a group of peers, apparently fellow subjects (but really "stooges" who are working with the researcher) uniformly respond to the task by selecting a line that does not match the target stimulus. Twelve-year-olds comply with the incorrect judgment of their peers approximately 23 percent more than 16-year-olds, who in turn conform more than adults.

Leadership Patterns in Adolescent Peer Groups

The leaders of adolescent peer groups possess the same characteristics as leaders of younger groups. They are self-confident, and with that confidence, they are able to contribute to others by making them feel acceptable and involved. The leaders also tend to be more intelligent individuals who are successful in school. Individuals who lack self- confidence are generally not selected as leaders, nor are they identified as popular people in the peer group. That lack of self-confidence may be exhibited either by withdrawal and social isolation or by overaggressiveness and attention-seeking behavior.

Career Decision-Making

One's identity is determined in part by one's vocational goals. Thus, the adolescent's search for identity involves a complete developmental process leading to occupational or career choice.

Over the years, not only have there been pronounced changes in the factors that determine the type of work one does, but cultural perceptions about working have also changed dramatically. Throughout history, a person's work was usually a consequence of his or her birth. Women, however, were not considered a part of the modern work world until the mid-twentieth century.

As democratic, industrialized societies evolved, large numbers of people found themselves with occupational options never before available. Coupled with this social change was an expanding technology that created new jobs considerably faster than old jobs were made obsolete.

Because the situation has changed so rapidly, it now requires quite a bit of self-assessment and cognitive adaptability for an adolescent to understand his or her relation to the working world. Many challenging questions arise as an adolescent thinks about the future: What skills, qualities, and interests do I possess that would be relevant to the world of work? What kinds of opportunities are available? What do I have to do to avail myself of these opportunities? What will work offer me, and what will it contribute to my life?

There is also the matter of choosing an occupational or educational level: Should I enter a profession, such as law, medicine, or pharmacy, which will require extensive training, or should I attend a two-year college to train for a position such as paralegal or medical assistant, which will enable me to earn a living sooner? Should I attend a vocational school to learn a trade? The choice between the so-called blue-collar and white-collar jobs, which in the past was usually determined by one's father's status, is now, for most adolescents planning ahead, a voluntary decision.

Such choices and options lead to complex levels of decision-making and many challenges of adjustment, especially for the adolescent. Many of the decisions made during these years of high school and college lead to career patterns in later life. Thus, appropriate career counseling interventions during the secondary (and even elementary) school years can have positive lifelong implications. In reality, whether one ends up at "just a job" or engaged in a career is often determined by the age of 18.

Working at a job one likes or does not like, whether for money, prestige or experience, the adolescent begins to come to grips with the multifaceted world of work. Different counseling perspectives may characterize this experience in somewhat varied terms. From the psychodynamic point of view, this phase of adolescence represents a breaking-free of the family, the beginnings of an economic self-sufficiency that serves as an integral part of the adolescent's quest for individual identity. Humanistic psychologists view the adolescent's work as a fundamental component of the self-actualization process, of fulfilling one's potentialities in life. To the cognitive psychologist, the first real work experiences change our entire way of thinking about ourselves and the world. And according to the behavioral psychologist, the meaning of money, as a method of achieving our goals and satisfying our needs, undergoes conditioning during this period.

Of course, the opportunities for growth and development through one's work are not limited to the adolescent years. Especially in our times, the world of work has become an important arena of development and adjustment throughout a life span.

Theories of Career Development

Underlying all serious efforts to understand career choice are a number of highly sophisticated and carefully developed theories of career development.

Super's Theory of Development

Donald E. Super has developed a theory of vocational choice based on the idea that one's self-concept influences one's occupational choice, as well as one's ultimate satisfaction or dissatisfaction with that choice. The vocational choice, according to Super, is the result of a developmental process that puts the individual's self-concept into practice.

He points out that people differ in their abilities, interests, and personalities and that they are each qualified, by virtue of these circumstances, for a number of occupations. All of these occupations require a characteristic pattern of abilities, interests, and personality traits, with tolerances wide enough, however, to allow both some variety of occupations for each individual and some variety of individuals in each occupation.

Vocational preferences and competencies, the situations in which people live and work, and hence their self-concepts change with time and experience (although self-concepts are generally fairly stable from late adolescence until late maturity), making choice and adjustment a continuous process.

The process of vocational development, then, is essentially that of developing and implementing the self-concept; it is a compromise process in which the self-concept is a product of the interaction of inherited aptitudes, neural and endocrine makeup, opportunities to play various roles, and evaluations of the extent to which the results of role playing meet with the approval of superiors and peers.

The process of compromise between individual and social factors, between self-concept and reality, is one of role playing, whether the role is played in fantasy, in the counseling interview, or in real-life activities, such as school classes, clubs, part-time work, and entry jobs. Work satisfactions and life satisfactions depend upon the extent to which the individual finds adequate outlets for his or her abilities, interests, personality traits, and values.

Super and his associates have developed these early premises into a comprehensive framework for assessing vocational choice and vocational development. They differentiate between the exploratory stage and the establishment stage of vocational development. The *exploratory stage* is characterized by fantasy, searching, investigating, experimenting, and testing out hypotheses. It is the period during which vocational images are molded and refined. The *establishment stage* consists of the period during which the individual actually begins to enact a career role and shape the career model into his or her own unique style. These stages may be considered maturational-psychological stages and may also be divided according to chronological ages.

Holland's Theory of Personality Types

John Holland also regards vocational interests and preferences as part of the total personality of the individual. Briefly, his theory consists of several simple ideas and their more complex elaborations. First, he assumes that we can characterize people by their resemblance to one or more personality types. The closer a person's resemblance to his or her particular type, the more likely it is he or she will exhibit the personal traits and behaviors associated with that type. Second, he assumes that the environments in which people live can be characterized by their resemblance to one or more model environments. Finally, he assumes that the pairing of persons and environments leads to several outcomes that we can predict and understand from our knowledge of the personality types and the environmental models. These outcomes include vocational choice, vocational stability and achievement, personal stability, creative performance, and susceptibility to influence.

Holland defines six character types that include most persons: realistic, intellectual, social, conventional, enterprising, and artistic.

The *realistic type* is physically strong, is basically unsociable and aggressive, has good motor coordination and skill, but lacks high-level verbal and interpersonal skills. Such a person prefers concrete to abstract problems, is task-oriented but not very social, and prefers to think through rather than act out problems. The *intellectual type* is even more task-oriented and prefers to think through rather than act out problems. The *social type* is humanistic, religious, needs attention, and demonstrates a high level of verbal and interpersonal skills. Such a person generally avoids intellectual problem solving and physical activity, and prefers to solve problems through feelings and interpersonal manipulations of others.

The *conventional type* enjoys structured verbal and numerical activities and feels comfortable in subordinate roles. The *enterprising type* has skills for selling, dominating, and leading, and generally avoids well-defined language or work situations requiring long periods of intellectual effort. The *artistic type* is asocial and avoids problems that are highly structured or require gross physical skills. He or she prefers dealing with environmental problems through self-expression in artistic media.

Holland has attempted to measure each of these personality types through a Vocational Preference Inventory, which ranks the subject's personal orientations in terms of these six categories. From this research, Holland concluded that people search for environments and vocations that will permit them to exercise their skills and abilities, to express their attitudes and values, to take on agreeable problems and rules, and to avoid disagreeable ones. In other words, a realistic personality type would function best in a realistic environment, while a social type would function best in a social environment, and so on. The choice and satisfactions of an occupation depend heavily upon the degree of concordance between the individual's type and his or her environment.

Roe's Theory of Needs

Anne Roe has developed a theory of occupational choice and job satisfaction based upon Abraham Maslow's ideas of the personality being formed around interacting levels of needs, arranged in a hierarchy of importance. One of Roe's more important insights concerns the relationship between the individual's family background, upbringing, and later occupational situation. Deficiencies during childhood, she suggests, may be compensated for through the work that one does. If one did not receive sufficient praise and respect from parents, one may attempt to elicit these through one's job and consequently seek jobs where such praise and respect would be forthcoming. Likewise, for all the needs that were unmet at earlier stages of development, one turns to work to find gratification.

Moral Development and Values

With the onset of adolescence, moral values undergo five characteristic changes:

1. Values and moral concepts become more abstract.

2. Moral values become focused more on what one should do—what is right and just—and less focused on what is wrong, what one should not do.

3. Moral judgments become more cognitive. Adolescents are inclined toward the analysis of society and the establishment of personal moral codes.

4. Moral judgments are less egocentric.

5. Because of the adolescent's potential to appreciate moral conflicts, moral judgments produce more psychological tension and anxieties.

Moral Subjectivism and Postconventional Morality

Moral judgments are influenced by the cognitive capacities of the individual as well as by his or her emotions. The development of formal cognitive capacities allows the adolescent to exhibit what Piaget called moral subjectivism and what Lawrence Kohlberg calls postconventional moral judgment. Morals are seen as relative to circumstances rather than as absolute. They are based on principles that go beyond adherence to an authority, avoidance of punishment, or search for approval. For a description of the characteristics associated with these forms of moral judgment, see Chapter 19.

While the cognitive capacities of adolescents and adults allow them to exhibit subjective, postconventional moral judgments, only 25 percent of individuals over 16 years of age demonstrate that level of functioning, and less than 10 percent of those individuals consistently exhibit the highest level of universal morality.

Values

Not only is the capacity for formal thinking reflected in the adolescent's potential to produce postconventional moral judgments, it is also demonstrated by the idealism of the adolescent's value system.

Adolescents tend to conceptualize the world as it might possibly be, and to feel frustrated by its incongruence with that ideal. This frustration is stimulated by their relationships with others, particularly their parents, and by the institutions of society with which they come in contact, particularly the school. In addition, the potential for abstract thinking allows the adolescent to develop an understanding of and concern for the political and economic values of his or her family and society.

This capacity is illustrated by one of the questions on the Wechsler Intelligence Scale for Children, Revised. The question is "Why is it important to have senators and congressmen?"   A typical response of a ten-year-old might simply be "To make laws." An adolescent, however, could be expected to answer the question by saying, "The population is too large for everyone to meet and make laws. By electing senators and congressmen, we have a group of workable size to make laws, yet one that is representative of a larger population."

Conflicts and Problems in Adolescence

Although the majority of individuals manage to make the transition from childhood to maturity and to discover a positive self-identity, for some young people the conflicts and confusions of that transition result in behavior that is even more deviant than is normal for of adolescents. In recent years, the rapid changes in society that have magnified the confusion of adolescents have also magnified the extent of this deviant behavior.

Adolescent Alcohol and Drug Abuse

One of the more refractory problems facing society today is the widespread abuse of drugs and alcohol by adolescents. Beginning in the mid 1970s and continuing through the late 1980s, alcohol emerged as the single most abused drug in adolescent culture. It is estimated that there are over three million teen-age alcoholics today, most of whom are in school.   One possible explanation for this is that it may represent an ironic adolescent rebellion against the prevailing adult acceptance of marijuana.

The manifest symptoms of alcohol abuse among teenagers are as evident or more evident than the symptoms of drug abuse, which at times may be obscure. The problem-drinking adolescent is likely to have a high absentee rate, may appear intoxicated in class, and will invariably fall behind in schoolwork.

Juvenile Delinquency

Juvenile delinquency is defined as breaking of the law by individuals under 18 years of age. There are two types of juvenile delinquency. The first includes acts that would be considered crimes if they were committed by an adult (such as, murder, assault, and robbery). The second type includes what are called status offenses: actions that are illegal for a juvenile to commit but not illegal for an adult to commit (such as curfew violations, running away from home, purchasing alcohol, and truancy). In the United States, reported juvenile delinquency has increased at a rate that far exceeds increases in the population. Increases in delinquent behavior are particularly evident among girls and the children of middle- as well as upper-class families.

Prediction of Delinquency

The single best predictor of delinquent behavior is the adolescent's relationship with his or her parents. Adolescents who identify with their parents, feel free to confront them with the frustrations of adolescence, and believe they are supported emotionally by their parents are less likely to engage in delinquent activity than those who do not have positive parental relationships.

Interestingly, adolescent delinquent behavior is predictable from observations of behavior patterns in kindergarten and the primary grades. This predictive power has led some school districts to establish teams of child development specialists whose task it is to discover potentially troubled children and work with both them and their families to alleviate the conditions that breed delinquency.

One of the predictors of delinquency is poor academic performance and dropping out of school. In Denver, Colorado, it was reported that 90.4 percent of the youths incarcerated for at least one year had experienced some form of learning disability that manifested itself in poor reading and mathematical skills.

Nationally, 40 percent of our youths drop out of high school before graduation. These high school dropouts have their own set of identifying characteristics, which include the following:

1.   Two years or more of retarded performance in either mathematics and/or reading.

2.   Failure in one or more grades.

3.   No participation in extracurricular activities.

4.   Feelings of not belonging.

5.   Resentment of authority.

Forms of Delinquency

Two forms of delinquent behavior have been identified: Individual and social. Individual delinquency results from the individual's being unable to cope with societal demands and his or her relationships with others. Because this form of delinquency is caused by the individual's inadequate socialization, it is difficult to rehabilitate adolescents exhibiting individual delinquency.

An adolescent was referred to a psychologist after being picked up by the police while robbing a car. In his discussion with the psychologist, the boy revealed that he was in constant conflict with his family and teachers and had no friends. He justified his robbery by saying, "I wanted a new stereo deck for my car and figured I'd just rip one off." Such a statement exemplifies individual delinquency.

Social delinquency refers to delinquency that results from an individual becoming socialized within a group whose societal norms sanction and encourage delinquency. Because these adolescents are capable of coping effectively within some societal system, they are receptive to rehabilitation that substitutes for their old social group a new social order with which to identify.

A second boy was referred to a psychologist by the police for repeatedly stealing from and vandalizing a school in a nearby community. In describing his crimes, the boy said that he and his friends were "just goofing off" and needed money to go to movies and have parties. They reasoned that they could get the money from desks and lockers at this school, which was a rival of their own high school, and that they probably would not get caught if they were careful. They reasoned further that this action would not hurt anyone they knew, so it was not as bad as stealing from their friends. While this boy's crime was not justified, it exemplifies social, rather than individual, delinquency.

Psychopathology and Adolescents

The conflicts and confusions that beset many adolescents create an atmosphere ripe for the development of psychopathology. The problems exhibited by adolescents include psychophysiological disturbances as well as withdrawal reactions.

Psychophysiological Disturbances

When the defenses against the conflicts of adolescence result in physical problems, they are referred to as psychophysiological disturbances.

Hypochondriasis. The chronic complaints about ill health typical of hypochondriasis may be stimulated by a conflict over the need to receive childlike attention from parents versus the need to exhibit independence. The adolescent who manifests the symptoms of hypochondria often receives the desired sympathetic attention from his or her parents without having to exhibit emotional dependence upon them. In this way, the behavioral characteristics of hypochondriasis are reinforced.

Anorexia Nervosa and Bulimia. Deliberate self-starvation, or anorexia nervosa, is also observed in some adolescents, particularly girls. This problem may stem from conflicts over poor appearance and the lack of personal acceptability that the disturbed person equates with being overweight. A compulsive attempt to avoid weight problems results in deliberate self-starvation. In some cases, the adolescent will eat but immediately vomit the food. This condition is called bulimia.

Enuresis. Bedwetting, or enuresis, is another psychophysiological reaction to the conflicts of adolescence. Although enuresis occurs in only 1 to 4 percent of adolescents, its impact on the self- concept can be devastating. Adolescents experiencing enuresis may avoid contact with others for fear that their problem will be discovered. Some older enuretics compensate for their feelings or personal inadequacy by engaging in delinquent behavior. Nineteen percent of the adolescent delinquents studied in one experiment were enuretic.

Withdrawal Reactions. The conflicts and confusions of adolescence are responded to by some boys and girls by withdrawal from the situations that produce those conflicts and confusions. The negative effect of these withdrawal reactions is that individuals reduce their potential for resolving the conflicts that are normally experienced in adolescence. The inability to resolve those conflicts perpetuates the need for pathological defense mechanisms and stimulates the development of severe psychopathology.

Depression. Depression is a form of withdrawal. In adolescence, depression is associated with prolonged states of physical fatigue, emotional disappointment, and sadness about circumstances that may not always be clearly identified. Often depression is accompanied by anger and conflict over how to express that anger. For adolescents to recover from a depressive state, they must develop realistic methods for confronting disappointment and resolving the conflicts concerned with the expression of anger. Reassurance that their feelings are normal also aids adolescents in recovering from depression.

Compulsive Behavior and Thoughts. The rituals of the compulsive act provide a rigid structure within which to function; thus, they serve as a defense against the conflict one faces in making important decisions about behavior—a conflict often faced by adolescents. The compulsion may be behavioral, as in compulsive neatness or hand washing, or it may be cognitive, as in uncontrolled thinking about stealing, sexual acts, cleanliness, and so on. Treatment for compulsive behavior may involve behavioral extinction and supportive acceptance of the adolescent's emerging decision-making capabilities.

Schizophrenia. While fully developed schizophrenia is not widely observed in adolescents, incipient signs of schizophrenia are common. The characteristics of this withdrawal reaction include (1) difficult interpersonal relationships, (2) reclusiveness and daydreaming, (3) withdrawal from work, (4) personal neglect, and (5) a tendency toward delinquency.

One may also observe the precursors of delusional patterns in adolescents. Typically the delusions of adolescents are more realistic than those of adult schizophrenics. Sometimes it is hard to assess whether an adolescent's beliefs are true delusions or misunderstood realities. Hallucinations may also be reported by adolescents. Typically, however, those hallucinations are logically related to the needs of the adolescent.

A 14-year-old boy reported hearing a voice that told him to engage in what the boy called "terrible activities." The voice was real to the boy and caused him much distress. After some discussion, it became apparent that the boy was angry with his parents, but was so fearful of the emotion that he could not directly express it. The voice was simply saying the things that the boy actually felt. When the boy was able to express those feelings openly in a therapeutic session, the voice went away.

Glossary

Accommodation Piaget's term for changing one's responses and thought structures to deal with new information provided by the environment.

Acuity The ability to distinguish details.

Adrenal cortex A portion of the adrenal gland which, among other functions, produces small amounts of both male and female sex hormones.

Allele One of a pair or group of genes that affects a trait.

Amniotic fluid The fluid in which the fetus is suspended while in the uterus.

Anal stage In Freud's theory of personality, the period when libidinal energy is expended to satisfy the conflicts created by being toilet-trained.

Analytical classification Classification based on shared physical properties.

Androgens A group of male sex hormones including testosterone.

Animism The attribution of animate qualities to inanimate objects—for example, believing that a rock or doll has feeling and is alive.

Anorexia nervosa A disorder characterized by deliberate self-starvation.

Areola The dark pigmented skin surrounding the nipple of the breast.

Artificial insemination. A process whereby sperm cells are placed mechanically into the vagina rather than being discharged during intercourse.

Assimilation Piaget's term for the ability to incorporate new information from the environment into already existing thought structures.

Attachment The relationship of a child to parents and other significant individuals; usually develops during the first six months of postnatal development.

Attentional flexibility The ability to shift attention from one characteristic of a problem to another when that shift if appropriate.

Authoritarian parents Parents who establish rigid standards of conduct that neglect the needs of the children and who enforce their standards harshly.

Authoritative parents Parents who are nurturing and loving, and who also establish and communicate behavioral standards for their children to follow. The establishment of those standards takes into consideration the needs of both the children and the parents.

Autosomes Cells that contain 46 chromosomes and compose all elements of the body except for the germ cells, or gametes.

Autonomy According to Erikson, it is self-control, and it is in conflict with shame and doubt at the toddler stage of psychosocial development.

Autostimulation theory A theory that suggests the prevalence of REM sleep in infants stems from their need for cortical stimulation to maintain neurological development, coupled with their need for sleep. REM sleep allows for the satisfaction of both needs.

Aversive conditioning Classical conditioning in which the unconditioned stimulus is distasteful.

Axon The single long fiber extending from the cell body of a neuron; carries the signal to the synapse.

Babinski response A normal reflex for healthy infants, in which the toes fan out when one strokes the middle of the sole of the foot.

Behaviorism A system of psychology which studied observable stimuli and responses only, and which denied the concept of mind.

Bilirubin A by-product of blood cell destruction which, if not adequately metabolized, creates a jaundice condition in an infant.

Binocular cues Cues for depth perception that result from the two eyes viewing a scene from slightly different angles.

Broca's area A brain structure in the front portion of the left cortical hemisphere that controls speech production.

Bulimia An eating disorder, characterized by eating binges, usually followed by self-induced vomiting or taking large doses of laxatives.

Case history An intensive study of an individual subject over an extended period of time.

Centration The focusing of attention on a limited portion of a problem.

Cephalo-caudal trend The tendency for the head to develop before and more quickly than the lower portions of the body.

Cerebellum The part of the brain primarily responsible for motor functioning.

Cervix The anatomical structure forming the mouth of the uterus and opening into the vagina. This structure must thin and dilate to allow the birth of a child.

Cesarean section A surgical incision through the wall of the abdomen and uterus in order to deliver a newborn, as opposed to vaginal birth.

Chromosomes Small bodies that contain genes; they occur in pairs within each body cell. Human body cells have 46 chromosomes, human germ cells have 23.

Chunking A memory strategy in which informational elements presented next to each other are grouped into larger units.

Class multiplication A concrete cognitive operation that allows one to classify objects and events on the basis of more than one characteristic simultaneously. Specifically, it allows for the creation of matrix classification systems.

Classical conditioning Learning procedure in which a previously neutral stimulus is paired with a response-producing stimulus until the neutral stimulus elicits the same type of response; also called respondent conditioning and Pavlovian conditioning.

Clustering A memory strategy in which elements to be remembered are grouped together on the basis of some property they share; for example, all the elements in a group are animals.

Codominant traits Characteristics that may be manifested simultaneously in the same heterozygotic individual.

Cognition Knowing. Used by psychologists to include the use of language, thought, reason, problem solving, and imagination.

Cognitive therapy A form of therapy in which illogical thinking is changed to produce more adaptive behaviors.

Common motion A gestalt principle of perceptual organization in which objects that move together are perceived to be a unit.

Communication theory of attachment A theory put forth by T. G. R. Bower according to which attachment, stranger anxiety, and separation anxiety occur because infants establish a nonverbal communication system with people to whom they become attached and are threatened by the potential loss of that communication system by the entry of a stranger or the removal of the person to whom they are attached.

Compound sentences Sentences that are combined to express more than one idea.

Compulsion An unwanted but unavoidable pattern of action that recurs often.

Conception The penetration of an ovum by a sperm, which results in the development of a child.

Concrete operational stage Piaget's third state of cognitive development—from approximately age seven to age eleven.

Concrete operations Piaget's term for a set of logical processes for analyzing information that is acquired by children at around six years of age. The processes are said to be concrete because they are capable of analyzing only concrete information, not abstract information.

Concrete thinking Thinking that is restricted to thoughts about objects and events that have a physical reality.

Conditioned response (CR) In classical conditioning, the response elicited by the CS; usually similar to the UCR.

Conditioned stimulus (CS) In classical conditioning, the stimulus that was originally neutral and comes to be response-producing.

Cones The visual receptors that function primarily in lighted conditions; they are located toward the center of the eye and operate for color vision.

Confounding of variables A condition that exists when an investigator attempts to introduce a single change into an experimental situation in order to assess its impact, and he or she discovers that one or more other changes are systematically associated with the change that is under study. When confounding of independent variables occurs, it is not possible to determine which change introduced by the investigator caused the effect on the dependent variable.

Conservation Piaget's term for the principle that if nothing is added or taken away from an amount, it remains the same.

Conservation of liquid The recognition that, other things being equal, pouring a liquid from one container to another does not change the amount of liquid.

Conservation of quantity The recognition that, other things being equal, changing the shape of an object does not change the amount of material contained in the object.

Conservation of weight The recognition that, other things being equal, changing the shape of an object does not change its weight.

Conventional morality The second period of moral development postulated by Lawrence Kohlberg in which the evaluative judgment of a behavior as good or bad is based on its conformity to social rules and the extent to which it protects or threatens social order.

Correlational method A research method in which subjects are assigned to groups because of a characteristic they possess prior to being included in the research. Cause and effect relationships cannot be assessed when the correlational research method is employed.

Cortex The most recently developed portion of the brain; involved with higher mental processes, such as thinking.

Cretinism A physiologically caused form of mental retardation resulting from a prenatal lack of iodine.

Critical period A state during which an organism is able to learn a new behavior; this state is limited in time: it has both a beginning and an end.

Cross-cultural research Research that attempts to compare psychological phenomena in different cultures and may use differences in those cultures to explain differences observed in the psychological phenomenon.

Cross-sectional study In developmental psychology, an investigation that makes use of subjects of different age groups to determine how age, the independent variable, affects behavior.

Cross-sectional/longitudinal method A compromise between a longitudinal and cross-sectional research design in which two or more short-term longitudinal studies are undertaken simultaneously with the oldest age at which measurements are taken in one group being the youngest age at which measurements are taken in another group.

Deductive reasoning The process of reasoning from the general principle to specific cases.

Deep structure An abstraction describing the logical grouping of ideas that convey the meaning of a sentence.

Democratic parents Parents who are accepting of their children and maintain a structured environment within which the child has some freedom of choice.

Dependent variable In an experiment, the response that is measured.

Depression A psychological state characterized by feelings of helplessness and/or hopelessness, which is often accompanied by prolonged physical fatigue.

Developmental approach The approach to studying psychological processes that explores the development of those processes rather than their mature functioning.

Developmental continuity Development that involves quantitative changes in a psychological process, but no fundamental changes in the mechanisms that underlie that process.

Developmental discontinuity Development that involves fundamental changes in the mechanisms that underlie the functions of psychological processes.

Deviation IQ The value of intelligence established by using normal probability distributions of scores obtained for various age levels.

Difficult children A class of children described by Stella Chess and Alexander Thomas as those who have difficulty adapting to new situations and exhibit negative attitudes and disruptive behavior when required to adapt.

Discrimination learning Learning in which individuals discriminate differences among stimuli and produce appropriately different responses to each stimulus.

Distributional analysis An analysis of sentence structure that emphasizes how words are distributed in sentences (where they are used), and de-emphasizes how the words are used (the meaning they are intended to convey).

Dominant traits Characteristics that are expressed in both homozygotic and heterozygotic genotypes.

Down's syndrome A form of mental retardation resulting from an extra twenty-first chromosome.

Ductus arteriosus A structure in the fetal circulatory system that allows blood to bypass the lungs.

Early maturers Children who mature physically at an age younger than the average of their peers. Early maturity has different effects on the personality of boys and girls.

Easy children A class of children described by Stella Chess and Alexander Thomas as those who approach situations positively and are regular in their biological functioning.

Ectoderm The outside tissue of the body that forms hair, skin, nails, the nervous system, and other structures.

Effacement The thinning of the cervix during the process of labor and childbirth.

Ego synthesis The state in which a person has achieved an independent identity that allows the development of comfortable and mature interpersonal relationships.

Egocentrism According to Piaget, the young child's belief that nothing exists outside oneself and that the self is the cause of all actions.

Embedded sentences Sentences that are used as component parts of more complex sentences.

Embryonic stage The period of time from approximately two to eight weeks after conception when the zygote has attached itself to the uterine wall, and the physical structures of the child differentiate.

Emotional dependence Dependence on others for affection and emotional support.

Empiricist One who stresses that a theory must concern itself with constructs that have the potential for possessing an objective reality.

Enactive representation A mode of representation characterized by motor actions.

Endoderm The tissues of the body that form internal organs such as the gastrointestinal tract, lungs, thyroid, and liver.

Engagement The lowering of the fetal head into the lower portion of the cervix a few days prior to a child's birth.

Enuresis The inability to consistently exert bladder control.

Epiphyseal ossification centers Cartilage, or epiphysis, located at the connecting points of some bones early in life, which changes to bone as a child grows. The change, or ossification, of these centers is an index of physical maturity.

Estrogen The female sex hormone that stimulates the development of female secondary sex characteristics as well as maintains the primary reproductive functions of the female body.

Ethological theory of attachment A theory postulating the development of attachment as a natural and spontaneous phenomenon that exists because it has survival value for the species and is triggered by a particular stimulus in the environment.

Experimental method A technique involving the controlled comparison of conditions to determine if the variable investigated affects the results obtained.

Extinction In classical conditioning, both the procedure of presenting the conditioed stimulus alone repeatedly and the result of this procedure, which returns the conditioned response to its original (preconditioning) level.

Extraneous variable A condition that may affect the outcome of an experiment but that is irrelevant to the experiment.

Eye movement reflex Eye fixations directed at any slow moving object or sharp visual contour.

Factorial design A research design in which more than one independent variable is systematically changed by the investigator so as to determine both the individual effects of those variables on the dependent variable and their combined effects.

Fallopian tube. Either of the pair of tubes connecting the ovary to the uterus. It is in one of these tubes that fertilization of the ovum takes place.

Fear of success The fear on the part of some women that success will result in being identified as nonfeminine and thus will result in rejection.

Fertilization The union of a sperm cell with the ovum (the egg cell) to form the zygote, the fertilized ovum.

Fetal stage The period of prenatal development extending from about eight weeks after conception until birth. This period is marked by continual growth and refinement of structures whose foundations were established earlier in development.

Follicle A small sac in the ovary that contains a developing ovum.

Follicle-stimulating hormone (FSH) A hormone produced by the pituitary gland that stimulates the female ovaries to produce estrogen, a female sex hormone. It also stimulates the growth of the male testes and in so doing, stimulates the production of sperm.

Fontanels The six points at which the bones of the skull have not yet grown together. The result of this immature development are soft spots.

Formal operational stage Piaget's fourth (and final) stage of cognitive development, from approximately ages eleven to thirteen.

Fraternal twins Two children conceived independently as two separate zygotes but born at approximately the same time.

Functional assimilation The repetition of actions or the repeated use of knowledge that has just been acquired, apparently in an effort to practice these skills.

Functional-locational classification Classification based on the fact that objects or events share a common location; for example, squirrels and birds go together because they both live in tress.

Gamete The female ovum and the male sperm cell. Also known as a germ cell.

Gene The basic element of genetic transmission, which is composed of DNA (deoxyribonucleic acid).

Genital stage Freud's highest stage of psychosexual development, in which individuals are capable of developing mature heterosexual relationships.

Genotype The genetic pattern inherited from parents and coded in the chromosomes of the individual.

Germ cells In the female, the egg; in the male, the sperm.

Germinal stage The first two prenatal weeks when the ovum has been fertilized but has not yet embedded itself in the uterine wall.

Gestalt psychology A system of psychology which adopted an holistic approach to the study of behavior.

Gonads Endocrine glands that control sexual and reproductive behaviors; the ovaries and testes.

Good continuation A gestalt perceptual principle in which an obscured portion of an object is still perceived to exist.

Growth spurt A rapid change in the rate of growth that typically occurs immediately prior to reaching puberty.

Habituation A change of behavioral pattern in which an organism ceases to respond with an fixed-action pattern (FAP) to an inappropriate stimulus.

Heterozygous Having different alleles for a trait.

Holophrase A single-word utterance used by a young child to convey the meaning of a complete sentence.

Homozygotous Having identical alleles for a trait.

Hypochondriasis A psychoneurotic disorder in which individuals chronically complain about physiological disorders.

Hypothalamus A small area of the brain that controls many of our basic drives, such as sex, hunger, thirst, and rage.

Hypothetical deductive reasoning Reasoning in which hypotheses are generated about the possible ways in which the elements of a theory relate to one another, deductions are made about the observations one would expect to make if the hypothesized theory were accurate, tests are made to assess the congruence between actual observations and the predicted observation, and finally, the hypothesized theory is modified to account for any discrepancies between the originally expected observations and the actual observations.

Iconic representation A mode of representation characterized by mental images.

Identical twins Twins who are the result of a single fertilization and therefore have identical genetic makeups.

Imitation The act of repeating a behavior engaged in by another person. For Piaget, imitation was a pure form of accommodation.

Imprinting Learning that occurs by instinct during a critical learning period.

Impulsivity The tendency to make quick judgments that are often inaccurate.

Independent variable A condition manipulated by the experimenter; the experimenter manipulates the independent variable to determine the effect of such manipulations on the dependent variable.

Individual delinquency Delinquency involving persons who are unable to cope with societal demands and relationships within society. These are poorly socialized individuals.

Inductive reasoning The process of arriving at general principles from specific cases or facts.

Inflection Alteration of the meaning of a sentence by changing characteristics of a subject or verb of the sentence; for example, by changing from singular to plural or from present to past tense.

Insecure attachment Attachment characterized by infants who fret and fuss whenever threatened by loss of contact with the person to whom they are attached.

Instrumental dependence Dependence on others to provide assistance in accomplishing objectives, for example, providing food, housing, and so on.

Intermediate expression A trait that manifests itself somewhere between the alleles reflected in a heterozygotic gene pair.

Intonation Rising and lowering of the intensity and/or pitch of the voice, which is used to differentiate the meaning of some verbal utterances.

Irreversibility The inability to think about how you have arrived at the state in which you find yourself.

Jaundice A condition caused by the overabundance of bilirubin in the blood. Symptoms include yellowing of skin and the whites of the eyes.

Juvenile delinquency Illegal activity engaged in by persons who are not legally adults, typically those under eighteen years of age.

Klinefelter's syndrome An abnormal condition occurring when a male possesses an additional female sex chromosome. Individuals with this genotype possess small testes, in many cases are mentally retarded, and exhibit a variety of personality and psychiatric problems.

Laboratory research Research that is undertaken in the highly controlled environment of the laboratory.

Latency stage In Freud's theory of personality, the period extending from the end of the phallic stage to the onset of puberty; during this period, libidinal energies are quiet.

Leydig cells Those cells in the male testes that produce the sex hormone testosterone.

Libidinal energy In psychoanalytic theory, the energy that underlies psychological activity.

Long-term memory A permanent memory system. Knowledge of the world, problem solving strategies, and memory for past events and experiences.

Longitudinal studies Psychological tests administered to the same subjects at different times, often with fairly long periods of time between testing sessions.

Luteinizing hormone (LH) A hormone produced by the pituitary gland that regulates the production of estrogen in the female and testosterone in the male.

Macula The portion of the retina at which visual images are primarily focused.

Maturation In development psychology, the physical development of the body.

Mediational deficiency A deficiency in the underlying cognitive or linguistic skills needed to employ a strategy to enhance memory. Mediational deficiencies are inferred when instruction in the use of a strategy does not improve memory task performance.

Meiosis The process of cell division by which germ cells are produced. Each germ cell receives half the number of chromosomes of the dividing autosome.

Menarche A girl's first menstruation.

Mental age A measurement of a person's performance on an intelligence test, expressed as a hypothetical age that has nothing to do with the person's real chronolgoical age. Rather, the mental age indicates how an average person of that age would typically perform.

Mesoderm The tissues of the body that form muscles, bones, the kidneys and gonads, and the circulatory system

Milk teeth The twenty teeth that erupt through the child's gums by about the age of two years: they are later replaced by permanent teeth, beginning at about age six. (Also called baby teeth.)

Minimal distance principle A grammatical principle that states that the noun associated with a verb is that noun closest to the verb.

Mitosis The process of cell division involving differentiation in which each chromosome in the nucleus is halved and each of the two resulting cells ends up with a full, identical set.

Moral realism A stage of moral judgment postulated by Jean Piaget and typical of middle childhood characterized by a belief that rules are rigid and cannot be changed, a tendency to evaluate actions as good or bad on the basis of their outcomes rather than the intentions of the actor, a view of punishment as an inevitable result of negative behavior, and a tendency to prescribe punishment that is retributive rather than rehabilitative.

Moral subjectivism A stage of moral judgment postulated by Jean Piaget and characteristic of older children and adults in which rules are viewed as subjective and alterable, value judgments about behavior consider both the outcome of the action and the intention of the actor, and punishment is designed to be rehabilitative rather than retributive.

Moro reflex A reflex in which newborns appear to reach out with their arms to grab themselves when confronted with a surprising event.

Morpheme(s) The smallest units of meaning in speech, including syllables, prefixes, words, or suffixes.

Motion parallax A cue for depth perception in which objects close to observers appear to move in the opposite direction from head or eye movements, while objects far away move with eye and head movements.

Multiple attachments The tendency for a child, once attached to a single individual, to develop attachments to a number of different people.

Mutation A spontaneous, sudden change in a gene pattern.

Myelin (myelinization) A fatty substance that covers many axons, usually surrounding the axon in a beadlike arrangement. Myelinization is the process by which this coating forms. This process enables the child's nervous system to effectively transmit the neural impulses that control many motor responses.

Natural setting research Research that is undertaken in the environment in which the behavior to be observed naturally occurs.

Nature-nurture controversy The dispute over the relative importance of heredity and environment in determining human traits.

Neonate Newborn human infant.

Neuron Basic unit of the nervous system: also called a nerve cell.

Norm(s) A statistical description of the test performance of a large group of individuals. Results become the guideline or standard against which to measure other test takers.

Normative data Descriptive statistics that denote the average characteristics of children at various ages as well as the diversity of those characteristics within a particular age group.

Object permanence The recognition a child develops that things continue to exist even when they are not readily apparent.

Occlusion A pictorial depth cue in which a near object blocks the view of objects behind it.

Oedipal complex In Freud's theory of personality, the period when the child has sexual desire for the opposite-sex parent and rivalry with the same-sex parent; successful resolution occurs when the child identifies with the same-sex parent.

Open-class words A large class of word used in the stage of language acquisition characterized by the use of two-word sentences.

Operant conditioning A learning process that involves changing the probability of a response by manipulating the consequences of that response; also called instrumental conditioning and Skinnerian conditioning.

Oral stage In Freud's theory of personality, the period from birth to the second year of life, when all libidinal energy is expended primarily to satisfy mouth-oriented activity.

Orienting reflex Changes in heart rate, galvanic skin response, and other automatic nervous system reaction that occur with the presentation of a novel or startling stimulus.

Ovaries The female sex organs that produce female germ cells (ova) and the female sex hormone, estrogen.

Overextension The use of a word to symbolize a much larger class of objects or events than the word typically symbolizes in adult speech.

Overgeneralization The use of semantic rules in situations where they logically should apply, but which call for exceptions to the rule in adult speech; for example, saying "I runned" instead of "I ran."

Ovum The human egg that, when fertilized, develops into a child.

Palmer reflex A grasping reflex stimulated in newborns when pressure is exerted on the palm.

Palpebral reflex The eye-blink reflex, a reflex that can be used to measure responsiveness to pure tones.

Partial reinforcement In classical conditioning, when the conditioned stimulus is presented on every trial, but the unconditioned stimulus occurs on only some of the trials.

Patellar reflex A reflex in which the lower leg kicks out when the tendon immediately below the knee is tapped.

Patent ductus arteriosus A condition in which the ductus arteriosus is not fully closed after birth, with the result that the blood of the baby receives inadequate oxygen.

Perception Basically, the interpretation or understanding of stimuli received as sensations.

Perceptual discrepancy hypothesis A hypothesis set forth by Jerome Kagan that individuals have a natural fear of objects and events that are greatly different from the schemata they possess, that is, are highly novel.

Perceptual dominance The tendency to focus attention on physical properties of a situation and to make judgments based on knowledge of those properties rather than mentally reflecting on the problem.

Perceptual recognition hypothesis A hypothesis set forth by Jerome Kagan that smiles are a sign of recognition on the part of an infant and are elicited by object or events represented by an emerging schemata.

Personal identity According to Erik Erikson, a sense of contentment about one's own physical, intellectual, and emotional attributes, a sense of purpose and objective, and the anticipation of recognition from other people who are considered significant.

Personality Those enduring characteristics that are representative of a person's behavior; they may be developed from unique or common experiences and the effects of environmental and hereditary influences.

Phallic stage In Freud's theory of personality, the period when libidinal energy centers in the genitalia; the period of the Oedipal complex.

Phenotype The actual characteristics possessed by an individual that result from an interaction of an inherited genotype and the experiences imposed on the person by the environment.

Phobia An intense, compelling fear of some situation or object; the fear is more intense than the circumstance appears to warrant.

Phonemes The basic sound or inflection components of a spoken language.

Phonetics The study of the identification and discrimination of speech sounds as well as their production.

Phonology The study of the perception and production of speech sounds.

Phylogenetic motor skills Motor skills (such as walking) that primarily depend on maturation for their development.

Pictorial depth cues Cues such as shading, linear perspective, or one object blocking the view of another that denote that one object is closer to the observer than the other. These cues can be used to produce depth effects in two-dimensional pictures.

Pituitary gland A major control mechanism for the endocrine gland system that, among other functions, stimulates physical growth, the activity of the adrenal cortex, and the growth and activity of the gonads.

Pivot-class words A class of words used in the stage of language acquisition characterized by the use of two-word sentences. The word class is small in number, members are not used in the same two-word utterance, and members are used either as the first or last word in word sentences but not in both positions.

PKU (Phenylketonuria) A disorder caused by a recessive gene, which prevents the metabolization of certain proteins (such as milk) usually resulting in mental retardation.

Placenta A network of capillaries on the uterine wall that delivers oxygen, nutrients, and other elements from the blood of the mother to that of the fetus, and waste products from the fetus to the mother. The blood itself does not mix.

Plantar reflex A reflex in which the toes grasp when pressure is applied to the ball of the foot.

Postconventional morality The highest stage in the development of moral judgment postulated by Lawrence Kohlberg; moral judgments of behaviors are made with a recognition of the subjectivity of value judgments and are based on whether the behavior enhances or interferes with interpersonal relations.

Preconventional morality A stage of moral judgment postulated by Lawrence Kohlberg in which evaluative judgments are based on whether the outcome is positive or negative.

Premoral judgment A stage of moral development postulated by Jean Piaget and characterized by the inability to make moral judgments. Typically thought to be present in children prior to age six.

Prenatal Before birth; the period of time from conception to delivery.

Preoperational stage Piaget's second stage of cognitive development, extending from the age of two through six. In this stage children can symbolize sensory and motor experiences, but are limited in the logical processes they can employ in thinking about those experiences.

Preterm infant Children born less than 40 weeks after conception.

Primary circular reaction The tendency for infants to stumble upon new experiences through their reflex actions and to then repeat these actions.

Primary class addition A concrete cognitive operation that allows one to analyze hierarchical classification systems.

Primary sex characteristics Those sex organs that are present at birth, including the penis, prostate, testicles, and seminal vesicles of the boy and the ovaries, uterus, vagina, and clitoris of the girl.

Primary visual system Those structures in the visual system that allow one to make fine discriminations among complex visual displays.

Production deficiency A condition in which the linguistic and cognitive capacities to use memory-enhancing strategies are available, but the strategies are not employed spontaneously.

Proximity The real or perceived distance between one person and another.

Proximo-distal trend The tendency for the central portions of the body to develop before and more quickly than the peripheral portions.

Rapid-eye-movement sleep (REM) The movement of the eyes during sleep; the period associated with dreaming.

Rationalist One who accepts theories and ideas that may not be demonstrated objectively, but which have a logical basis.

Rationalization Acting because of one unacceptable motive while crediting that action to some more acceptable motive.

Realism The tendency for young children to conceptualize everything as being real.

Recall memory Memory that involves the construction of a mental representation for a missing object or event. As a measure of retention, the ability to arrive at the correct response with a minimum cue statement.

Recessive traits Characteristics that are manifested only when a gene pair critical for the expression of that characteristic is homozygotic.

Recognition memory Memory that requires individuals to identify an object or event with which they are currently confronted as one they have been confronted with before.

Regression Acting in a manner appropriate to someone of a younger age.

Rehearsal A strategy to enhance short-term memory in which the material to be remembered is repeated over and over.

Rejecting and autonomous parents Parents who exhibit little love for their children, and do not care about trying to exert any control over them.

Rejecting and controlling parents Parents who exhibit little love for their children but who insist on rigid control over them.

Relational addition (transitivity) A concrete cognitive operation that allows one to analyze the relative positions objects or events may possess in a sequence and to recognize that logical relationships exist among those positions.

Reliability The extent to which a test provides consistent results from one testing time to another.

Repression The use of psychic energy to keep anxiety-producing memories from conscious recognition; motivated forgetting.

Retina That part of the eye containing the receptors for vision; located at the back of the eyeball.

Reversibility The ability to mentally retrace one's steps so as to determine how the state at which one finds oneself was arrived at.

Rods The visual receptors which function primarily in dim or dark conditions; they are located toward the periphery of the eye and operate only in a black-and-white dimension.

Rooting reflex A head-turning reflex stimulated by stroking the cheek of the infant.

Schema As used by Jean Piaget, a term for an organized system of actions that forms the basis of thinking.

Schizophrenia The most common of psychotic reactions, often characterized by delusions, hallucinations, and pronounced loss of contact with reality.

Secondary appraisal An interpretation of the causes of an emotion; may change the explanation from the one that was first proposed.

Secondary circular reaction The tendency for infants to stumble on actions that produce interesting consequences and then to repeat those actions.

Secondary sex characteristics Physical changes that are dependent on the increased levels of sex hormones in the blood following the onset of puberty. They include body hair, voice changes, breasts, and so on.

Secondary visual system Those systems of the visual system that allow one to see with some clarity and discriminate colors and brightness, as well as patterned and nonpatterned visual displays.

Secure attachment Attachment characterized by infants who can leave the individual to whom they are attached in order to explore new experiences.

Selective attention A sensory state in which an organism attends to certain aspects of the environment while ignoring others.

Semantics The study of the meaning of words.

Sensorimotor stage Piaget's first stage of cognitive development, from birth to about age two.

Sensory memory The sensory trace that lingers for about one-quarter second after a stimulus is terminated.

Separation anxiety The anxiety and accompanying crying and tantrum throwing that occurs when children are separated from, or anticipate separation from, an individual to whom they are attached.

Sex-linked genetic transmission Genetic characteristics that are transmitted on the sex chromosomes.

Shape constancy The perceptual ability to realize that an object's shape remains constant even if the appearance of the object changes before the perceptual field.

Short-term memory Memory storage lasting approximately 30 seconds after the termination of a stimulus and from which material may be transferred to long-term memory.

Size constancy The perceptual phenomenon whereby objects are seen to retain their shape even though the form of their retinal image changes when the objects are rotated in space.

Slow-to-warm-up-children A class of children described by Stella Chess and Alexander Thomas as those who have difficulty adapting to new situations and who withdraw from new situations.

Social delinquency Delinquency that results from an individual's becoming socialized within a group whose societal norms sanction and encourage delinquency.

Sound localization The ability of an individual to locate the spatial position of a sound source.

Specific attachment An infant's attachment to a specific person, typically the mother.

Specific motor skills Those motor skills (such as ice skating) whose development is dependent primarily on practice.

Spectrographic analysis A visual analysis of the sounds that combine to form a sound pattern such as speech.

Sperm The male reproductive cell that can fertilize an ovum and, in so doing, initiate the development of the child.

Status offense An action that when committed by a juvenile is illegal but when committed by an adult is legal.

Stepping reflex A reflex in which newborns make steplike movements when their toes brush against the floor.

Stranger anxiety The anxiety characteristic of infants about seven to nine months of age when they are in the presence of a stranger.

Sublimation The process whereby individuals experiencing needs whose satisfaction is socially forbidden substitute for that need one that is acceptable.

Sucking reflex A sucking response stimulated by placing any object in the mouth of the infant.

Superordinate classification Classification based on the sharing of an abstract attribute; for example, dogs and cats are both animals.

Surface structure The arrangement of words in a language.

Swimming reflex A reflex in which newborns engage in swimminglike motion when held horizontally.

Symbolic representation The highest form of representation characterized by verbal labels and language.

Syntax The way in which words and phrases are put together to form meaningful sentences.

Telegraphic speech Speech that uses only those words that are essential for the communication of a message.

Temporal conditioning A classical conditioning procedure in which the unconditioned stimulus occurs at regular intervals; these regular intervals are treated as the conditioned stimulus.

Tertiary circular reaction The tendency for an infant to accidentally initiate an action and then repeat systematic variations of the act so that new cause-effect relations can be discovered.

Testes The male gonads that produce both germ cells (sperm) and the male sex hormone, testosterone.

Testosterone The male sex hormone responsible for the development of male secondary sex characteristics as well as sex drive.

Texture cues A pictorial cue for depth in which fine details of near objects are more easily seen than those of objects far away.

Thyroid gland An endocrine gland responsible for controlling the body's rate of metabolism.

Thyroxin A hormone secreted by the thyroid gland that controls metabolism.

Trance alternate A sleeping state characterized by EEG patterns alternating between comparative silence in cortical activity and bursts of irregular slow activity mixed with rhythmic theta waves.

Transductive reasoning Reasoning in which it is concluded that one event always accompanies another event because the two events have been experienced together in the past. Transductive reasoning moves from the particular to the particular rather than from the particular to the general or from the general to the particular.

Transformational rules Linguistic rules that are applied to translate the deep structure of a sentence (its meaning) into an appropriate surface structure (the produced sentence of speech).

Twin study method A method for testing the extent to which a characteristic is influenced by genetic factors. The method compares the similarity of the characteristics of identical and fraternal twins. Genetic causation can be inferred if identical twins are more similar with respect to the characteristic than are fraternal twins.

Umbilical cord A lifeline connecting the wall of the mother's uterus to the fetus. The cord allows the blood of the fetus to receive oxygen and nutrients from the blood of the mother and in so doing sustains life.

Unattached children Children who exhibit a lack of concern for the presence of others and who do not develop interpersonal bonds.

Unconditioned response (UCS) In classical conditioning, the response elicited by the UCS.

Unconditioned stimulus (UCS) In classical conditioning, the stimulus that is response-producing on the first and every other trial.

Underextension The use of a word to denote a much smaller class of objects or events than the word typically symbolizes in adult speech.

Uterus The female organ in which the prenatal child develops.

Vagina The external opening to the uterus into which sperm are discharged and begin their journey to the ovum.

Valve of foramen ovale A valve in the fetal circulatory system that allows blood from the interior vena cava to move directly to the left atrium rather than first circulating through the right portions of the heart and lungs.

Visual cliff An apparatus used to test depth perception. It consists of a glass table, one side of which appears to be a drop-off or cliff. If animals or human infants avoid crawling to the cliff side of the table, it is inferred that they can perceive depth.

Visual constancy The perceptual phenomenon whereby the characteristics of objects are seen as remaining constant in spite of changes in their retinal image.

Warm but restrictive parents Parents who are warm and loving towards their children but often overcontrol them.

Wernicke's area A brain structure that controls language comprehension.

Wh words The English words, "What, why, when, who, where, which," and "how" that are used to ask questions.

Withdrawal reflex A reflex in which the foot is withdrawn when the sole is pricked.

Yes/No questions A question that can be answered with either a "Yes" or a "No" response and requires no further elaboration.

Zygote The single cell formed by the uniting of a sperm cell and an egg cell at the moment of conception.

Index